C000229803

21st Century Marketing

What it is
Why it matters
and
How to do it

Chris Kent

Forward Marketing
Isle of Man

First published in 2017 by 21st Century Marketing, Douglas, Isle of Man IM1 5BY, British Isles

British Library Cataloguing in Publication Data

A catalogue record for this book is available from the British Library

Library of Congress Cataloguing in Publication Data

A catalogue record for this book has been requested

ISBN: 978-0-9956893-0-5 (Hardback)

ISBN: 978-0-9956893-1-2 (Paperback - Colour)

ISBN: 978-0-9956893-3-6 (Paperback - Black and White)

ISBN: 978-0-9956893-2-9 (eBook)

Typeset in the Isle of Man by Forward Marketing

Cover design and illustrations by Forward Marketing, Isle of Man, British Isles

Visit the companion website at www.21stCentury.Marketing

Dedication

This book is dedicated to the 25 entrepreneurs and micro-business owners who so generously gave their time during my research for a Master's Degree in Digital Marketing Communications.

Without their detailed insights, frankness and heart-warming honesty into the real marketing challenges and struggles they face on a daily basis in the 21st century, neither this book, nor my Master's dissertation (on which this book is based) would have been possible.

Foreword

I started my first business over thirty years ago with a dream, a great idea, a bank loan and virtually no clue about marketing — and it cost me dearly! Fortunately, a wealth of practical experience guided by some pretty incredible teachers and mentors, both in the commercial world and in academia, have helped me rectify my early failings and shaped who I am today.

Many of the 5.3 million micro-business owners who, at the end of 2016, accounted for 96% of all UK private sector businesses, also started their entrepreneurial lives with limited marketing knowledge, but in a far more demanding and complex modern marketing landscape. They realise that the internet and digital technology is no longer an optional extra, but a key driver to growth, yet the global digital marketing skills shortage often means they have to fend for themselves.

The 25 entrepreneurs and micro-business owners I interviewed as I conducted the research for my Master's Degree in Digital Marketing Communications, frequently expressed sheer frustration at the modern marketing challenges they face. Some told me:

> "We found plenty of people who could build us a website, but no-one could really tell us how to use it to properly market our business. We discovered there is so much more to digital marketing than just having a website and, without even a basic understanding of the bigger picture, it was extremely frustrating and we made some very expensive mistakes!"

> "If there was only someone to guide me and tell me what to do and how to do it when I started out, it would have been so much easier."

> "Even with quite a bit of marketing knowledge I really struggle to understand how it all fits together and you can waste a lot of time and money on marketing – it's all a bit hit and miss."

> "It's a real jungle out there and it's all so complex – what with digital marketing, social media and everything else. Plus there are so many self-proclaimed experts talking about so many different things it's impossible to know who to trust and where to start."

What was needed was a simple solution to this complex problem. It was only when I really started to analyse the data from the many detailed interviews, that I fully understood the enormity of the challenges they faced-and the lack of real support out there to help them start their entrepreneurial marketing journey. This reignited a fire in my belly that had been simmering for many years – to finally solve the modern marketing puzzle that had eluded me for so long. That solution is "The 21st Century Marketing System" and it has been specifically designed to help me and these 25 heroes of the modern economy – as well as the millions of entrepreneurs and small business owners up and down the country – get to grips with the modern marketing challenges we face, turn opportunity into reality, realise their dreams and make the world a better place.

If you want to join them, then this is a great place to start.

Enjoy the journey!

Chris.

Chris Kent MSc

Acknowledgements

I'd like to start by thanking Jim Moore, my early accountant, who found me in a right mess, sorted it out, and pointed me in the right direction as a young and budding entrepreneur who was very much "wet behind the ears". Without Jim's initial support and advice, my journey may never have started and this book would never have been conceived, let alone written.

I am indebted to my many mentors and teachers over the last thirty years. In particular, my early mentor copywriting genius Ted Nicholas, who taught me the craft of writing sales copy — a skill I treasure and am so grateful I discovered early in my career — and Stuart Goldsmith who introduced me to direct marketing. I'm grateful to Stephanie Hale for her coaching at the start of my journey as an author, and to Andy Harrington for his "Speakers University" where the concept of the M.A.G.I.C. Marketing Matrix was born back in 2013.

My sincere thanks to Colin Gundry, Heather Blackley, Marina Corkill, Peter Ginty and Karen Greatbatch from the Isle of Man International Business School who reintroduced me to the academic scene in my early forties after many years in the entrepreneurial wilderness and who guided me through my professional qualifications with the Chartered Institute of Marketing and Chartered Management Institute. I would also like to thank Sam Sloan, my mentor at the Learning and Performance Institute, who taught me how to share my knowledge with impact.

I extend my thanks to David Bird, my Master's course leader at Manchester Metropolitan University and my other tutors and mentors including Jeff McCarthy, Brendan Keegan, Dr David Atkinson, Professor Cathy Urquhart and Dr David Chaffey. I would also like to thank Lily Barton, my Master's Dissertation supervisor, who skilfully guided me through every step of my research and kept me on track. A huge "Thank You" to Professor Jenny Rowley, my PhD Supervisor, whose insights, guidance and encouragement helped me extend and refine my ideas into a concise solution to the problem that's been bugging me for years.

I am truly grateful to the 25 entrepreneurs and micro-business owners spread throughout the Isle of Man, Jersey and Guernsey, who so generously and willingly gave up their time, shared their frustrations and reminded me of some of the serious challenges we face, as we venture into the unknown world of entrepreneurship. University ethics and data protection preclude me from naming them, but I can honestly say that without their frank and candid input we would not have discovered — nor been able to articulate — the very real marketing challenges entrepreneurs and micro-business owners face in the 21st century.

I would like to thank June Stead and the team at Jersey Business and Tony Brassell and the team at Startup Guernsey who pulled out all the stops to help me identify suitable interview candidates back in December 2014 when everybody else was thinking about Christmas. Their willingness to take up the challenge to help some bloke they'd never heard of from the Isle of Man identify ideal research candidates with tenacious enthusiasm is very much appreciated, as were the facilities they provided for a student on a limited budget! Their help and support before, during and after our visit in January 2015 was a major contribution, not just to my Master's dissertation, but also to this book — and for that I will be forever grateful.

My gratitude also extends to the many government officials and associated experts in the Isle of Man, Jersey, Guernsey and the UK who generously gave their time and insights to help me understand the full picture from both sides of the fence. All of whom in one way, shape, or form contribute to the supporting ecosystem that helps nurture small businesses and builds a strong modern economy.

I would also like to thank my book production team including: Simon Barron, my structural editor, Michelle Dotter, my copy editor, and Rob Attree who painstakingly proof read every single word of the final manuscript and checked every dot and comma before we went to print. My thanks also go to my good friends, Dick and Anna Horsnell, who diligently proof read my early manuscript and who provided continual support over many years — way beyond the limits of this project. I would also like to thank my advanced reading team for their feedback and a big "Thank You" to Daren Ward of Forward Marketing whose knowledge of marketing, artistic flair and technical skills were critical to producing the final book.

I'd like to also extend my thanks to my close friends and family who got used to me saying "I'm not going out tonight because I have to work on my book" over the last two years, but were always there in the background to support me through life's ups and downs. And, of course, to Oksana, my harshest critic and soul mate, whose tenacious attention to detail and willingness to challenge me every step of the way pushed me to make this book the best I possibly could.

I could not finish without saying a special "Thank You" to Dr Rod Stables and his team at the Liverpool Heart and Chest Hospital who literally saved my life, not just once, but twice. Being diagnosed with a potentially killer heart disease is one thing, but being given a second chance to make a bigger contribution somehow makes it all the more worthwhile.

Finally I'd like to thank you, my readers. I sincerely hope the 21st Century Marketing System and the rest of the knowledge shared in these pages helps you master the art and science of modern marketing. I also hope one day we will meet in person. In the meantime, please check out our website www.21stCentury. Marketing where you can access other resources mentioned in this book and keep up to date with the latest developments, as we continue to discover and share new ways to help you build your business and turn opportunity into reality.

The journey continues...

Contents

Introduction

"It's time to go," Jim said in a soft, but firm tone, as he returned his coffee cup precisely to its saucer.

I accidentally nudged the leg of the tiny blood-red bistro table as I stood up, more as a reflex to his voice than a conscious response to his command. Cold brown liquid vomited from my cup, splattering the innocent white tablecloth that had been my sole focus for the last twenty minutes. Am I really THAT nervous? Clearly! In truth, I'd been shaking for days — or was it weeks? — as the inevitable dreaded day approached. And now it was time to face the music. Things had started badly and were about to get a whole lot worse.

Inside the banker's lair, I waited nervously for my fate. Mr Cleason purposefully marched toward us; a tall, well-built, stocky and formidable character who could have captained any rugby team. Introductions, pleasantries, a bone-crushing handshake and with a powerful, yet eloquent wave of his arm, directed us to the door of the small office in the corner. We were directed to sit on the opposite side of the small oak desk. Two versus one — but there was no competition. My heart raced, my palms were sweaty and my throat was as dry as a bone. I wanted to run, but the wall of muscle was guarding my escape.

"Well," boomed Cleason, "I guess things aren't looking good, if you've brought your accountant with you!"

"No", I croaked. "I...I...I..." I painfully stuttered but failed to get a word out, before Jim thankfully interrupted and took over.

"I have advised my client to cease trading, as his company is now insolvent," he announced, his tone so very matter-of-fact he could have been ordering another coffee.

Jim had been my accountant for about two months and I'd had more sound advice and help in that time than the last accountant had given me in the previous two years. Jim could make an unintelligible set of accounts tell a human story with ease and finesse — which was what he was doing right now. But as good as he was, he could not avert the inevitability of this meeting or its outcome. It was far too late for that.

"I see," Cleason replied. "Well, we'd better..." and I honestly don't recall hearing the rest. It's almost as if I wasn't there. I heard the voices. I saw the indulgent smiles and impatient gestures. I saw them both making notes. But I didn't hear a word.

How had it come to this? It was such a great plan. The builders who bought the software package I'd spent over two years developing were delighted; we had a nice small office in a converted farmyard; and I had a salesman — well, sort of. Two years before, everything was set to go and the future looked so rosy. Even Mr Cleason had approved my plan and "was happy to provide the facility" I'd requested. Of course, there was just the small matter of signing the personal guarantees. "Standard practice, you understand."

I'm not sure which frightened me most. Was it the excruciating embarrassment of failing in my first business venture — the loss of face after telling anyone who would listen what a wonderful idea it was? Or was it the shame of having no income and struggling to survive and put food on the table? Letting down my friends and family who had lent me money to chase my dreams? How could I face them? And what of the future? Decades of repaying my now very real mountain of debt? The prospect of having to declare myself bankrupt and suffering the public humiliation that followed? Or losing our home and having nowhere for my young family to live? What would become of us? What would, could, or should I do next?

My head was ready to explode as I tried to make sense of all these nagging questions. And it was all down to my failure. I wasn't feeling sorry for myself — not entirely — but I did feel overwhelmed by the enormity of it. I was beyond exhausted — way beyond. I'd worked so hard for so long... and for what?

Cleason's booming voice brought me back into the room. "That's the formalities dealt with. You'll be hearing from our securities department in due course to arrange liquidation of the assets and settlement of the debt. All I need right now is for you to sign here and, of course, I'll need your chequebooks and cards returned immediately so I can freeze your accounts." He offered me a toothy, unfeeling smile. Like a shark.

"Of course," I replied submissively.

And like a shark, having nibbled at the carcass of what was left of my dreams, he granted my escape with one more knuckle-crushing handshake. "We'll be in touch," his parting shot.

The dazzling light blinded me as I stepped back onto the street. But there were no paparazzi with their flashing guns to capture my moment of doom; just the intense rays of the summer sun, interrupted by the leaves gently dancing in the breeze. People all around me were going about their usual daily business. For them, it was another beautiful summer's day, but not for me. Today, I became a government statistic. I was now officially one of the many start-up micro-business owners who fail within the first two years. Friggin' great! At least I'd achieved something! The 4th July 1990 was a day I would — and could — not forget.

"Everything happens for a reason, Chris," Jim said cheerfully, clapping me on the shoulder. A gesture, in other circumstances, that might have been congratulatory. It was something he'd told me many times in the last two months. "And remember what I said: you might have some of the skills you need to run a business, but you need to gain an understanding of bookkeeping and marketing before you have another go."

Another go! After what I'd just been through? You have GOT to be kidding!

Deep down, I guess I knew it wasn't the end, but it sure as hell felt like it!

"I'll give you a call when I've made an appointment with the Insolvency Practitioner and then we can discuss the bankruptcy route." We shook hands and he headed back to his office, leaving me alone on the side of the street.

Fast forward a quarter of a century and I'm sat in seat 14B in the second row at the Bridgewater Hall in Manchester. "If you can quietly move to the right of the stage", the usher whispered, directing us to join the diminishing queue. I rose to join my fellow students, also decked out in cap and gown. I stood in the darkness in front of the steps, calmly waiting for my call to mount the stage for my handshake of triumph.

"OK, you can go now," whispered the usher, as the announcement came: "Vice Chancellor, may I present to you Christopher Anthony Kent, Master of Science in Digital Marketing Communications — with Distinction!"

The Vice Chancellor's enthusiastic handshake accompanied his warm smile — the exact opposite to Cleason's all those years before. I was no longer a failure, but a specialist in my field.

The audience politely responded with the customary applause. A quick glance to the auditorium and a wave at the camera and then I was trying not to fall down the dimly lit steps on the other side of the stage, having stupidly left my glasses in the car.

During the intervening years, I'd taken Jim's advice. Some great teachers and amazing mentors guided me to my fair share of well-deserved successes and, of course, I'd also had the inevitable failures along the way.

The Internet was taking over the world — well, kind of — and new opportunities were leaping out from around every corner. How was technology going to change the face of marketing? There were many questions, much speculation, a huge amount of stubbornness, but no real answers.

At the turn of the century, no one really knew how to use the emerging phenomenon of the Internet as a marketing tool. A rapidly growing band of "self-proclaimed experts" were quick to offer their "training solutions" to becoming an "Internet marketing guru". These early adopters fed the hungry masses at weekend seminars, where they'd reveal their "secrets" in exchange for a few thousand pounds/dollars a seat.

These events usually turned into "pitch fests" for more training by other slick "experts" with an equally highly polished sales pitch, claiming to hold the key to a different part of the new Internet marketing puzzle. All promised the world, but the picture always remained stubbornly incomplete, as they peddled the same old nonsense.

With the benefit of hindsight, this era was akin to one massive digital Ponzi scheme, run by a bunch of digital snake oil salesmen.

Einstein said, "Insanity is doing the same thing over and over but expecting different results." By the summer of 2007, it was time to quit the asylum.

Enough was enough! There had to be a better way. I just had to find it.

And find it I did — through a more formal and academic approach to digital marketing enlightenment, which finally led to seat 14B.

Today, as I write these pages, further advances in technology have created an even bigger, global digital skills shortage. Digital marketing skills are in huge demand. Many of my fellow Digital Marketing Masters have already been tempted by large corporates with deep pockets to work on exciting, cutting-edge projects.

But what about those poor souls at the bottom of the digital marketing food chain? People like John, Nigel and Angela and the other twenty-two micro-business owners I'd interviewed during my Master's research project. They had all started their own businesses and were struggling to make sense of their modern marketing challenges. Who was going to show them the way?

Every single one of them had told me, "If I only knew how it all fits together and how I can apply it to my business, life would be so much easier." And they were right. The very harsh reality is that entrepreneurs and micro-business owners must also be their own marketing managers. Consequently, they need their own set of marketing skills, fit for today's marketing environment — and therein lies the problem! The vast majority just don't have anywhere near the level of marketing skills they need, if they're to avoid humiliation at the hands of their own Mr Cleasons.

What entrepreneurs and micro-business owners actually need is a simple and practical solution to this complex problem. A solution that empowers them to make the right decisions for their business and avoid falling prey to the myriad of digital snake oil salesmen out there, who promise the world and deliver very little.

That's where the 21st Century Marketing System I've developed over the last two years, to use in my own business, comes in. You see, as an entrepreneur and micro-business owner myself, I'm not interested in anything that doesn't directly contribute to helping me achieve my business goals. What I am interested in is what's relevant, applicable, realistic and practical to helping me develop and refine my own marketing strategies and tactics to build my business today. Strategies that get results by turning opportunity into reality — and reality into profit. Had I known nearly 30 years ago what I know now, my 4th July back in 1990 would have been just as beautiful as everybody else's.

My purpose in writing this book is to help entrepreneurs and micro-business owners — the heroes of the modern economy — get to grips with the complex world of modern marketing and compete on an equal footing with the "big boys". I want to help everyday heroes like John, Nigel, Angela and the millions like them up and down the country, who risk everything and put their neck on the line in pursuit of their goals and dreams. Their biggest challenge, without doubt, is to master and apply the art and science of modern marketing to their business. Why? Because marketing is so very fundamental to everything we do in business. It determines our success and ultimately defines our fate.

The 21st Century Marketing System is a leading edge, yet simple and comprehensive flexible marketing framework, designed to guide you through every step of your own modern marketing journey, to get the results you deserve. Most importantly, it's a system that's easy to use and addresses the real business and marketing challenges of the twenty-first century.

Its primary purpose is to give you that "helicopter view" and a solid grounding in all the things that actually matter in the micro-business marketing context. The 21st Century Marketing System is the complete picture and is shown in figure 1.1.

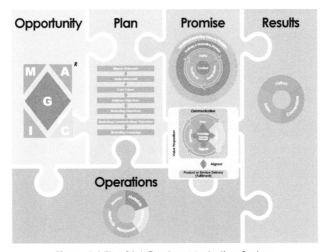

Figure 1.1 The 21st Century Marketing System

Don't worry if it looks a bit complicated, or if you don't understand it. At this stage, you're not expected to!

There are five parts to the jigsaw and, as we progress through the book, we'll examine each one in turn. We'll pull them apart, examine them in detail and build them back up, so you have a good understanding of exactly what 21st Century Marketing is, why it matters and how to use it. I'll even give you a set of tools you can use to apply the system to your particular business context, regardless of which industry or sector you're in.

The 21st Century Marketing System is the simple solution to the complex modern marketing problems every entrepreneur and micro-business owner faces in our complex, inter-connected and technically driven modern world.

This system will help you create and update your business and marketing plans, to secure the resources you need from your own Mr Cleasons. You'll also discover what the modern marketing landscape really looks like, why the old methods no longer work, how you can take advantage of it and leave your competitors in the dust. We'll examine digital marketing and social media and how to use modern marketing tools to promote your business and build a loyal band of happy customers.

Whether you want to start your own business, or you've been trading for a while, the information in these pages will tell you everything you need to know to succeed in the 21st Century.

If you're now flicking through this book trying to decide whether or not to take it to the checkout, perhaps one of the biggest benefits within these pages will persuade you. If you want to know how hugely successful businesses generate lots of cash through "word-of-mouth", we'll cover that, too — step-by-step.

My hope is that this book will serve as an invaluable guide and trustworthy companion, as you build your business, take it to the next level and achieve your business goals.

So let's get started!

Why it matters

Your 21st Century Marketing Journey Starts Here

There are three sections to this book, each one designed to deliver on the promises made in the title: WHAT 21st Century Marketing IS, WHY it matters, and HOW to do it.

We'll start by explaining WHY 21st Century Marketing matters, because if you have an appreciation of the challenges you face in marketing your business in the twenty-first century, the reasons WHY we need a whole new approach become crystal clear. We'll then take a detailed look at the five elements of the 21st Century Marketing System — the WHAT — before explaining HOW you can apply them in your business context.

Sound good? OK! Let's crack on.

The New World Order -
WHY 21st Century Marketing Matters:

There are essentially three reasons why twenty-first century marketing matters, and these are the result of:

1. *Changes in the ENVIRONMENT brought about by the rapid rise of the Internet and how it has infiltrated every aspect of our daily lives.*

2. *Changes in TECHNOLOGY, which allow us to take advantage of everything the Internet has to offer.*

3. *The resulting changes in peoples' BEHAVIOUR, and consumer behaviour in particular.*

The New World Order

All this has made the world a very exciting and, some would say, much smaller place, as barriers are broken down and we embrace the global society we now live in.

Let's take a quick trip down memory lane and just remind ourselves how we got to where we are today...

A Brief History of Modern Marketing

The "Good Old Days"

Once upon a time there was no such thing as the Internet. There was no Facebook, no email, no websites, no online banking and no instant messaging service. In fact, when I started my career back in 1984, we didn't even have PC's or mobile phones. I bought my first PC — an Amstrad 1640 with 640K RAM and a 20MB hard disk — in 1987 and I had to wait until 1993 to buy my very first mobile phone — which was only any use in a few highly populated areas covered by the emerging network.

When I started my first business in 1986, I had very few marketing channels available to me compared to what we have today. Back then, the emphasis was on advertising and promoting my product, to sell as many 'units' as possible. Placing adverts in newspapers, magazines and trade journals was very expensive for a small start-up business. Particularly when I was competing with much larger companies, who could afford to pay a premium to place their adverts in the prime locations. This meant my ads were often relegated to the lesser read pages deeper in the publication. They could also afford to complement their print ads with TV and radio advertising — which was way beyond my budget. Their advertising budgets allowed them to shout, whereas mine barely bought me a whisper.

Hiring an exhibition stand at trade shows was also very time-consuming and hugely expensive, especially when accommodation, travel and other costs were added to the bill. Then there were the endless hours of "telephone bashing" following up "hot" prospects after the show and, of course, the endless trips up and down the country trying to close deals.

I also spent a fortune on direct marketing, sending out literally thousands of sales letters trying to promote my product. Finally, public relations (PR) was the last tool in the toolbox where I invested hundreds of hours trying to get free exposure for my business in relevant magazines and trade journals. It was very expensive and very time-consuming.

And for what? The reality was the greatest "share of voice" was always awarded those who had the biggest marketing budgets — not the best products. I was constantly drowned out by the larger companies who simply threw more money at their marketing campaigns than I could ever dream of. The power was truly in the hands of those with deep pockets. It was simply a case of the more money you had, the louder you could shout at your target audience, by buying more print ads, billboard space, TV and radio airtime — and sending out tons of direct mail.

Back then, marketer's focus was on selling their products and/or services — not the customer — and for that they needed to interrupt their target audience, to tell them what they had to offer. This is referred to as a product (or sales) orientation and can be traced back to the late 1800s.

The Old Broadcast Paradigm

This one-way communication model is referred to as the Old Broadcast Paradigm as it relies on marketers bombarding their target audience with as many messages (typically adverts) as they can get their hands on. The problem is that it does not give the recipient of the message the opportunity to have a conversation, at least in marketing terms, and this is a big difference with how things are today. The Old Broadcast Paradigm is represented by the model shown in figure 1.2.

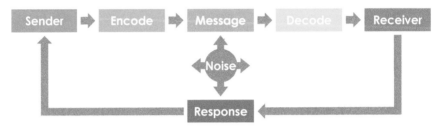

Figure 1.2 The Old Broadcast Paradigm

The essence of this model is that the marketer (sender) creates (encodes) a message and then sends that message via some means, be it advertising in the press, direct mail, or through some other broadcast means such as TV or radio. When it's received, the recipient (receiver) has to interpret (decode) the message to discover its meaning. If they interpret it correctly (i.e. as the sender intended) and if it resonates with them (i.e. it's relevant), they may take the action (response) suggested by the message sender (the marketer). That message has to be heard over and above all the other messages in the marketplace (the noise). It is, therefore, important that the receiver decodes the message as the sender (or encoder) intended, in order for the message to be understood and, hence, "heard".

In this example, the marketer is only able to measure the effectiveness of the message by the actual response received. This is typically measured by the number of sales or replies to the message — be it a direct marketing piece or advertising campaign. There is no mechanism for the recipient of the message to provide any kind of feedback, other than to place an order, buy the product, or request an information pack. Therefore, to a large extent, the marketer is working blind, just going by "gut feel", or being guided by experience. It's no wonder marketing is sometimes referred to as a "black art"!

What this Means to Micro-Business Owners

Starting a business is hugely risky and if you do not have the resources to have a fair crack of the marketing whip, then you really should not start. Why? Because if you don't know how to design, create and execute an effective, coordinated marketing campaign then you could be burning cash on adverts and other marketing tactics faster than you ever thought possible.

I certainly did!

Thank You Sir Tim!

Whilst I was happily playing on my Amstrad 1640, a lot of seriously clever technical stuff was going on in the background and the first commercial Internet Service Provider (ISP), known as "The World", was introduced in 1989. That was the "technical bit", but it wasn't very usable. Not until Tim Berners-Lee, a micro-business founder and later a CERN scientist, developed a hypertext system, known as HTML in 1990. This was the first graphical interface and it opened up a new world of opportunity because it made it easy for ordinary people to communicate with technology. To use a historical analogy, it was the Internet equivalent of inventing the wheel. He revealed the first website to the world on 6th August 1991 and is credited with inventing the Internet — the World Wide Web (WWW) — as we know it today. In 1993, CERN released the Web to the public, thus making it available to the masses.

The Queen gave Berners-Lee a knighthood in recognition for his "services to the global development of the Internet" on 16th July 2004 and the rest, as they say, is history. Incidentally, Sir Tim put in an appearance during the opening ceremony of the London 2012 Olympics which celebrated great British achievements and the scale and importance of Sir Tim's contribution to the development of the Information Age should not be underestimated. Incidentally, he also continues to steer the development of the worldwide web.

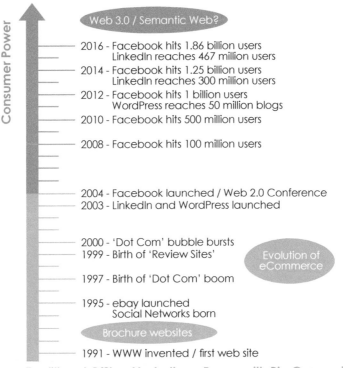

Figure 1.3 The Evolution of the World Wide Web

The Power Shift

The marketing landscape has changed significantly in the last quarter of a century and we have witnessed a massive shift in power. We are now in an era where the power has been taken away from the marketer and is well and truly in the hands of the consumer. There are a number of key events that have led us to where we are today — but how exactly did it happen?

When the Web was first developed, the physical infrastructure was extremely slow and had yet to be developed. It used the standard (and some would argue ancient) traditional copper telephone line with a modem. I still remember driving up the motorway in 1996 to get my hands on one of the latest high-speed 33.6K portable modems as soon as they were released. It was a far cry from the fibre optic network and 4G mobile broadband we take for granted today!

Figure 1.3 identifies some of the key events that shaped the modern marketing landscape. It's worth spending just a few minutes discussing this history, because it has a significant impact on how we — as modern marketers — have to change our behaviour to respond to consumers' new demands, if we are to maximise our opportunities in the twenty-first century.

As the Internet became more popular, more websites went online, but the technology was still very limited and hence restrictive. What really happened in the early days was that print brochures were put online to create brochure websites, if for no other reason than they were easy to keep up-to-date and represented a healthy cost saving over traditional print, whilst still maintaining current and accurate information. That was the primary benefit of companies' websites; it was just another one-way communication channel and this saw the birth of what we could term the "brochure website era".

It didn't take too long for things to develop and eCommerce really started to take shape around 1995 when eBay was launched. This was the first real step in putting the power of the Internet into the hands of the consumer because eBay allowed individuals to trade with other individuals. It was a "peer-to-peer" trading platform allowing anybody to sell anything to anyone—conceivably anywhere in the world (as long as they had a PC and an Internet connection, of course!) At around the same time, social networks started to spring up (Geocities (1994), TheGlobe (1995), and SixDegrees (1997)). These gave consumers and individuals the opportunity to communicate with each other, again without restrictions or physical barriers.

The subsequent flurry of activity saw a huge rise in the use of the Internet, particularly as technology advanced at an exponential rate. 1997 saw the birth of the Dot-Com boom, and many entrepreneurs persuaded investors to part with huge amounts of cash to "get in early" with this new trend of buying online. This further fuelled the development of the Internet and the evolution toward eCommerce was in full swing. But there was a problem. In fact, there were several problems.

Many of the early Internet entrepreneurs did not fully appreciate the need for the traditional back-office infrastructure and assumed that the Internet was the "be all and end all" to all their problems. In reality, the Internet was a means to reduce part of their marketing budget (and hence cost base) by being more efficient with their front-end activities. Struggling companies needed more investment and began to fail. This created lack of trust in the Internet as a marketplace and, around 1999, Review Sites were born. This gave disgruntled Internet-based consumers the opportunity to share their frustrations and poor experiences with other members of the Internet community, by leaving reviews on independent review sites.

The importance of these review sites was that they were truly independent and could be trusted because they were unbiased. Entrepreneurial characters started creating sites to review pretty much anything; one early review site I remember subscribing to many years ago reviewed "business opportunities", a.k.a. get-rich-quick schemes (or scams). Sadly, the business opportunity seekers market was riddled with schemes and scams, whereby the opportunity providers got rich by selling their "opportunity" to the opportunity seekers, who all too frequently didn't make any money from their investment.

Not all were bad; there were some genuine business opportunity providers out there, but they were all tainted by the less scrupulous operators. This meant that if you were looking for a business opportunity, it was very difficult to separate the good from the bad. An independent review site gave members the opportunity to share their experience for all to see and gradually the scammers could be exposed before you wasted — err, invested — your hard-earned cash into their retirement fund.

Trust was a key factor and obviously a highly valued commodity. Many companies started to suffer due to their inability to gain customer trust. In around the year 2000, the Dot-Com bubble burst and there were many high-profile casualties; Boo.com, an online fashion retailer, and Pets.com, to name just two.

One of eBay's early critical success factors was its ability to build trust within the system, by encouraging honest feedback between buyers and sellers and making it available for all to see. The system was supervised and overseen by eBay themselves and, where necessary, they also acted as arbitrators in resolving disputes. "Feedback" was a key element of eBay's success; buyers and sellers could leave feedback based on their trading experiences and the higher your score, the more trustworthy you were (and the same still applies today).

Technology continued to advance after the Dot-Com bubble burst and the Internet took a significant turn, as entrepreneurs saw the opportunity for sharing information. LinkedIn was born in 2003 and Facebook launched in 2004. These social media platforms allowed Internet users to socialise and freely communicate with each other. They chatted and shared information about themselves on a dedicated platform that was specifically designed to facilitate peer-to-peer communication. This was a huge step forward in facilitating global communication at a personal level — not least because it was FREE!

It's also worth noting that WordPress was launched in 2003. This is an Open Source project that created a platform originally designed for blogging. This put a huge amount of power into consumers' hands, as they could literally write as much as they liked about anything that took their fancy on their own dedicated blogs. Think review sites on steroids!

WordPress also allowed users to create their own websites and, hence, also put some of the development capability into the hands of "the man on the street" — the average Internet user. Coding was no longer just for the technically elite. Just over a decade later, WordPress was by far one of the most influential and largest platforms for developing websites and blogs on the Internet. Being an Open Source platform, it did not suffer from the highs and lows of commercialism (although there is a commercial aspect to it). Basically, being Open Source means it is developed by a community of like-minded people — rather than a commercial enterprise — for the good of the community it serves; it is therefore a philanthropic project. Many contributors participate in developing the platform merely for the fun of it and the feeling of satisfaction that comes from helping others.

In 2004, the first "Web 2.0" conference was held and I suppose you could say that led to the prolific rise of social media, which encouraged user participation and communication using Internet-based technologies. Now, here's the thing. When you put the power of communication into the hands of the individual and give them the tools to express their views, they grasp it with both hands and willingly spend hours sharing their points of view on any number of topics — especially the products and services they buy both online and offline. And that includes the products and services they buy from you!

Over the last decade, review sites and social media platforms have developed and matured. They are now an established part of the decision-making process (key point) and an essential part of the eCommerce trading lifestyle (another key point). For example, when you're looking for a new product, such as a new smart phone, it's no longer sufficient just to believe what the manufacturers or retailers say about their wonderful new gadget. There is an increasing probability that consumers will also seek out the views of other consumers and find out what their experiences were like, before committing to purchase the product. Think about this for a second. What do you do? Do you check things out online before you part with your cash, or do you blindly believe everything the seller tells you?

This is hugely significant, because it is other consumers who now have the loudest voice — via social media and review sites — and it is they who can influence potential customers far more effectively than the manufacturers and retailers themselves, no matter how clever their marketing departments or the size of their marketing budgets. This is a seismic shift!

The implication here is that, over the last decade or so, the power of influence has shifted from marketers to consumers. This has significantly changed the way that marketers need to behave. It is no longer acceptable to ignore the voice of even the smallest vocal customers. Why? Because they can influence the decision-making process of many of your potential customers — and this can have a significant impact on your business.

But it doesn't stop there. By 2008, Facebook had 100 million users worldwide, half a billion users by 2010, 1 billion users by 2012, 1.25 billion users by 2014, and a massive 1.86 billion by the end of 2016. That's nearly a quarter of the population of Planet Earth! This prolific rise in the use of social media by individuals consolidated consumer power. Wherever you look, somebody somewhere has something to say about pretty much everything — and they will probably post their thoughts on Facebook. It is impossible to escape the Facebook effect! As a company, you may not even use Facebook, but Facebook (and other social media and review sites) will have an impact on your business. Someone somewhere will mention your product or service in the social sphere and there's not a damn thing you can do about it. Your only defence is to behave in a way that encourages them to say positive, not negative, things about you and your business.

Social media has the power to make or break a brand (literally) overnight. If people love what you do, it's great! When they can't stop talking about you because you've done a great job or have a fantastic product, this generates your ultimate marketing tool: positive word-of-mouth. But if they don't like what you do and the keyboard warriors take to social media, you could have a crisis on your hands quicker than you can log into your Twitter account.

The only way for businesses to keep pace and stand some chance of gaining a little of the power back, is to consistently monitor what goes on in the social media sphere. This is hugely resource intensive, requires a big budget, takes a lot of time and requires a particular set of skills, many of which do not exist in most small and medium-sized companies.

By 2012, there were over 16 million WordPress blogs on the Internet. People were embracing the chance to express themselves at every opportunity. Blogging also became big business because, as a company, if you can get somebody to write a positive blog post about your product or service, they could potentially influence a large number of people who could become your customers. Social media, blogging and video-based websites, such as YouTube and Vimeo, were all rising in popularity as technology advanced at an ever-increasing rate. Smart phones and tablets allow users to access these new platforms 24/7 and share their thoughts and post comments whilst on the move during the day. They no longer have to wait until they get home in the evening to fire up their PC before posting what they think online for the world and his dog to see.

Whilst many of the social media platforms focus on the consumer market, business social networks, such as LinkedIn, also became more and more popular. By 2014, LinkedIn had over 300 million users worldwide; by the end of 2016 this had risen to 467 million. Now that's a huge business network! And if you're in the B2B marketplace, this is a platform you cannot afford to ignore.

The only way forward for the enlightened marketing professional — or anybody involved in marketing, for that matter, including entrepreneurs and micro-business owners — is to engage with this new process or be left out in the cold.

In recent years, we have seen the power of social media in action and how it can change global events. For example, the Arab Spring is one example where tens, if not hundreds of thousands of people were mobilised and encouraged to demonstrate and, hence, change the political landscape of their country. Whilst we as individual entrepreneurs and micro-business owners may not be able to use social media to such a great extent, we cannot ignore its power, in terms of its ability to reach and influence our target audience.

We will talk more about exactly how to harness the power of social media a little later, but for now, I hope you have an appreciation of how technology has achieved a seismic shift in stealing the power to influence away from the marketers with huge budgets and placing it firmly in the hands of the consumer.

This really has levelled the playing field. As an entrepreneur or micro-business owner, it should be music to your ears. The big corporates have lost their power over the consumers and this has opened a fantastic opportunity for entrepreneurs and micro-business owners with limited budgets. By learning to harness the power of digital marketing and social media, individual entrepreneurs and micro-business owners can engage with large audiences right across the globe and compete with the "big boys" on equal terms. All they need are the skills, resources and desire to be able to do it. The tools are already there and, for the most part, free to use.

No longer does the massive marketing budget directly equate to maximum influence. This means that the "one-man band" can compete on equal terms with multinationals and global competitors on an equal footing. Why? Because it is the consumer that decides what and who to believe and they have the whole world at their fingertips to help them decide. They can now choose who they listen to and how to react to the information they are provided with. To buy or not to buy — THAT is the question! To a greater extent consumers now create the "noise", not marketers. Therefore, it is becoming more and more important that you focus on generating both online and offline positive word-of-mouth for your business using all channels at your disposal, including digital and social media.

So how do we do it?

Rather than keep interrupting our target audience at random points in time, we need to ask them for their permission to respectfully present our offering, but this takes time. We are therefore more interested in starting and developing longer term, mutually beneficial relationships with our customers, because we want them to say nice things about us after they have used our product or service, because this will influence others who may become our prospects. It is most definitely not about make a sale, grabbing the cash and running off, never to be seen again. These days, it is all about making sure your customers have a great experience before, during and after the transaction takes place, because a positive experience usually generates positive word-of-mouth. It is also worth noting that as more people join the social sharing ecosystem, many feel they have to say something to maintain their online social status. Many will write the first thing that comes into their mind — whether it's good or bad. If you make them feel good, then you're in with a chance of a positive mention — which could tip other prospects' decision making scales in your favour. But if you make them feel bad — well...

Market Orientation

It is now all about the customer, not the product, so to be successful in modern marketing entrepreneurs and micro-business owners need to adopt what's known as a "market orientation". This is significantly different from the product orientation, because absolutely everything is focused on the customer and, hence, the customer's needs and wants take centre stage.

For some, this may seem like an obvious statement. However, the shift from a product orientation to a market orientation has been developing for many years. I guess you could say it's one of the evolutionary factors of modern marketing, encouraged by technological development and the adoption of the Internet as an integral means of communication.

In fact, a product orientation is incompatible with a market orientation, for the simple reason that they have different primary focuses. To put it bluntly, a company with a product orientation takes the view of, "We have these great products — who can we sell them to and how can we sell as many as possible?" By comparison, a company with market orientation asks questions like: "What is it that our customers need and want? What will they pay for? Do we have the resources and capability to provide what they want and serve them well?" Only then will the organisation develop a product tailored to meet the specific wants and needs of their ideal target customers. This often involves close contact with the customer during the development process, by getting feedback — a.k.a. two-way communication — as they can provide valuable insights both very early in and throughout the entire product development cycle.

Historically, in many organisations, the marketing department has either been part of, or played second fiddle to, the sales department because generating revenue —and hence profit — has been seen as the organisation's primary goal. As marketing has become more complex and the benefits of digital and social media marketing improve results, whilst cutting the traditional cost base, the role of marketing has been elevated to the "top table" and sits at the core of the business.

Respectful Interruption Initiates Permission Marketing

In a perfect world, your ideal customers will seek you out and naturally give you permission to start a long and mutually beneficial relationship. However, the world is seldom perfect and certainly in the initial stages, when nobody knows who you are, you have to resort to more traditional means, in order to create initial awareness for your product or service.

Therefore, at the very beginning of the relationship life cycle, we have to resort to techniques and tactics which are firmly embedded in the Old Broadcast Paradigm, because you must first "interrupt" your prospective customers, to encourage them to take note of what you have to say.

Advertising, telemarketing, unsolicited mail and email are the most common forms of interruption marketing; we see common examples all the time in newspapers, magazines, on television and on radio. The idea is that the marketer "interrupts" the natural flow, or pattern, of their target audience in order to create the initial awareness, by saying something like, "Hey, we just wanted to let you know we exist and here's a real cool product or service we offer that might be of interest to you!"

Now, because you want to build a relationship with members of your target audience, you must interrupt them in the manner that is respectful and quickly demonstrates the benefits of establishing a relationship with you. It should be appropriate to your offering and congruent with your brand values. For example, just standing up and shouting "SEX" at the top of your voice in the middle of a crowded post office is hardly appropriate behaviour to promote a special offer at your family-run coffee shop!

This interruption has a single purpose: to encourage members of your target audience to give you permission to start a relationship with them. That's it! Note I did not say "sell to them". Once you have permission to communicate with them, you can then move to the next phase, which is to start building the relationship in a way that's mutually beneficial.

In terms of digital marketing, gaining permission is most commonly done through an exchange, whereby members of your target audience give you permission to contact them by email. For example, you will give them a free report (or something else of value) in exchange for their email address and their permission to communicate with them on a regular basis. This is the second stage of engagement and it is, therefore, very important to build a database, or list, of members of your target audience who have given you permission to enter into some kind of relationship with them. Unfortunately, too many marketers abuse this permission by spamming their database on a daily basis, sending them a whole host of unrelated emails designed to sell just about anything they can get their hands on. This is a real shame, because it gives email marketing a bad name. I'm sure you are well aware of the irritations of having an inbox full of useless, uninteresting and irrelevant spam every time you open your email.

All content and, hence, all of our marketing messages, should be designed with a fixed purpose in mind. If it is to interrupt a prospect to gain permission to start a relationship, then that's one specific purpose (or aim)of a piece of communication. If it's to introduce a product or service to somebody who has only recently established a relationship with you, then you will probably speak to them slightly differently than if you'd been in a relationship with them for years. If you think of the relationship a business has with its customers in a similar vein to a personal relationship — for example, between a man and a woman — you won't go far wrong.

This serves as a very good basis on which to explain how the relationship develops and how your behaviour will change over time, as you build that relationship. Typically, the most successful, personal human relationships take time to develop and go through a number of steps; from initial introduction, to establishing rapport, developing some depth through conversations and ultimately to some form of long-term, mutually beneficial, rewarding interaction that both parties value and enjoy. You should make every effort to apply the principles of good, respectful relationship development in the personal world to the business world — especially online. Because at the end of the day, what we as entrepreneurs and micro-business owners are dealing with, is other (real) people. It's people who make up our target audience and it is people who consume our product, or service and relate to and connect with our brand.

This leads us onto to another key factor of relationship management: the personalisation of communication. If you know precisely who you're talking to, what their names are and what their interests are, you can talk to them on a far deeper, more personal level than if you're talking to a group of several hundred. We all want to be treated, and respected, as individuals. We give greater credence to those who treat us with respect. This, in turn builds trust, which is the cornerstone of every successful relationship, business or otherwise.

As a modern marketer, the importance of building meaningful, lasting relationships with your target audience cannot be over-emphasised. This should be the focus of all of your marketing communications; everything you do should contribute to building, maintaining, or enhancing your relationship with your target audience. The more personal these relationships can be, the more they are valued and, hence, the harder it is for them to be broken — which, in business terms, means your customers going to an alternative supplier. There is a direct business benefit here, because it is far more costly to acquire a new customer than to retain one. Therefore, everything you do should focus on retaining customers to maximise their lifelong value to your business.

Let me give you two examples: one where there is a long-term relationship opportunity and another that is short-term. It is quite appropriate for accountants to have an extremely long-term relationship with their clients, as they have a regular need for help with their accounting and tax administration process. The lifelong value of an accountancy client could be many thousands of pounds and last several years. By comparison, if your product or service is something that the customer will consume once, and only once, then their lifetime value could be significantly shorter. An example might be the service provided by a luxury hotel in a remote holiday destination, you know you're only ever going to visit once in your lifetime.

Now, bearing in mind that your ultimate objective in terms of marketing is to get people talking about your business, brand, products and the services you provide, you want to leave a lasting impression on everybody who has any kind of experience with your business. This creates the greatest opportunity to encourage them to talk about their experience and recommend you to their friends, colleagues, and other associates, thereby generating ongoing word-of-mouth, which results in new (free) customers for your business.

You must, therefore, view the relationship as starting way before you actually acquire the customer and finishing well after the customer has stopped using your product or service. You should be continually looking for ways to promote your business through word-of-mouth. I, therefore, encourage you to seriously think about how you can enhance the relationship with your customers and your target audience, at every step of their journey with your business and your brand.

This is what's meant by placing the customer at the centre of everything you do. Building relationships is central to the concept of a market orientation.

So when and how do you respectfully interrupt them to ask for their permission to start a relationship?

The Zero Moment of Truth

Search engines know exactly when you should interrupt your target audience because it is the precise moment they tell you they are ready to listen to what you have to say. Google define this as the "zero moment of truth" and it occurs when the consumer tells you precisely what they are looking for when they type a search phrase into the search box. This is the single most important change in consumer behaviour in the last decade.

Advances in technology, particularly mobile, have made information much more accessible and, more importantly, available whenever consumers demand it. I'm sure many reading this book have either a smart phone or tablet connected to the Internet within an arm's length for 90 to 95% of their waking hours, 365 days a year!

Access to the Internet via mobile devices has literally put a world of information at the fingertips of hundreds of millions of people. When humans need to make decisions, particularly purchasing decisions, it's natural to search for information to ensure the decision they're about to make is the right decision in any given situation. Before the proliferation of the Internet, consumers used to go into retail stores and speak to the sales staff and product specialists to gather information about any particular product. Printed material such as product specification sheets and brochures also played a large part in information research, as did other sources including friends, colleagues, or specialist publications such as Which? The important thing is that the store was probably the first port of call in the information gathering process. Nowadays, the first port of call is most likely a search engine, such as Google, Yahoo, Bing, or YouTube.

Stimulus ➡ First Moment of Truth (Shelf) ➡ Second Moment of Truth (Experience)

Figure 1.4 The First and Second Moment of Truth

Marketers go to enormous lengths to understand how their consumers behave and, many years ago, Procter & Gamble identified a three-step process they claimed all buyers went through. These are: stimulus, shelf, and experience as shown in figure 1.4. Consumers would initially have some kind of stimulus, such as seeing an advert on TV or in a magazine, which sparked some interest in a particular product. They would have followed this up with a trip to the store to speak to the salesperson and gather more detailed information before making a purchase decision. Traditionally, this was the first way marketers could influence the buying decision process.

Procter & Gamble called this the "first moment of truth". The final step in the process was when they consumed or used the product and would reflect on their experience. If it was positive, maybe they'd purchase again; if it was negative, they'd probably look for an alternative. Procter & Gamble called this the "second moment of truth". Consumers also tell their friends of their experiences, thereby generating either positive or negative word-of-mouth.

These three steps are still as important today as they were when Procter & Gamble first defined them several decades ago. However, there is now an additional step directly after the stimulus. It's becoming increasingly common for decisions to be made during the "zero moment of truth", as shown in figure 1.5, and there are many factors that can influence it, ranging from what the manufacturer and retailers have to say about the product, to what other consumers have said, by sharing their thoughts on the many review and social media sites across the Internet.

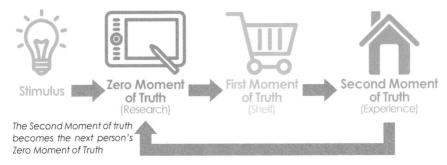

Figure 1.5 The Zero Moment of Truth

Here's an example of what really happens these days. You may receive a stimulus for a product during a commercial break whilst watching your favourite programme on TV. You reach for your smart phone, tablet, or laptop and go straight to Google and type the product or company name into the search box. Before the adverts have finished and your favourite programme comes back on, you've already checked out the manufacturer's website, several retailers' websites for price comparisons and skimmed several reviews on Amazon for the product you saw just a few moments earlier. Literally, within a matter of minutes, you have collated a significant amount of information and already formed an opinion, which may well shape your purchase decision without even getting out of your armchair!

Other stimuli could be when you notice an advert in a magazine or newspaper, on a billboard or the side of a bus, or just by good old-fashioned word-of-mouth when a friend of colleague tells you about a product they think you might be interested in. Whatever the stimulus, the next step in the information-gathering process is likely to involve a battery-powered device, rather than wearing out shoe leather walking to the nearest store.

Whilst this may be exceptionally cool for the user, it really does present an absolute nightmare for the marketer. If the marketer does not have some kind of presence at the "zero moment of truth", there is no way they can have any influence over the consumers' decision-making process. It is, therefore, absolutely critical to not only have an online presence, but ensure your online presence is visible to the consumer at the precise point they are looking for the information they require — i.e. the "zero moment of truth".

During my Master's research, it was reassuring that the majority of entrepreneurs and business owners I spoke to recognised the need for an online presence. In fact, one guy I interviewed expressed this most eloquently when he said, and I quote, "If you're not online, in my world you don't even exist!" What this essentially means is you simply must be online — 24/7. Many of my interviewees had a website and those who didn't at least had a Facebook page. However, that online presence is absolutely worthless in marketing terms if it is not presented at the "zero moment of truth". This was a vibrant source of frustration for everyone I interviewed, as their success at being present at the "zero moment of truth" ranged from limited to non-existent.

The best way to be present at the "zero moment of truth" is with your own website (rather than just relying on social media platforms), because this gives you far more power to influence the consumer during the "zero moment of truth" — particularly if you use a landing page which has been specifically designed to answer their specific questions at this crucial moment. Given that consumers search for information at this point in their decision-making journey, it stands to reason that having a search engine friendly website gives you the greatest opportunity to respond to their stimulus and hence influence their decision — preferably to use your solution to solve their problem!

This is why having a good appreciation of modern marketing and, in particular, digital marketing, is so important to the success of your business and why you absolutely must have an effective digital presence if you are to survive and prosper in the digital age.

Earlier I said that you need to interrupt your potential customers before you can gain permission to start building a relationship with them. Interrupting them by providing relevant information at the "zero moment of truth" is a very, very effective way of starting a mutually beneficial relationship by demonstrating the value you can offer — and that should be one of your primary modern marketing goals.

Just presenting your potential solution to their problem at the precise moment they are specifically looking for a solution, shows not only that you are listening to what they are saying, but you are prepared to take the necessary action to show them how your solution can improve their lives when it most matters to them. But be warned! This is a long-term investment and there are rarely "quick wins" when it comes to digital marketing, especially in the early stages. You absolutely must understand how this works in order to make the right decisions to build a meaningful and effective digital presence — at the very least, a search engine friendly website — to give your business the greatest chance of success.

It would be ideal if all our prospects just used a search engine when they wanted to find information — but they don't! They also ask their friends directly on social media platforms and many readily share information they feel may be of interest to their friends and contacts. This, in turn, can initiate a new stimulus and/or serve an informational need at the "zero moment of truth" from a trusted source.

The Old Broadcast Paradigm is no longer totally valid and I hope now you're beginning to see why merely attempting to just sell to your target audience is no longer sufficient. As consumers become more educated and, therefore, more demanding, you need to fully engage with them to satisfy their information and emotional needs and assist them in making the right decisions. For that, we need a new model and this is where the New Engagement Paradigm comes in.

The New Engagement Paradigm:
The Marketer's Secret Weapon in the Digital Age

The New Engagement Paradigm (see figure 1.6) consists of four elements: content, traditional marketing, digital marketing and social media. It is important to understand how this differs from the Old Broadcast Paradigm, which focuses on the sender broadcasting messages aimed at interrupting people to attract their attention. On the contrary, one of the most important success factors in modern marketing is to fully engage your target audience, so they voluntarily give you their attention. Their "attention" is a very precious commodity, something you need to work hard to get — and keep.

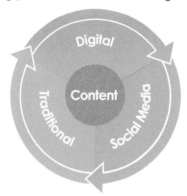

Figure 1.6 The New Engagement Paradigm

We'll discuss each element of the New Engagement Paradigm in a lot more detail when we look at the modern marketing landscape but, for now, a brief overview will suffice to start comparing it with the Old Broadcast Paradigm.

> *Effective marketing is all about getting the right message in front of the right audience at the right time using the right tools.*

Effective marketing is all about getting the right message in front of the right audience, at the right time, using the right tools. Your message(s) will be "wrapped" in your content and each piece of content will have a specific objective, which could be to create awareness, create some kind of exchange, or build your brand.

Delivering content that your target audience finds valuable is the secret to creating engagement, as this ultimately generates word-of-mouth — your primary goal. Therefore, content is placed at the very core of the New Engagement Paradigm. Everything you do will focus on creating messages that fully engage your target audience and satisfy their informational needs. What you say and how you say it depends on your particular situation.

Once you've created your message, you need to deliver it, so the outer layer focuses on "using the right tools". You need to use traditional, digital and social media tools (channels) to tell your target audience that this new content exists and where they can find it. Not all of your target audience will be in the same place at the same time and their "zero moment of truth" may happen whilst they are using different platforms. This means you will inevitably use a combination of tools to make sure your message is delivered appropriately. In marketing circles, this is known as "multi-channel marketing" and it's important because the advances in technology and changes in consumer behaviour demand your message be in multiple places if you want your voice to be heard far and wide. That pretty much sums up the challenge of modern marketing: creating this coherent, congruent omnipresence that delivers a consistent message across all platforms that is heard by as many of your target audience as possible.

The New Engagement Paradigm works very differently to the Old Broadcast Paradigm and is virtually impossible to turn off once the word is out. It is important to have your content at the core and then to use all the channels available to encourage your target audience to consume your content. This is because you want to build a long-term relationship with your customers and for that to happen effectively, you need to have permission to engage in a mutually beneficial relationship. You, therefore, have to convince them that you have something of value to offer on a regular basis which will justify them giving you their ongoing attention.

Search Engine Friendly Website

Now that you have a good appreciation of the modern marketing environment and an understanding of the events that led us to where we are today, the limitations of the Old Broadcast Paradigm should be evident. The need for a new approach to respond to these modern marketing challenges is addressed by the New Engagement Paradigm, as it lays the foundation for everything you need do to market your business in the twenty-first century.

The only way you can truly respond to the insatiable information demands of your target audience is to have a customer-focused marketing strategy, supported by a search engine friendly website that presents your solution to your prospects' problems at the all-important "zero moment of truth" and encourages them to willingly enter into a mutually beneficial relationship with your business and your brand.

Your search engine friendly website should be at the heart of your digital marketing strategy (see figure 1.7) and your digital marketing strategy should be a key component of your overall marketing strategy, which integrates your content into the two other key components of social media and traditional marketing.

Figure 1.7 The New Engagement Paradigm with Search Engine Friendly Website

What this Means to Micro-Business Owners

Entrepreneurs and micro-business owners must develop and optimise an effective digital presence, if they are to take advantage of this new level playing field and compete with their larger rivals on an equal footing. Being ready to service the informational needs of your target audience at the "zero moment of truth" is essential to initiating relationships at this optimal time and, hence, having a search engine friendly website is a critical success factor for your business.

So!

▲ How do you make sure you're found at your ideal customers' "zero moment of truth"?

▲ How exactly do you design a search engine friendly website from a strategic perspective — one that sits at the heart of your online marketing strategy and actually delivers results?

▲ How do you build a highly tailored marketing strategy that's absolutely perfect for your business?

▲ How exactly do you integrate traditional marketing with digital and social media to give a consistent message across all channels?

▲ How do you choose the right marketing tools and why are they appropriate for your business?

▲ And most importantly, how do you create that all-important. positive word-of-mouth and encourage your customers to become excited vocal advocates for your business and your brand?

I'm sure at least a few of these questions will be buzzing round inside your head and you'll probably also have many more.

Whether you're an experienced entrepreneur or business owner, or whether you're still planning your new business venture, you need a marketing plan that's fit for purpose. Your purpose. And that purpose is to support your business every step of the way.

My goal in this book is to help you build that all-important, rock-solid foundation for your business — whatever line of business or industry you're in. No two businesses are the same, hence no two business or marketing plans will ever be the same. But they will share many common elements and address many similar challenges along the way.

What you, and every business owner — existing or potential — needs is a bulletproof system to create a highly tailored marketing strategy and supporting marketing plan that plays to your strengths and minimises your weaknesses. A strategy that allows you to quickly and efficiently evaluate new opportunities and react swiftly to emerging threats, without wasting valuable time on lengthy re-planning exercises. A strategy that you can continually build on with ease and minimal effort — and, most importantly, that saves you time.

The 21st Century Marketing System helps you create that strategy step-by-step and easily keep it up-to-date. It takes you through the entire process from beginning to end, so by the end of this book, you'll understand how it all fits together and have a full and comprehensive set of proven tools to design and build your own 21st Century Marketing Blueprint specifically tailored to your business — and most importantly, tailored to your level of resources and skills.

You have already seen how the New Engagement Paradigm has replaced traditional broadcast marketing and how both technology and changes in consumer behaviour have changed the marketing landscape forever. We've also discussed how having a search engine friendly website that presents your solution at the "zero moment of truth" is an essential weapon in your modern marketing arsenal.

Where to find stuff in this book

Before we get too deep into this exciting journey, let me give you a quick heads up of what's in store and where to find it…

Section 1: 21st Century Marketing - Why It Matters

▲ One of the biggest mistakes novice marketers make is going straight for the sale. In the next chapter of this section you'll discover why building relationships with your prospects and customers is so vitally important in the twenty-first century. Building trust is a key element and an area where many novice marketers (and, surprisingly, many experienced marketers who should know better) just don't "get it". We'll cover the three-step formula to creating trust both online and offline and how to integrate this formula with all your online and offline marketing activity.

▲ There are so many tools out there that you could use to promote your business, it's all very confusing. Many entrepreneurs and micro-business owners just don't know where to start. In fact, this was a key finding from my Master's primary research. Every micro-business owner I interviewed — without exception — said if they knew what was available to them when they started out and why they should use it, it would have helped them to make far better decisions and, hence, save a lot of time, money and sheer frustration.

We'll take a detailed look at all the tools available to you at the end of Section 1, by which time you'll have a good understanding of precisely WHY 21st Century Marketing actually matters to every entrepreneur and micro-business owner, regardless of what business or industry they're in. We'll conclude by showing how these tools fit into the New Engagement Paradigm before we continue into Section 2 and the real "guts" of this book.

Section 2: 21st Century Marketing: What It Is

Section 1 sets us up nicely to get our teeth into the real "meat" of the 21st Century Marketing System which consists of five key elements:

1. the Opportunity
2. the Plan
3. the Promise
4. the Operations, and
5. the Results.

Each element has a dedicated tool, or set of tools, to help take you through the entire process step-by-step.

The 21st Century Marketing System Toolkit

1. **Opportunity:** The M.A.G.I.C. Marketing Matrix is a simple yet powerful and proven tool to help you think strategically about every aspect of your business. If you're already in business, it will help you analyse, audit

and evaluate your business without the need for expensive external consultants. This tool alone is "worth its weight in gold" and will help you see every aspect of your business from a new perspective.

If things aren't going well, it will help you identify the key areas you need to focus on. If things are going well, it will help you identify and take advantage of new opportunities without overstretching your limited resources. But what if you don't yet have a business but are currently thinking about starting one? Don't worry! The M.A.G.I.C. Marketing Matrix has been specifically designed to help you evaluate new opportunities and build a business to take advantage of them.

2. **Plan:** The Seven Point Plan helps you turn your strategy into realistic, practical and powerful marketing tactics. The Seven Point Plan also makes a major contribution to the design and development of your all-important search engine friendly website that puts your solution in front of your prospects at the "zero moment of truth".

What we entrepreneurs want is to get on with turning opportunity into reality, not keep talking about it. That's the purpose of the Seven Point Plan: to create a usable, coherent plan of action that sets out precisely what we need to do and start TODAY!

Not turned on by planning? Me neither! That's why the Seven Point Plan focuses on just the seven essential elements you need to make the 21st Century Marketing System work for you, in your situation, to achieve your goals.

3. **Promise:** The Value Proposition Communicator is a vital element of your marketing toolkit because every business needs to communicate its promise (or "Value Proposition") to their target audience.

Successful marketing is all about getting the right message (your promise) in front of the right audience, at the right time, using the right tools.

The second tool here is the Message Development Matrix; a simple yet efficient and effective tool designed to help you develop meaningful marketing messages that really "hit the spot". Making sure you deliver — and keep delivering — powerful messages to your target audience is a vital step in building that all-important trust and encouraging positive word-of-mouth for your business and your brand.

4. **Operations:** The Operations Performance Optimiser has five components; each one focuses on a key aspect of your operational capability, to ensure you actually deliver on what you promise.

This is critical, because people relay their experiences to others, which ultimately results in that all-important word-of-mouth. Unfortunately, over-promising and under-delivering is all too common and here we'll discuss what you need to do to make sure you get the balance right, with the limited resources available to you.

5. **Results:** The Dynamic Results Dashboard is all about monitoring your results to keep your finger on the pulse of your business. Whether you use a simple spreadsheet, or a more complex cloud-based Business Intelligence Dashboard, measuring success (or the lack of it) is vital to the survival and growth of any business.

Knowing what to measure and why and when you should measure specific key performance indicators, are all essential activities in managing your business. To specifically help entrepreneurs and micro-business owners, the three key performance indicators you should take particular note of are explained in detail, so you know exactly where to start. These three numbers will tell you instantly if your marketing is working, or whether you're wasting your money. Once you've mastered these three simple key performance indicators, you can expand your feedback mechanism, to gain deeper insights into your business and gather valuable information to help you make even better decisions.

Although this section may sound a little complicated, don't worry! Like the rest of the 21st Century Marketing System, every element has been designed specifically for the entrepreneur and micro-business owner with limited time and resources. You can make it as complex, or as simple as you need to meet your individual business requirements. My focus is on helping you create a solid marketing-focused foundation for your business that you can actually use and implement quickly and easily, not to bamboozle you with science.

By the end of Section 2, you'll know WHAT 21st Century Marketing is and how to create your own highly tailored, strategically focused 21st Century Marketing Blueprint for your business. This alone will put you way ahead of the game, because you'll be focusing on precisely what matters to turn your opportunities into reality

Section 3: 21st Century Marketing: How To Do It

▲ The final section is to understand HOW to do it. Here we discuss a detailed two-part case study which takes you through the whole process — from beginning to end — and covers both the initial business start-up phase and a detailed example of how this differs once the business is established. Starting with a business idea, we'll develop a strategy using the M.A.G.I.C. Marketing Matrix. We'll then turn it into a Seven Point Plan and start building our 21st Century Marketing Blueprint.

The piece most people struggle with is integrating the tactical marketing elements with the strategy. This is where the New Engagement Paradigm comes into its own and sets us up nicely to start developing our physical marketing campaigns using the Value Proposition Communicator. We'll also use the Message Development Matrix to create some content before deciding which online and offline tools to use to deliver that content. We'll quickly review the operations side of things, before we focus our attention on how we'll monitor our performance using the Dynamic Results Dashboard.

▲ If you want to take the extra step, you can also turn your 21st Century Marketing Blueprint into a full-blown 21st Century Business Plan. The beauty of the M.A.G.I.C. Marketing Matrix and the Seven Point Plan is that they force you to think about all the important areas related to your specific business in a structured manner. This means that when you come to "the numbers", you have already thought about a lot of what you need to include in your business plan. You just need to add a little extra detail around the "financials" so they are meaningful to your bank manager, investor, or accountant.

With all that in place, you'll be in a very strong position to create a high-level design for your own search engine friendly website that you can use to either develop a website yourself, or if you prefer, have a meaningful discussion with a website developer so they can develop it for you.

The 21st Century Marketing System has been designed to help you develop a holistic (and realistic) approach to your modern marketing challenges, by focusing on what really matters to you and your business. As we go through the book, I'll teach you everything you need to know — step-by-step — so by the time you finish your journey you feel enlightened, empowered and motivated to apply the system to your business.

But it doesn't stop there! I want to support you in your marketing journey and invite you to visit this book's companion website at www.21stCentury. Marketing and become a member of the 21st Century Marketing community.

Here you'll find a vault of additional resources to help you get the best out of the 21st Century Marketing System and we'll be adding new material to it regularly, to make it easy for you to keep up to date. You'll also be the first to know about other training and networking opportunities, as well as live events to support you on your entire entrepreneurial marketing journey.

Are you ready to continue? Let's start by taking a look at relationship marketing and how to build that all-important cornerstone of success — **TRUST**.

The Golden Goose - Relationship Marketing
Acquiring and Retaining Customers

Relationship marketing is an essential marketing discipline for entrepreneurs and micro-business owners because it saves time and money — and lots of it. The bottom line is this: if you want to maximise the return on your marketing investment, you must embrace relationship marketing with your heart and soul. But what exactly is relationship marketing? Put simply, it is all the steps you need to take — and manage — to consistently satisfy your customers' wants and needs every time they deal with, or even think about, your business and what you have to offer.

The value of relationship marketing in the twenty-first century cannot be overstated. In a global digital world, we now have more opportunity to buy from pretty much whoever we want, whenever we want. The choice facing the consumer is huge — for example, it is now entirely possible to buy a packet of tea from either your local supermarket or direct from the producer in China via eBay! That was inconceivable just twenty short years ago, but now it is an everyday reality that all too often gets taken for granted.

Here's the key thing: finding alternative suppliers takes time and energy, but once we have found a good supplier, we, as consumers, often stick with them for a very long time. In fact, it does not take much on the part of the marketer to make their customers feel special; it just takes a little effort. A good example of this is the multitude of loyalty schemes that cross our path every day, such as the store "Club Card" or "Premium Membership Card" we are asked to present every time we do our weekly shopping or visit the gym.

The reality is, relationships go through a number of stages and are often discussed by marketers in terms of a normal human relationship along the lines of "when boy meets girl". Every business owner and every marketer must think strategically about the relationships they want with their ideal customer. The harsh reality is you cannot serve, or satisfy, everybody all the time. It is simply impossible and, if you try, you will inevitably end up satisfying no one particularly well. The result? Your customers will go elsewhere, where they are made to feel special, valued and loved.

This implies you must really know your customers so you can satisfy their ever-changing needs. And here we touch on the vital importance of understanding your customers' entire interactions with your business over time — the concept of the "Customer Journey".

When you fully understand your customer and how you can best serve him or her through every step of the relationship, you create a strong bond your competitors will find nearly impossible to break. This underlines one of the key concepts of relationship marketing: the best relationships are built up over time and they go through many stages as you nurture, build and support your customers along their journey, for as long as they remain your customers.

According to the Chartered Institute of Marketing, it can cost up to twenty times as much to get a new customer as it does to keep an existing one. Yet many business owners throw stacks of cash and other resources at acquisition and leave their existing customers to fend for themselves, or at best serve them badly. Can you then blame your customers for transferring their business to alternative suppliers? And remember this; once they're gone, they're usually gone forever!

Therefore, you must pay attention to and invest a significant amount of your limited resources into "retention marketing" so your customers not only stay, but also tell others how great you are. This is simply the pinnacle of relationship marketing and can reduce your acquisition costs substantially. How much would your marketing costs reduce by if all your new customers were acquired through word-of-mouth? What if all your customers were also your unpaid sales team?

Building profitable relationships really is "The Golden Goose" so we'll start by exploring exactly why relationships are important to every business and how you can evaluate the types of relationships that are ideal for your business. Not all businesses are the same and you should take the time and effort to understand the types of relationship that work best for your business, before you start spending any money on marketing. Many pay lip service to relationship marketing to get that warm, fuzzy feeling that they're doing the right thing. In reality they are just kidding themselves into thinking that their version of "relationship marketing" is highly customer focused, when in reality it is no more than a codename for the traditional "hard sell" and then wondering why they struggle to build a sustainable business.

When you understand relationship marketing — and in particular how satisfaction, commitment and trust work — you'll find it a lot easier to convert your prospects to customers and eventually turn them into raving fans! Commonly quoted phrases include "your customers should know, love and trust you". But how do you do it? How does it work? Why does this work and how can you do it online, to maximise your chance of success? How do you achieve modern marketing utopia: positive word-of-mouth from raving fans who deliver hot new prospects to your door whilst you sleep? An interesting topic — so let's get started.

The Importance of Relationship Marketing in the Digital Age

The Internet has created the opportunity for many people to trade part-time, undercut the main suppliers and still make a profit, because many of them work from home and have such low overheads. In fact, it happens on eBay all the time. As we discussed earlier, the Internet has levelled the playing field and allows even the smallest "one-man band" to compete with the biggest global traders.

Very often, the product is the same product, from the same manufacturer, from the very same factory. The only two differentiating factors are typically the price and how the customer "feels" about their purchase. And, of course, this is heavily influenced by how the customer "feels" about the people representing the business they purchase the product or service from. Obviously, some people will always buy on price, but for many, the emotional experience of the purchasing process fulfils part of their satisfaction needs.

People (a.k.a. your customers) much prefer to buy from people (a.k.a. you, as either a supplier or service provider) they like. If your customers "like" you, you're on to a winner. But you must do much more than that; you must consistently satisfy your customers' experiential and emotional needs because that's what keeps them liking you. Satisfying your customers' experiential and emotional needs is a key element of successful marketing because people often make decisions based on emotion and justify with fact — much more often than most would admit.

Ted Nicholas, one of my former mentors, used a great example. The story goes like this: Imagine you just bought yourself a brand-new brightly coloured sports car and your friend says, "That's a lovely car. Why did you buy it?" If you're totally honest, you'd tell them the real reason: because it makes you feel sexy, virile, young, exciting and you want people (probably the opposite sex) to notice you. Whilst you may allude to some of these things, you'll probably start justifying the logic of your decision. You'll tell them about how economical it is, how the insurance isn't "that bad really", how it holds its value and why bright canary yellow or flame red is easy to see on the road and therefore safer!

The reality is, we often make our decisions based on emotion and then justify them with fact. And I'm sure we all know when somebody is doing this to us — don't we? Once you understand this basic principle of human behaviour, it will help you with your marketing enormously, particularly in creating and building successful relationships.

So how can you influence how people "feel" about your business?

The primary tools you have at your disposal are the quality of the service you provide during any transaction — and indeed any interaction your customer has with your business — and how well your product or service solves the customer's problem. If they like you, but the product is substandard, or if the product is great, but your customer service sucks, your customers are not going to feel loved and cherished.

Assuming that either your service or product satisfies their needs, the only thing left is the human element. This is the primary opportunity you have to build a connection with your prospect or customer. The personal level of communication and emotional connection creates a human bond. This is also reflected through your brand, which communicates your core values and should be an extension of who you really are.

These factors create a connection with your prospect or customer that is unique between you and them. Nobody can replicate it. You, therefore, need to ensure your bond is as strong as it can be and you should work on strengthening that bond at every opportunity. That way, you create a differentiating factor and price becomes less of an issue. In the twenty-first century, it's very likely you will have customers outside of your immediate locality. Therefore, you must build this emotional connection with "the tools of distance" — typically on the Web, via digital marketing and social media.

With so many potential competitors all vying for your customers' attention, your biggest weapon — and the thing that can make you stand out from the crowd — is to create a strong emotional connection. This, in turn, helps build a solid foundation on which to build a relationship. If the customer wants a relationship with you, you are in a very strong position, especially if you sell a product with a long lifespan, such as a car or any other item that subsequently needs looking after or servicing.

For example, many years ago a friend of mine dreamed about owning a Jaguar car. He couldn't afford a new one and bought a fairly old one privately which needed a bit of work. He then proudly took it to his local Jaguar dealer and asked them how much it would cost to bring the car "up to scratch". The reception he got wasn't particularly wonderful; it was almost as if it was an inconvenience because his car was so old. Understandably, he decided he did not want any form of relationship with them, especially as he'd spent a long time saving up for his beloved Jag and the local dealer did not make him feel good about his purchase (second moment of truth).

He then went to see the Jaguar dealer in the next town, which was about thirty miles away. From the minute he walked through the door, the service manager treated him as if he was someone special. It didn't matter that the car was "so old", what did matter to the service manager was to give good service to his new customer because he understood the value of long-term relationship management.

The service manager treated my friend as if he bought the car from them brand new and my friend often recalls this "wonderful experience" (a.k.a.

positive word-of-mouth). The inconvenience of an extra thirty miles was a price worth paying to maintain that relationship and continue enjoying that special feeling. The service manager understood this and made every effort to look after both the car and my friend to an exceptionally high standard. On one occasion, my friend turned up to collect his car after a routine service and it wasn't quite ready so he was given coffee and biscuits in the customer lounge whilst they finished the complimentary valet. His car always came back cleaner than it went in, which made him feel good.

He owned and loved that car for several years and the service manager obviously relieved him of large amounts of cash on a regular basis. But that didn't matter because he found a garage that loved his car as much as he did. They had a "connection" — a special bond!

A couple of years later, my friend's business was doing well and he wanted to buy a brand-new Jaguar. Do you think he went to his local dealer? No chance! They were on his "blacklist". He still remembers and talks about the way they treated him on his first visit several years previously (a.k.a. long-term negative word-of-mouth). His loyalty was firmly attached to the dealer thirty miles away, because not only did he get the impression they valued his custom, they also valued him as a person. He subsequently bought a brand-new Jaguar from them for nearly ten times what he paid for his first second-hand Jag.

Thinking in terms of the lifelong value of the customer, this garage maintained the new car for many years and probably got half as much again out of him in servicing costs. Every time he went in, they made him feel special and the emotional connection was, once again, reinforced. He subsequently bought two more cars from them and still talks about his initial experience today — over twenty years later. I'd guess the emotional bond in this example resulted in a lifetime value of well over £150,000 and all this is attributable to the way my friend was treated when he was first looking for a relationship with a Jaguar dealer. That's over £150,000 worth of business that could have been placed with his local dealer, or anybody else for that matter.

I'm sure you have similar stories to tell from your own experience of buying a car or some other major item, or at least know somebody who does. We hear about good stories and bad stories all the time. The point is that the initial stages of any relationship are a great determinant in deciding the direction that relationship may take and also how long it will last. The initial stage is crucial to the success of the relationship, so let's take a closer look at the acquisition process.

Acquiring Customers Is Your Biggest Expense

Acquiring new customers can be a hugely expensive and time-consuming activity and a lot of your marketing budget will need to be allocated to customer acquisition. It is, therefore, very important to understand the acquisition process before you choose the tools you will use to acquire new customers. All too often, we get emails about new trends, like video being the best acquisition or conversion tool, or maybe this week's flavour is Facebook, LinkedIn, Twitter, a blog post, or a new style of landing page, or whatever the latest "sure-fire" traffic generation technique may be, or...or... or — the list goes on and changes all the time.

All of this is worthless if you don't understand the process and end up stabbing in the dark, trying to "catch" anyone who may come past your (virtual) door.

You should start your customer acquisition process by describing your ideal customers and create "personas". These are detailed descriptions of your ideal customers and you can have as many as your business needs. For example: "Brian Smith, forty-seven, a car mechanic for a Ford main dealer. Married to Mary; they have two teenage daughters and a dog. They live in a three-bedroom, semi-detached house on the outskirts of Birmingham and go on holiday in their caravan three times a year during the school holidays. Brian enjoys car rallies and has a classic Ford Escort RS Turbo which he shows regularly at local events. He is also fed up with being a car mechanic and has dreamed about being his own boss and starting a coffee shop with Mary."

Or how about a separate persona for Mary, his wife: "Mary Smith, forty-two, wife and mother of two teenage daughters, likes to keep fit and plays badminton twice a week. She likes fashion and make-up and spends around £250 a month on clothes for herself and her two daughters. Mary also enjoys the three family caravanning holidays they take each year and works twenty-five hours a week as a nurse in a residential care home for the elderly."

Two different perspectives of the same family. In this example, it might be appropriate to promote caravan holidays to either Brian or Mary (or both), but inappropriate to promote badminton equipment to Brian or a classic car magazine to Mary.

The point is simply this: you need to define precisely who you're marketing (talking) to and how your product or service solves their problem. Do not make the mistake of trying to talk to "everybody", because you will dilute your message so much, it will be drowned out by your competition and you'll end up talking to nobody. You should always aim to talk to one specific group, and if others pick it up and respond to it too, that's a coincidental bonus — not an objective!

Your objective is to speak to as many members of your specific target audience as possible and deliver a consistent message that resonates with them, so they want to start a relationship with you. Note the key idea is "relationship", not "buy a product". Hopefully, they will buy something, but probably later. Step One is to establish the relationship and for that you need to master the first part of the Know | Love | Trust Framework, shown in figure 1.8.

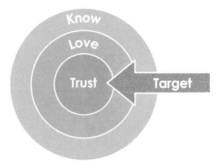

Figure 1.8 The Know | Love | Trust Framework

Know: Your prospects and customers must first know you exist; this is often achieved by creating awareness of your product or service.

Love: When they have purchased and tried your offering, you want them to not just like but love your product AND love the way you treat them by making them feel special.

Trust: If you deliver what you promise (and perhaps just a little more), they will begin to trust you and they will be happy for the relationship to develop and maybe buy again.

The acquisition process relies on your potential target audience knowing you exist. A good marketing model to help you develop your customer acquisition process is AIDA, which has been designed to take your prospects and customers through a proven sequence towards a desired outcome.

The AIDA Model

A	Awareness	The first step of the process is to create AWARENESS of your product or service amongst your target audience. It is now on their radar.
I	Interest	Once they are aware your product or service exists, you need to generate INTEREST in whatever it is you have to offer.
D	Desire	The third step in the process is to turn interest into DESIRE: they should now want whatever it is you have to offer.
A	Action	Taking ACTION is the final step in the process. Whether placing an order to buy or downloading a free report, this last step involves your prospect or customer actually doing something.

Here's a quick summary of the process:

It starts with initially creating awareness for what you have to offer. In the offline world, advertising is a very common way to create that initial splash of awareness. Online, using your search engine friendly website to present your solution to your prospect or customer's problem at the "zero moment of truth" is a great way to create that initial awareness.

Once you have their attention, you need to quickly generate interest in your offering by explaining how they will benefit from your product or service. They need to understand what it will do for them and why they need it to create desire. This is where they see themselves using your product or service and enjoying the benefits you've described. Each step of the process deepens their involvement, to the point where they realise they cannot do without it. This is where you present your "call-to-action" and ask them to make a decision. That's how the acquisition process works in a nutshell.

It is quite common to have an acquisition goal of getting the customer to just register their interest in what you have to offer, by collecting a name and email address. This is the indicator that your prospect wants to have some kind of relationship with you and has given you permission to contact them by email. That's a great start!

However, many believe getting traffic to their website is the key to successful acquisition. In fact, it's not! Getting the right kind of traffic to your website is far more important, because traffic costs money and it takes energy to convert people from merely being prospects into paying customers.

By focusing on attracting your ideal customer, you stand a far better chance of converting prospects or website visitors into customers, because what you have to offer is relevant to them. And it's probably the right time too — particularly if they've found you at the "zero moment of truth"! Take a simple example of Brian and Mary Smith; if you attract Brian to your Badminton Equipment website, there's little chance of converting him — unless he's looking for a present for Mary. However, if you attract him to your Ford Escort RS 2000 Accessories website, it's probably going to be much easier to establish a long term-relationship with him.

Key Point: *Relevant traffic is the key — not just any old traffic.*

You must also have a clear idea of what you want to happen when Brian visits. What does "conversion" mean to you, in your business context, at this stage of his customer journey? Is it to collect his name and email address so you can continue to build a relationship via email? Is to sell him a product straightaway? Or do you just want to provide some information to start building Brian's confidence in your brand?

Whatever your desired outcome from these visits, you should be looking for your visitor to make a decision and then act upon that decision. The decision your prospects and customers make at each point in their journey with your business should bring them closer to you and your brand. If they choose not to continue, you need to understand why and make the necessary changes to stop it happening again in the future. Could it be you are attracting the wrong type of prospects? Is your offer actually relevant to them? Is there something else that is putting them off and causing them to leave?

Customers are not only acquired through your website. Social media platforms and traditional marketing methods are equally important. However, if you choose to have your website as your "hub", it makes a lot of sense to direct as many potential customers to your website as possible, so they can start interacting with your brand at their convenience. As part of your acquisition process, you should be directing your prospects to specific landing pages that are highly relevant to what they are looking for. This should occur at the "zero moment of truth".

In the offline world, meeting people face to face, sending out direct mail, or good old advertising are all good ways to identify new prospects. Your website and social media presence should complement and support all your offline activity. If you tell a prospect you meet in a lift "The details are all on the website" as you hand them your business card, you'd better make sure those details are actually on your website, otherwise the relationship will get off to a rocky start.

In the complex digital world we now live in, you simply do not know where your prospect will first encounter your offering or your brand. It may be your website, Facebook, or even offline; but regardless of where the relationship starts, you must give a clear and consistent message across every channel you use.

Once your customers "know" about you and how you can help solve their problems, they must take the next step and buy from you. After all, money makes the world go round and, in business, "cash flow is king". So you must have it coming in as well as going out — hopefully more of the former than the latter! Your prospects must like your offer (in the purest sense of the word) and trust you enough to part with their hard-earned cash, in the hope that you can deliver "what it says on the tin" and solve their problem. Therefore, at some point in the journey you must "convert" them from a prospect into a paying customer. This is "the first moment of truth" discussed earlier.

In the past, this was where many companies stopped their marketing activities. Once the sale had been made, that was it — job done! However, in the digital age, the communication (marketing) process must continue because what happens next is equally important.

What these new customers say about you and their newly acquired product, or the service you have provided, may encourage others (new prospects) to seek you out, too. This is "the second moment of truth" and a lot of it will happen in the "social space" on social media and review sites. Comments left here will be available for the rest of the world to see for a very long time — so you really cannot afford to ignore this step.

Just remember, your acquisition process does not stop as soon as you've banked the cash; after-sales support is becoming particularly important in the digital age. Even if you don't have anything else to sell your customers, how you look after them and what they say about their experience has the power to influence many future prospects.

It is very common for businesses to be able to provide additional products and services, so maintaining a relationship with your customers, once one has been established, also becomes a very important part of your marketing process.

Retention Marketing:
Your Key to Long-Term Profits

Let's start our detailed discussion on retention marketing by defining exactly what it is. Retention marketing involves all the communication activities any business invests in, which deepen and strengthen the bond with their customers and maximise their lifetime value.

If it costs up to twenty times as much to acquire a customer, then why do so many companies invest so little time, money and effort in retaining them? The DRIP model is a really useful tool to help you craft retention-based marketing messages. DRIP stands for Differentiate | Remind (or Reinforce) | Inform | Persuade and it can be used in a similar manner to AIDA, to take your customers through a sequence towards a desired result or outcome, that rekindles previous positive emotions and reinforces connections to your brand.

The DRIP Model

D	Differentiate	To explain how your offering differs from your competitor, you need to DIFFERENTIATE it so it stands out as unique.
R	Remind	Even though people may be aware of your product or service, you need to REMIND them about what you have to offer to keep it "top of mind".
I	Inform	You may want to INFORM your customers about enhancements or new versions of your product or service, or maybe new ways they can benefit from using it. All this strengthens the bond with your brand.
P	Persuade	The final step of the DRIP process is similar to the ACTION in AIDA; you want to PERSUADE them to make some kind of decision or take a particular course of action.

There are some industries where the nature of their product or service implies you will consume their offering just once. Two examples that spring to mind are: a luxury hotel at a resort on the other side the world, which you will never go back to, and an undertaker. But guess what? Even an undertaker should have a retention marketing strategy, because if you think about it, the customer is not the person inside the box; it's the person outside the box who is still around after the funeral to pay the bill. One day they too will need the services of an undertaker — we all will! More importantly, though, they will also know people who will require the services of an undertaker, as the cycle of life sadly claims their loved ones too.

As for the hotel on the other side of the world, they must also have a retention marketing strategy, because everybody talks about their holiday. I bet you've been asked by at least one friend upon your return, "How was the hotel?" Is that an invitation for word-of-mouth or what? Generating word-of-mouth, which translates into repeat business, is as important for these types of businesses with seemingly "one-off" purchase cycles, as it is for your local butcher, baker, grocery store, or even your local plumber, who relies on their reputation to build and sustain their business.

The bottom line is this: every business needs a customer retention marketing strategy — whether they like it or not! And whilst many show signs of having one, they probably don't actually realise it. Retention activity far too often tends to happen by accident, rather than being a carefully planned and executed strategy.

We know marketing is all about communication and. as marketers, we spend our time communicating messages to our target audience. When we think in terms of retention marketing, our target audience is usually our existing customers. The purpose of our communication is to strengthen that warm, fuzzy feeling they have about our product, service, business, or brand. In a nutshell, we want them to think of us regularly and, when they do think of us, we want them to smile. Again, we're back into the realms of emotions and feelings, not necessary selling the next product. This is all about strengthening your brand in their eyes. When they decide they are ready to consume more of what you have to offer, you hope the bond between you is so strong they won't even consider talking to one of your competitors. Think back to the example with the Jag — who do you think my friend will call when he's ready to buy his next car?

Finally, you want your customers to give you all the money they spend on the type of thing you have to offer, not share some of it with your competitors. For example, the Jaguar dealer took my friend's entire car maintenance budget for many years — and he was happy to give it to them, because they solved his private transport problems.

Think back to the KLT model (Know | Love | Trust) we discussed a little earlier. Retention marketing is all about keeping and building the love and trust. It also allows you to introduce new products and services, because you already have an established relationship with this section of your target audience (your existing customers) and you have their permission to let them know of your latest offerings.

Do you think the Jaguar dealer let my friend know when a new model was launched or they had a special event, such as a Track Day? Damn right they did! Do you think he opened the envelope with XYZ Jaguar printed on the top left corner? Of course he did! He had to see what "his friends" were up to and the information they sent him was always relevant — because it was about Jaguars. Every time he opened the envelope and saw their logo, it rekindled those positive emotions for the brand they spent so much time and effort cultivating. And that, my friends, is an excellent example of retention marketing. Did he buy every new car that came onto the market? Of course not! But when he's ready to buy the next one, they will be at the top of his list, because they kept reminding him of "the good old days".

This is why branding is so important. It establishes your core values and consistently communicates them to your target audience. A classic example I often use when teaching marketing is this. Try it for yourself — if I said, "Tell me the first thing that springs into your mind when I say these words: 'fast, red, expensive luxury sports car,' what image do you get?" Most people respond with "Ferrari". That's because Ferrari "owns" that part of your brain associated with "fast red expensive luxury sports car". Similarly, XYZ Jaguar owns the "Jaguar" space in my friend's brain and the same applies to every other strong brand.

Here are a couple of my own examples:

▲ Avis "owns" the "car rental" section of my brain,

▲ easyJet owns the "cheap flights" bit,

▲ Loakes "owns" the "formal business shoes" section, and

▲ Aldi "owns" the "cheap good-value food"' portion.

What brands do you associate with? Who's living inside your head?

They will be different for all of us, but like it or not, it is a reality. What we want to do as marketers of our own business is to occupy the space in our target audience's brain that associates our solution with their problem.

Once you've won that valuable space, you need to work doubly hard to keep it. Why? Because someone else wants it too! This is why you must invest in a retention marketing strategy. Think of it as paying the rent on a valuable piece of real estate and if you skip a single payment, you will be evicted!

So how does a retention marketing strategy differ to an acquisition marketing strategy?

That's a good question and one that not many businesses seem to understand.

When you want to acquire new customers, your target audience would typically not know who you are. Therefore, you have to initially "interrupt" them to make them aware of your presence. This may happen by interrupting their normal "pattern", which is often achieved through advertising which, incidentally, is the most common interruption tool. Alternatively, in the digital world, you also have the option of a much softer approach, which is to present them with your solution at the "zero moment of truth".

The whole process can be likened to the guy asking the girl for a date in the "boy meets girl" story. In both examples, the objective is to start some form of relationship — however short it may be. Without this initial "interruption" interaction, nothing has a chance of starting. In the real world, he may use a "chat up line" to attract her attention; in the online world, she may be advertising the fact that she's ready to meet someone on a dating website. Having declared herself as being "in the market", potential suitors offer themselves as solutions to her "single status" problem. In both cases, the interruption is the starting point to get the show on the road.

Once the "permission" has been granted to allow the relationship to start, it is not so appropriate to keep interrupting. Therefore, we move to the next phase of permission marketing. In the twenty-first century, there are more products and options available than ever before, so rarely is exclusive supply of product the key issue. Just think about buying a new laptop from PC World, or one of the many other stores you could choose that are full of them. So why do you ultimately buy from PC World, or any of the other main retail outlets, or even direct from a manufacturer, such as Dell? It really boils down to how you feel about the supplier and whether they can offer anything extra that will help solve your particular problem more effectively and efficiently. It's all about that extra layer of benefit over and above the basic product.

Let's go back to our "boy meets girl" story and add a couple of names to make it a little more entertaining. When Brian first asked Mary for a date, he had to interrupt her thought pattern somehow. When she said, "Yes", permission for the initial request was granted. Both parties were happy with the initial encounter — the asking and acceptance. Let's assume things went well, i.e. both parties were happy with the "transaction" or "exchange" — say, meeting for coffee and a chat one lunch time. Toward the end of their first date, Brian asked Mary what she was doing on Saturday evening and would she like to go out again. They got along pretty well and agreed to a second encounter, then a third, fourth, fifth, etc. etc. etc...

Pretty soon, they have forgotten all the other potential partners, cancelled their Internet dating subscriptions and become "exclusive" (or monogamous). At this point, neither is even considering looking for anyone else, as the relationship works both ways and fulfils both their wants and needs. Over time, their bond strengthens and this makes it harder for any potential alternative partner (think competitor) to attract Brian away from Mary, or Mary away from Brian. If things continue to go well, the relationship deepens and strengthens and they get engaged and, ultimately, married. If things don't work out, i.e. they want different things, or identified there is a mismatch between their core values, the relationship will deteriorate to the point where something happens and they go their separate ways. At this point, they will either hate each other's guts or remain "just good friends".

I'm sure we can all identify with Brian and Mary's generic story. The same basic principles of human relationship development also apply in marketing because, at the end of the day, people in business deal with people who are the consumers of what all businesses provide.

At different stages of the development of a relationship, different messages will be exchanged, often relying on the result of previous exchanges of communication and experience. For example, if Brian asked Mary on the third date when her birthday was, she'd be pretty upset if he asked the same question eight months later and then totally forgot it!

Here's the key point: the communication (a.k.a. marketing messages) must be appropriate to the stage in the cycle of the development, or maintenance, of the relationship.

Let me give you a quick example. One thing that really annoys me as a customer is when a company has a pretty good acquisition process but completely ignores the retention cycle, especially when I've entrusted them with sufficient data to help them understand my needs, wants and problems. A while ago, I bought some Internet marketing–related training DVDs on a specialist topic from an "expert" company in the US. In fact, I bought product one, a few months later product two, then product three, then a few more products. After about a year, I had pretty much the complete set. They were pretty good and the company seemed to know what they were doing — until, that is, I was bombarded with sales material for product one, followed by product two, then three, four, and five! I couldn't believe it! I'd spent nearly $2,000 with this company in almost a year, and now they were trying to sell me stuff I already had — and from them!

They did not walk their talk. They lost all credibility in my eyes — and my trust. Everything they did to make me feel special as the relationship developed was destroyed quicker than I could turn on my laptop. Despite their claims, they clearly viewed me as a number, not a person, and after twelve months went back to marketing message number one.

I promptly terminated the relationship and began looking for an alternative supplier for the $5,000 "Advanced Mentoring Programme" I almost signed up for. In this example, one fundamental mistake cost them two and a half times the revenue they could have easily extracted from me! Plus, and here's the real kicker, I'd been telling several friends and acquaintances how brilliant this company was (read: positive word-of-mouth) and that stopped dead! I then started telling the story of how they didn't "walk their talk" — enter negative word-of-mouth. Not good!

This really does emphasise the need for a retention marketing strategy, to follow on from a customer acquisition strategy and to ensure you look after your customers properly through their entire lifecycle with your business. The impact of not doing this can be colossal. Once I stopped recommending this company to my friends and acquaintances, the flow of new leads from me dried up. Who knows how many of my referrals would have spent the same as me — or more? And what about their potential referrals? The loss of potential business from this one incident, of not having a retention strategy, could be substantial.

That's why retention marketing is so important. Please don't make the same mistake in your business and do have a separate retention marketing strategy which places your existing customers at its core. Listen to what your customers are telling you and adapt your business accordingly, to make sure you keep solving their problems. If you do, you will keep them as your customers and maximise their lifetime value to your business.

Maximising Your Customers' Lifetime Value

Before we go on to discuss lifetime value, I'd like to share a great quote that stuck with me ever since I first saw it many years ago: "People come into your life for a reason, a season, or a lifetime". Let's apply that to your business.

Thinking in these terms helps us focus on the realistic length of the relationship we can expect our customers to have with us. What are your expectations? What are theirs? The answers will determine how much energy and resources you put into building, managing and maintaining these relationships. This also depends on the nature of the problem you can help your customers solve. This is what your business is all about and should be articulated in your mission statement (more on this later).

For example; let's think back to Brian and Mary, who are now happily married and celebrating the birth of Emma, their first child. If you are in the baby supplies business, you would have been looking for Mary to come onto your radar when she was about three months pregnant. You would have sent out marketing messages aimed at interrupting Mary (and Brian) to attract their attention and make them aware you can solve their new "baby supplies" problem.

You'd hope to have a good share of their available budget before Emma was born and will certainly work very hard to get as much of this baby budget before it tapers off around Emma's second or third birthday. In this example, the relationship will last approximately two and a half to three and a half years, at which point it drops off. You'll notice this because your key metrics —your KPIs —tell you that their order frequency and average order value has decreased significantly in the last three months and you know Emma is growing up (after all, you have her date of birth on record).

The Smiths are hitting the "average active purchase length" of three years and two months (or whatever your data tells you the average is). You know there is no point in sending out marketing messages for nappies now Emma is potty trained — which, by the way, is reflected in the Smiths' purchase history in your database. After all, six months ago you sold Mary the potty, the parents' training DVD and, subsequently, the "little person's adult bathroom kit", comprising of a little pink stool and miniature-size layover toilet seat. The Smith family's pattern fits the average customer profile (because you know your customers), so you now scale back your "relationship serving activity" to "relationship maintenance activity". Your retention marketing objective is to keep your brand in Brian and Mary's mind, until they get news of child number two. From your database, you estimate this will be sometime in the next eighteen to twenty-four months.

Your retention marketing campaign could be as simple as sending out a leaflet in the post, or sending an email offering 10% discount on this month's special promotional product, which Mary can either use herself or give to one of her friends (the coupon, by the way, has Mary's customer code on it so you can track it!). Alternatively, she could save them for herself and convert them to "premium customer purchase vouchers", which she can spend any time in the next two years (of course, terms and conditions apply). When Mary breaks the delightful news to Brian that Emma is going to be "big sister" before Christmas, the three-year cycle starts again and Brian can't wait for another round of sleepless nights.

In this example, do you see how really knowing your customer and keeping a little relationship retention marketing bubbling along in the background keeps you "top of mind" and keeps paying the rent on the "baby supplies" part of Brian and Mary's brains? When little Lucy is born, you have a huge advantage over your competitors and Lucy represents an extension to Brian and Mary's customer lifetime value of another two and a half to three and a half years. Cool!

After Lucy's third birthday, you can once again scale back your retention marketing activities and perhaps have a similar cycle, as you know from the Office of National Statistics that the average family size in the UK is on the rise and three or more children is quite common. So it really is worth keeping in touch and looking for those clues that suggest Lucy may become "the middle one". If the family moved to a bigger home, for example (note: your clue may be the change of address notification), you may want to increase your retention marketing activity. However, if the Smiths purchase nothing for the next ten years, it might be worth assuming Brian has had enough sleepless nights!

If you had only focused on selling Mary the initial products when she first knew about Emma, you would have sold maybe £200-£300 worth of products in one month and never seen her again. However, if you understand your customers and focus on building a relationship with Mary and Brian, by applying both a relationship marketing and retention marketing framework, you can easily lay claim to £2,000-£3,000 of their baby budgets per child purchase cycle — two, three, or even four times — depending on the number of children they have. That means that as customers, Brian and Mary could potentially have a lifetime value of over £10,000 in revenue — which I'm sure you'll agree is a lot more lucrative than the £200 or £300 you could have achieved as a "one-hit wonder".

How Relationships Are Developed:
Satisfaction, Commitment, and Trust

There has been a lot of research into the "Know, Love and Trust" area and many academics have published papers based on their extensive research. One word is at the centre of this: trust.

All lasting relationships are based on trust and this has to be earned over a period of time. For example, whilst Mary may have wanted to trust Brian on their first date when he said "she was the girl for him", he needed to prove it over a period of time, by demonstrating his values through a series of behaviours that Mary found acceptable. Only then could Mary gradually begin to trust Brian — and, of course, the same applies to Brian building his trust in Mary.

So how is "trust" built?

Extensive research shows that trust is built through numerous incremental interactions, or transactions, that satisfy a particular need for both parties and where the outcome is equally valued by both parties. In short, it's a three-step process starting with satisfaction, which leads to commitment and ultimately trust — the most precious commodity.

Working back from trust, there are a number of stages and components that contribute to this ultimate goal, one of which is "commitment". In our "couples" example, it may have been when Brian asked Mary to marry him and they got engaged. But Mary wouldn't have gone straight from not trusting to trusting Brian — it would happen over a period of time, when enough commitment had been demonstrated (by both sides) to formalise that commitment, which was built on the foundation of many little episodes (or transactions) of mutual satisfaction.

Research by Morgan & Hunt (1994) and Hess & Storey (2005) shows multiple satisfactory transactions ultimately lead to increased trust. It also identified several components that lead to commitment and trust: cooperation, shared values, mutually compatible goals and cost of change, just a few of which we can easily apply to our own businesses. This had a huge impact on developing what we now refer to as "relationship marketing".

In summary, multiple transactions, or interactions, that result in both parties feeling satisfied, creates a "win-win" scenario, which then becomes a great starting point for another, slightly more risky transaction, where both parties may have a little more to lose if it goes wrong. The more experiences of total satisfaction, the greater the commitment to have another go. These individual transactions, or exchanges, take time. Trust is therefore built up over time.

In essence, we can break down the Know | Love | Trust framework a little more by replacing the "Love" with "Satisfaction" and "Commitment", as shown in figure 1.9, as this more accurately depicts the progression, particularly from a marketing perspective.

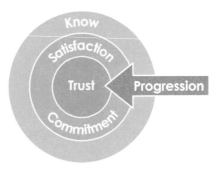

Figure 1.9 The Know | Satisfaction | Commitment | Trust Framework

Once your customers truly trust you and you've built a strong bond with them — a strong commitment — it becomes very difficult for your competition to steal your customers away from you, as long as they remain satisfied, of course.

When it comes to satisfaction, it has to work both ways; your customers may be delighted they benefit from your solution at a fair price, but if they never pay their bills, you will not be satisfied. It has to be a two-way street. That's the basis of a "win–win" relationship.

When one party takes advantage and tries to change the terms of the relationship or manipulate it in their favour, it becomes a "win–lose" scenario. Dissatisfaction begins to fester and starts to eat away at the goodwill that's been built up. This is because, ultimately, there is a mismatch of core values on which the commitment — and hence trust — has been built in the first place. Gradually, this destroys the trust and the relationship suffers, often to the point of irretrievable reconciliation, at which point it's time to "move on" and find a more compatible partner (or supplier). Even if the relationship does "recover", it will never be the same again, because once the seeds of doubt have been planted, they tend to live forever and are virtually impossible to root out, no matter how hard you try.

For example, if one partner cheats and the other finds out, they are usually pretty upset. This is because the foundation of the relationship — the trust — has been damaged. The offending partner may ask for forgiveness and the hurt partner may consent and agree to "try again". However, they will never forget how the abuse of trust made them feel. "They can forgive, but never forget" — as the saying goes!

So what does this mean to you as an entrepreneur and micro-business owner? Simply this: you should work hard to attract your ideal customers who share your core values. Your brand and your behaviour play a huge role in this. Once you have attracted your ideal customers, you need to nurture the relationship through multiple interactions, or transactions, where each party comes out just a little better off (and satisfied) than before they started the exchange (or relationship). "Continuous win–win" should be your motto and you should aim to consistently under-promise but over-deliver. Even if it's just by a small margin, it's worth making the effort to go "beyond the call of duty" or "go the extra mile", because this creates goodwill — and people love to talk about good things that happen to them. This can only help create positive word-of-mouth, as your customers will tell their friends about the extra bonus or extra help you gave them. At the end of the day, you or people in your company, made them feel special.

However, if you over-deliver by too wide a margin, you'll project the message that you don't have faith in what you offer and you'll end up encouraging others to take more than they rightfully should. As a rule of thumb, I'd say over-delivering by 3-5% is enough to "wow" your customers — and if you do it when they least expect, it can have an even greater impact!

The whole process can be represented by the following formula:

Satisfaction of initial transactions plus repeated satisfaction of subsequent and larger transactions, equals commitment and ultimately trust.

Understanding Your Customers: Why Maslow Was Right

Abraham Maslow was a famous psychologist who did extensive research into human behaviour, to help understand why human beings do the things they do. In 1943, he published a paper in Psychological Review explaining his "Hierarchy of Human Needs" theory. It was a real breakthrough in understanding human behaviour and is often used in marketing circles because, quite frankly, it is pretty relevant.

Maslow came up with a pyramid of five core human needs as shown in figure 1.10.

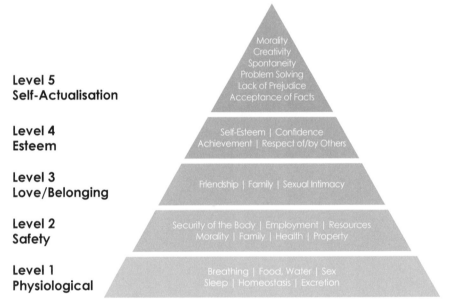

Level 5
Self-Actualisation

Level 4
Esteem

Level 3
Love/Belonging

Level 2
Safety

Level 1
Physiological

Morality
Creativity
Spontaneity
Problem Solving
Lack of Prejudice
Acceptance of Facts

Self-Esteem | Confidence
Achievement | Respect of/by Others

Friendship | Family | Sexual Intimacy

Security of the Body | Employment | Resources
Morality | Family | Health | Property

Breathing | Food, Water | Sex
Sleep | Homeostasis | Excretion

Figure 1.10 Maslow's Hierarchy of Human Needs

There is plenty of material on the Internet that explains this in more detail, if you are interested in looking into this further — just search for "Abraham Maslow" or "Hierarchy of Needs". However, the short story, according to Maslow, is that we humans have five levels of "needs". These are:

Level 1: Physiological needs — Air, food, water and all the other basic elements of survival, without which we cannot properly function as human beings.

Level 2: Safety needs — We need to know we are safe, otherwise we are constantly running away from some kind of danger. We also need security of income and somewhere to live and bring up our families and, of course, our health. When we have achieved these needs, Maslow argued, we have created the "base layer" of our survival needs in a modern society.

Level 3: Belonging needs — In order to be fulfilled as human beings, we need to feel we fit into some kind of social structure. That social structure can take many forms: family, friendships, work and personal relationships, being just a few examples.

Level 4: Esteem needs — Maslow argued that when we have all our basic needs fulfilled, we can then pursue our "higher-level" needs, including self-esteem, respect, confidence and achievement. Maslow suggested we are put on this earth to make a contribution to society, so we all want to feel that our contribution is of value and that others respect us for what we achieve.

Level 5: Self-Actualisation — The highest level of need Maslow referred to as "Self-Actualisation", which essentially means being the best you can possibly be and working toward your "ideal self". Ultimately, this means truly understanding the meaning of life, how it applies to you and where you fit into the universe.

Maslow's research led him to the conclusion that the lower-level needs must be satisfied before the needs of a higher level can be addressed. Basically, there's no point in trying to satisfy your higher-level needs, such as fulfilment and self-actualisation, if you have nowhere to live and you're starving to death! For example, only when you have somewhere to live and a full belly can you consider satisfying your belonging needs. If you don't satisfy these lower-level needs, you cannot focus — and hence commit (key word) — to satisfying (another key word) your next higher need.

Why does this matter to us? Why should we care?

Simply this: you need to satisfy your customers' basic needs first (in terms of building the relationship) before you can move them up Maslow's pyramid and satisfy their more advanced (relationship) needs. If we apply Maslow's lessons alongside the advice for building relationships, by fulfilling our customers' needs — particularly for belonging and esteem — we develop strong, deep relationships that are difficult to break.

Pulling It All Together with the Loyalty Ladder

The "Loyalty Ladder" (see figure 1.11) is another marketing model that helps us understand where the customer is on their journey with our business and also help us understand how strong that relationship is —which, in turn, helps us understand what we need to do to strengthen (or abandon) the relationship.

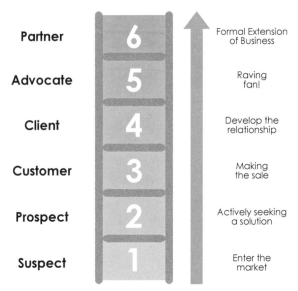

Figure 1.11 The Loyalty Ladder

You want your ideal customers to start at the bottom and climb up to the top as quickly as possible. The ladder highlights the process, from targeting your ideal customers and identifying prospects, through converting them into customers and, subsequently, into long-term clients. From that point on, it is very important to encourage them to become a supporter, and an advocate, of your business, as this leads to much more positive word-of-mouth. This is because they have a greater vested, emotional interest in the success of your business; they are demonstrating they share your values and beliefs. Remember, this is the ultimate goal of marketing: to have your customers introduce new, qualified prospects to your business and help build your market share. By the way, advocates typically introduce more people to your business than the lower levels.

When the key building blocks of relationship development discussed earlier are seen alongside these enlightening concepts, you have the basis for an extremely powerful marketing strategy that takes members of your target audience from mere prospects and turns them into advocates for your products, services, business and, ultimately, your brand.

If you have a business and marketing strategy to actually develop long-term advocates for your brand, do you think your business will survive and prosper? The more people that talk positively about what you have to offer, the greater chance you have of creating a long-term sustainable competitive advantage. Think about it for a second. If you have a large number of unpaid salespeople telling all their friends, acquaintances and other contacts (who incidentally trust them) how wonderful your offering is, do you think that would help build your business? Would it be worth the effort in maintaining relationships with these valuable "influencers"?

Of course it would! If you can achieve this, then in marketing terms you've "made it!" Congratulations!!!

But how will you know? When you achieve this, you will probably have new prospects contacting you out of the blue, saying something like, "Mr Smith is a client of yours and told me how wonderful you are — can you please help me too?" You'll be spending very little (notice I said "very little", not "nothing") on marketing. You will still have to maintain your investment in retention marketing to keep your brand "top of mind" and activate your advocates'/influencers' brains. Remember, you cannot afford to stop paying the "rent" on this valuable piece of marketing real estate.

Before we finish on relationship marketing, there's just one last point.

Dealing with Humans:
The Drive for Personalisation

Successful relationships in business are ultimately relationships between people — people who like each other. Respect is also one of the elements of any successful relationship and one way to show respect is to address people correctly. For example, if you meet Pete who prefers to be addressed as Peter, then using "Peter" is a mark of respect, whereas "Pete" may annoy him.

I remember one of my sports teachers at school called a friend of mine "Ginger" because he couldn't remember his name (or couldn't be bothered because he wasn't on the school football team). My friend absolutely hated it and consequently loathed that teacher. I'm sure many of us can think of similar examples and one thing I discovered during my research into psychology is the aural reception of our name actually creates a physiological response (Carmody & Lewis (2006)). What this means is that one of the most important (and sweetest) things we humans like to hear is our own name. So if this triggers emotional responses and, if our name (or preferred label) is pronounced correctly, it stimulates positive emotions. If it is not, then negative emotions are triggered. This is actually pretty important when we understand that decisions are based on emotion and justified with fact, because the more positive emotions we can generate, the stronger the bond — and hence the relationship — becomes.

> "There is unique brain activation specific to one's own name, in relation to the names of others. In addition, the patterns of activation when hearing one's own name relative to hearing the names of others, are similar to the patterns reported when individuals make judgements about themselves and their personal qualities and include the regions of the medial frontal cortex and superior temporal cortex near the temporo-parietal junction."
>
> Carmody & Lewis 2006

As a simple example, think of emails you might receive: when you get an email that addresses you correctly, e.g. "Dear Peter," your natural response is, "They're talking to me". If the same email is addressed "Dear JTPeter1903@ something.com" or "Dear Smith (surname)," it hardly evokes the same emotional response, does it?

Therefore, if you want to build and maintain strong relationships, you absolutely must address members of your target audience correctly — at every stage and by every method. Consistency is key. If you use "Dear Peter" in an email, make sure you address him as "Peter" when you're on the phone or when you send a letter, unless "Mr X" (where X is the surname) is more appropriate in your specific context.

Think about how this might apply to your business. Are you addressing your prospects and customers correctly? Is your customer data accurate? If not, how can you update it to make sure you don't inadvertently offend your prospects or customers and damage your business?

The key point I'm driving home here is to make sure you get remembered for what you want to be remembered for, not something else. If you remember you're dealing with humans and strive to build personal (human) relationships, then personalised communications can only help your cause, not hinder it.

The Modern Marketing Landscape: How It All Fits Together

The New Marketing Ecosystem

With the power now firmly in the hands of the consumer, their ever-increasing demands put more pressure on marketers and stretch budgets to the limit. The digitally dominated marketing landscape in the twenty-first century is becoming increasingly complex and confusing. Even the simplest business needs to implement a multi-channel marketing strategy, if they are to maximise their return on marketing investment. Merely keeping up-to-date with all the latest developments is near impossible — even for the experts!

> Multi-channel marketing is the ability to interact with prospects and customers on a variety of platforms. In this sense, a "channel" might be a print ad, a radio commercial, a retail outlet, a website, a promotional event, a social media page, or even word-of-mouth.
>
> The benefit of multi-channel marketing is that it increases the target audience's "opportunity to see (or hear)" the marketers' messages, thus increasing the likelihood of them being noticed.

In this chapter, we'll explore the modern marketing landscape and discuss what tools are available to you and why you should consider using them. One of the biggest challenges facing the modern marketer is understanding how all these new digital techniques, innovations and endless supply of daily tips can be applied to create sustainable competitive advantage and generate additional revenue.

Very often business owners and marketers are too eager to jump straight to the tools without really thinking through which tools are most appropriate. They don't consider how these tools may be used in any given situation to solve a particular communication problem and, ultimately, satisfy a customer's unfulfilled needs.

It is not necessarily the latest fad or employing state-of-the-art cool video techniques that makes the biggest difference. Whilst the techies may relish developing cool cartoon-style marketing videos and posting them on YouTube, it may not be the best thing for your business at that precise point in time. Occasionally, these may work well for a while, but once the novelty has worn off, you're back in search of the "next big thing". And so the never-ending cycle of trial and error, and hit and miss, continues…

A key finding of my research was that without a solid foundation in the fundamentals of marketing, it's near impossible to apply modern digital and social media marketing techniques effectively and efficiently. Many entrepreneurs and business owners tried applying and adapting whatever marketing activity had previously worked to their new and emerging challenges, but rarely generated favourable results. It was a consistent battle of trial and error. Some hit a "rich seam" of marketing almost by accident; it works for a while and then spluttered and eventually stopped, just like a car running out of petrol. However, finding enough of "the right fuel" to get it going again seemed almost as elusive as the Tooth Fairy.

One thing that was absolutely clear from my research and, incidentally supported by the work of other researchers and practitioners, is that "digital" marketing cannot exist in isolation. Whilst I did find some examples of businesses who claimed they did "everything online", when I dug deeper I discovered that they, too, relied on a mix of traditional (offline) marketing methods, as well as digital and social media (online) marketing methods. They just didn't realise it, or perhaps didn't consider it to be marketing, because it was "just what they did".

By the end of this chapter, you'll have a good understanding of what the modern marketing landscape looks like and how you can apply the available tools from a strategic perspective. You'll then be far better placed to decide which tools are most suitable for your business in any given situation.

Essentially, the New Engagement Paradigm requires tight integration of traditional, digital and social media to deliver valuable content focused on building relationships and brand equity. Its effective use is one way of differentiating your business from your competition, through a variety of methods and channels, all aimed at strengthening your bond with your customers by creating multiple opportunities for them to engage with your brand — not necessarily always aimed at generating a sale.

The modern marketing landscape is built on a foundation of the four central elements of the New Engagement Paradigm and it's essential to understand how they all work together, as well as making individual contributions to the overall process.

Delivering content that your target audience finds valuable is the secret to creating engagement, as this ultimately creates word-of-mouth — your primary goal. Therefore, it is placed at the very core of the New Engagement Paradigm; everything you do will focus on delivering a message to your target audience in a way that fully engages them.

Your messages will be "wrapped" in your content and each piece of content will have a specific objective.

The "New Engagement Paradigm"

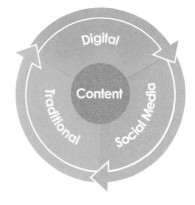

You'll notice that traditional, digital and social media form the outer layer of the New Engagement Paradigm. This is because, when you have created your content, you have to create some form of "noise" to alert your target audience that this new content exists. The traditional, digital and social media channels are the way you alert your target audience to this new (valuable) content and tell them where they can find it.

Let's take each of the four elements of the New Engagement Paradigm (content, traditional, digital and social media) in turn and examine them in more detail.

Content

Everything you produce which can be read, seen, heard and shared is your "content". All content should be created with a specific purpose in mind and should also directly contribute to achieving specific business and marketing objectives. For example, let's say your objective is to create initial awareness for your product or service; you could create a short video demonstrating how it works and explain the benefits it brings to your customers. You might even include some testimonials from your satisfied customers saying how your offering has solved their problems. It will be quite reasonable to post this on YouTube and send some emails describing the video with a link to "click here to view".

Your content can take many forms and refers to anything you create to engage with your target audience. It can be written material in the form of downloadable PDFs, such as special reports or white papers; videos which you may post on YouTube or Vimeo; blog posts that actively encourage discussion; or pictures that may be shared on Instagram or Pinterest. Even social media postings that result in interactions with members of your target audience can form part of your content library. It could even be argued that this type of content is preferable because it encourages people to voluntarily and directly interact with your brand.

If the product is quite technical, you could create a "White Paper" or "Special Report" explaining the technical specification in detail and give a description of how the product solves your customers' needs. It could even include a case study as an example. You could also create a video demonstrating how it works, so your prospects can see the product in action and make it downloadable from your website, possibly in exchange for their email address. Both the report and video are "content" and their main objective is to inform your prospects and help them make a decision — not apply the "heavy sell". Each item of content should be stand-alone, but there's no reason why several pieces of content cannot support or refer to each other. For example, a series of blog posts that discuss particular issues, could all point to the same video or special report.

Content Location

You may be wondering where the best place to store content is. Unfortunately, there is no simple or definitive answer to that question, as it really does depend on the nature of your content. For example, any videos you create could either be an integral part of your website (which you host and manage yourself) or you could post them on YouTube and let Google take care of the technical issues. Any documents you create could be stored on your website as PDFs, so your prospects and customers can download them and consume them at their convenience; equally, you could deliver them by email or give access via your Google Drive.

Here's my take on the issue. I prefer my own website to be the central store (hub) for all my content (except for large files) because I can retain control of pretty much everything I create. However, videos I prefer to post on YouTube or Vimeo because it's a far more efficient use of my limited resources (video files can be huge). If you don't have your own website, but get on well using a social media platform, you may choose to store the majority of your content on another platform — such as Facebook, LinkedIn, or somewhere else (or even a combination). This alleviates the need, and expense, of maintaining your own independent platform.

However, the risk you run in this scenario is that if Facebook (or whichever platform you choose to use) changes the way they do things, or start to charge for their services, or place any kind of restriction on you in the future, then you really are at their mercy. It is quite conceivable that something which is free to use now might cost something in the future, as that platform develops and they enhance their business model. I would, therefore, strongly encourage you to seriously consider having your own website as the "hub" for all of your content — except, that is, for things like videos, where there are advantages in having them stored on a third-party platform. Something for you to think about!

Content Marketing

What actually is "content marketing"? The simplest definition is, "regularly creating and publishing engaging material that is relevant to your target market and contributes to building long-term relationships". All content you create should be both relevant and worth sharing; it has to be relevant to your target audience, otherwise they will gloss over it or ignore it altogether. Equally, it has to be high-quality and engaging so your target audience will want to make a comment about it (or "remark" on it) — which is great for you because it encourages "sharing" (a form of word-of-mouth) — and helps build your brand. Every piece of content should support a specific objective and help move your prospect, or customer, one step further along the "customer journey" within your business.

Creating regular content can be a very time-consuming activity and, as Halligan and Shah note in their excellent book 'Inbound Marketing', the role of the modern marketer is "half marketer and half publisher". This eloquently positions and describes the role of the modern marketer in the digital age! They also say that any content you create should be "remarkable" — and that's also an excellent piece of advice. First of all, it emphasises the importance of creating something of great value. The second thing creating "remarkable" content does, is to naturally encourage it to be shared with others. If you read a blog post or watch a YouTube video that you find interesting, engaging and entertaining, there is a high probability that you will tell somebody else about it; i.e. you will remark on it, or, in social media terms, "share" or "like" it. This, in turn, encourages others who respect your opinion to look at the things you like or have chosen to share, thereby resulting in positive word-of-mouth.

One final comment…

As a small business owner, you'll probably have very limited resources, so creating a small amount of high-quality content is far better than regularly publishing any old rubbish, which, of course, will be of no real value to anyone — especially your target audience. What you do publish could be there for a very long time, so make the effort to ensure it shows you in the best possible light and contributes to your business goals and objectives.

The Traditional Marketing Landscape

If you're old enough to remember "the good old days" before the Internet, then cast your minds back to the dim and distant past; if not, then imagine the Internet has been turned off and there is no access to any website or social media platform. I know some "youngsters" would cringe at the thought of not being able to chat with their friends on Facebook with their iPhones, or keep up-to-date with the latest developments from one of the multitude of websites that feed their insatiable need for up-to-the-minute information — but once upon a time, the online world didn't exist and, back then, things were very different!

The offline world we'll refer to as the "Traditional Marketing Landscape" — that is, everything that is not digital or social media. Back then, marketing was still a very expensive process but arguably far less complicated. It was also largely based on interruption marketing and, traditionally, had a major focus on selling product rather than building relationships. Organisations typically had a product (or sales) orientation and their primary focus was to sell products at a profit, to survive and prosper.

The motto of these companies was "find a need and fill it". A couple of good examples include Tesco. , who were originally in the "cheap groceries" market; their strategy was to "stack them high and sell them cheap", i.e. they shifted lots of products at a small margin. Gillette was in the razor blade business; their business model was to "give away" the razor and sell the blades — the consumables — to generate repeat sales. Unilever sold Dove soap, claiming it helps keep skin soft and beautiful; its aim was to sell as many bars of soap as possible.

I'm sure you can think of many other examples, but the key point is that with a product/sales orientation, the product is created first and then it's Marketing's job to find the customers to buy it. Of course, many manufacturers would have conducted some form of market research first to establish that there was a need for the product they had in mind, but when it came to marketing, the focus was heavily on sales. Nothing essentially wrong with that, especially when demand exceeds supply.

To communicate with their target audiences, marketers used advertising extensively. TV, radio, newspaper and magazine ads, outdoor advertising on billboards and buses, even cinema adverts, were all used to interrupt the target audiences (be they local or national), at huge expense. The poor entrepreneurs and start-up micro-business owners were competing for advertising space in all these media. However, there were two distinct disadvantages. The ads were short-lived, only twenty-four hours in the case of a daily newspaper or, at best, monthly in a magazine. Billboards and other outdoor advertising could have a longer "shelf life", whereas TV and radio ads could be over in just a few seconds — now that was a very fast way to spend money!

The other disadvantage was the cost. Advertising is very expensive and well beyond the reach of most start-ups and micro-business owners. The "big boys", however, could afford these huge advertising costs. Coca Cola, for example, spent many millions annually advertising their soft drinks to encourage consumption; consequently, ad space was dominated by those with very deep pockets.

Once you have decided on the location of your content hub, you can advertise your content on all of your traditional media very easily, in the knowledge that it is extremely unlikely to change in the future (unless, of course, you change it). So, for example, on your business cards you can quote your website address and when you give your business card to potential customers, you can encourage them to visit your website, in the knowledge it is exactly as you left it. By comparison, if you only use Facebook or another platform as your main hub, you will first have to quote a rather longer web address (URL) — which would not look so impressive on your printed material — but more importantly, it will be more complicated for your target audience to type in and, potentially, get wrong.

If you engage in other forms of traditional media such as TV, radio, or good old adverts in the local press, then you can also include links to your website in all other aspects of your offline marketing activities.

The other thing to consider is the lifespan of your material. Printed material such as business cards, letterheads and compliment slips, typically last six to twelve months (or even longer). Equally, when you have your website domain name, it's also likely to be under your control for a very long time. One of the greatest things about having your own website is that you can update the content as regularly as you like, so as your business develops and you add new, engaging (remarkable) content, all of your offline material is still valid and up-to-date.

Printed Material

At the very least, most business owners had to produce brochures, stationery and business cards to "get their name out there" and tell the world what they had to offer. Flyers were a good tool for attracting attention (and still are) and a favourite of many of the fast-food outlets, such as pizza home delivery services.

Public Relations

Public Relations (PR) is another mechanism to "get your name out there" and, again, extensively used by the bigger players, whose deep pockets enable them to appoint PR agencies. PR can also be done in-house, but PR itself does not guarantee exposure, as it is the newspapers and other media executives who decide what they want to publish or broadcast. PR can be quite a time-consuming activity and best left to those who have the specialist skills and contacts to maximise its effect, if you can afford to pay a professional. If not, it's still worth your while talking to your local paper or radio station, because they are always looking for fresh stories to fill their pages or broadcast. Nonetheless, PR was, and still is, a popular channel to gain exposure and create awareness.

Trade Events

Trade events such as trade shows, conferences, and exhibitions are other traditional routes to market. Many a time, I've attended trade shows in search of new products or services, as well as having been involved as an exhibitor. Again, a time-consuming and costly activity, but usually quite productive because it's often a place where buyers meet sellers, as they are both in the same place at the same time. After the show, there is a lot of follow-up work that goes on to convert leads into sales.

Personal Selling

Personal selling is the most personal, traditional method, as it involves either face-to-face communication or conversations over the telephone. Obviously, personal selling is just that — selling —and the focus is often on creating a "sale" or some kind of transaction or exchange. Again, this was (and is) an expensive and time-consuming activity and devours a large part of any organisation's budget. Professional salespeople are worth their weight in gold to any organisation and great sales skills don't come cheap.

Direct Marketing

Direct marketing can be an effective means of communication and can be quite personal if the material is addressed to specific recipients. Sometimes direct marketing is referred to as "junk mail" and, as a bit of an expert in this area, I think it's worth pointing out the differences between good direct marketing and junk mail. It all boils down to relevance. For example, if you identify yourself to me as being interested in what I have to offer (maybe by responding to an advert or by sending back a coupon), if I'm smart enough, I'll send you mail that piques your interest and, hopefully, that may result in a transaction or sale. That's good direct marketing. By contrast, if I send you something that's completely irrelevant on the off chance you might be interested, then that's junk mail — especially if it ends up in the bin! The junk mail operators often send out hordes of stuff in the hope that some of it may "stick". Typically, 1% is received favourably and the other 99% wasted. Direct marketing does have an advantage over other traditional methods because it is measurable, which means promotional material can be tested before being rolled out to larger audiences.

Again, direct marketing is an expensive method. I can recall some of my own direct marketing projects racking up the costs and feeling like a real gamble. One project in particular costly just over £1.50 per letter by the time I'd had the material printed, stuffed the envelopes, stuck the label on the envelopes from a list I'd rented, licked all the stamps and taken them to the post office. £1.50 may not sound like much, but multiply by two thousand letters for a minimal test and that's an awful lot of expense to reach just two thousand prospects (and twenty years ago, £1.50 per direct mail letter was quite a lot of money — about £3.00 in 2017). Fortunately, that particular project achieved a 10% success (conversion) rate for an expensive product, but it could easily have gone the other way had it not hit the mark!

Sponsorship

Sponsorship is another traditional marketing method that could quite easily drain your marketing budget. It's very difficult to measure and many finance directors could be forgiven for feeling like they're pouring money into a black hole. It basically involves throwing large amounts of cash at a cause or event that attracts a wide viewing audience for an extended period of time. Banks, airlines, or drinks manufacturers sponsoring sports teams for several seasons would be a good example.

Here's how it works: When a popular team plays at their home ground, all their fans are subjected to multiple impressions of the sponsor's message for the duration of the event. In the case of a football match, fans may be subjected to these messages for several hours on a regular basis. For the bigger televised events, such as the final of a football competition, this could result in audience figures in the millions, as the match is beamed into fans' homes and sports bars across the globe. This creates a huge amount of what marketers refer to as "opportunities to see" (OTS) their marketing messages and generate brand exposure.

For the micro-business owner, this type of sponsorship is way out of their league; however, the same principles can be applied to much smaller local events. For example, sponsoring your son or daughter's swimming team for a season might be worth considering, if they get a fair amount of exposure in local press or on the local radio (or TV). This works especially well if your target market includes other parents whose children are involved in the sport you sponsor, or people who are just generally interested in reading about the sport. Of course, one of the hidden benefits is you are investing in your local community, which in itself buys you goodwill.

There are a couple of other traditional marketing methods and techniques I could mention, but these are the main ones that make up most of the traditional marketing landscape.

During my research, I asked business owners which traditional marketing tools they used or felt comfortable with when they:

a) started up, and

b) once they were more established

I presented them with the following list of prompts.

Traditional/Offline Marketing Tools

Advertising	Direct Marketing
Television	Direct Mail
Radio	Selling 'off the page' using
Newspapers	coupons
Magazines	Telemarketing
Trade Journals	Mobile Marketing
Outdoor Advertising	e.g, SMS Texting
Others?	Others?
Printed Material	**Events**
Business Cards	Trade Shows
Brochures	Conferences
Flyers	Exhibitions
Leaflets	Networking & Social Events
Others?	Others?
Sales Promotion	**Corporate Image**
Special Offers	Corporate & Social Responsibility
e.g. BOGOF	Cause Related Marketing
Time limited introductory discounts	Community Contribution
Others?	Others?
Point of Sale	**Sponsorship**
Displays stands at the till	Sponsoring events
Discount Vouchers	Sponsoring community activities
Others?	Others?
Personal Selling	**Guerilla Marketing**
Face to face selling	Fly posters
Selling over the telephone	Sticker bombing
Others?	Others?
Public Relations	**Product Placement**
Press Releases	
Publicity Articles	**Referrals**
Guest Interviews on Radio and/or Television	
Others?	**Word of Mouth**

Most of them admitted to using at least a few from this list. What was really interesting was that they all used the traditional tools to initially interrupt their target audience and create awareness for their new venture at the point of start-up. Several placed adverts in the local paper, a couple used the radio, flyers were quite popular to create that initial "splash" and everybody tried to get some form of PR by inviting the local paper to do a feature on them.

One thing that came through very strongly was that despite the claims of some "experts", traditional marketing is not dead. Far from it! In fact, it's not just "alive and kicking". It's just as important now as it always was — and possibly even more so!

Sergio Zyman, the former head of marketing at Coca-Cola, claimed in his book, 'The End of Marketing As We Know It', that traditional marketing was "as dead as Elvis". That grabbed a few headlines back in 1999, when it was published! He argues that the traditional marketing methods will always have a place in the digital age; however, the role they play in the overall marketing mix has become more complex. This is because traditional marketing methods must be integrated into the new digitally dominated landscape and used alongside other marketing tools and methods, to communicate with your target audience(s) and to maximise their overall impact.

In short, you cannot afford to forget traditional marketing methods and assume everything can be done online. The traditional marketing landscape is alive and well and most definitely here to stay!

The Digital Marketing Landscape

There is absolutely no doubt that the Internet has made marketing much more complicated. It didn't happen overnight, but it has morphed into this complex ecosystem which many struggle to get to grips with. So what exactly is the "digital marketing landscape" and what does it look like? For the purpose of this discussion, we'll define "digital" as anything that happens online which does not include social media — we'll cover that separately in the next section.

The main digital marketing tools are websites, search engine marketing, online partnerships, display advertising, email marketing, online PR, webinars and mobile. Let's take a closer look at each of these.

Websites

Your business' website should be your online "shop window" and be at the heart of your digital marketing strategy. The main benefits are that it should be available 24/7, it leaves you in total control and it's also very easy to add new content on a regular basis and to manage efficiently.

Having the website as your hub makes it very easy to direct your target audience to your content. For example, if you've got a great offer for a new product or service and send your subscriber list an email, it is very quick and efficient to just include the link in your email to a dedicated landing page on your website rather than send the full content.

As your business develops and you create more content and, hence, additional dedicated pages, you can easily include the link to these new pages in all of your communications. Let's say that you have an offer you want to run for the month of June; you can easily create a dedicated landing page specifically for that offer and only have it available on your website for a fixed period of time. This makes it very easy for all of your communications, both online and offline, to point to this new dedicated landing page for as long as you require. For example, your ads in your local paper and every email you send in June can point to www.<yourwebsitename>.com/june-offer.

You should take great care when you develop your website to ensure it correctly projects your brand values, communicates your online value proposition and gives the visitor a good experience. This can all have a positive effect on customer satisfaction and loyalty which, in turn, creates positive word-of-mouth. "Usability" is a hot topic in website development circles and is primarily concerned with designing a website that's easy to use, meets users' expectations and contributes to your business goals. Designing and building a good, usable website is a specialist skill and not something anyone can just knock together in a couple of hours on a Friday night.

> A great customer experience increases satisfaction and hence loyalty. This should be one of your website's key outcomes.

Other benefits of a good website include:

▲ The ability to integrate tools of engagement and create a more personalised user experience, such as a blog; opportunities to leave user ratings, reviews and other feedback; and links to other content to give a consistent message to reinforce your brand proposition.

▲ It can provide a wealth of analytical data, which can assist with understanding your visitors' behaviour and give you a deeper understanding of your customers and the way they use your website. You can then tailor your website to more closely match their needs.

▲ It gives you the opportunity to gather qualitative and quantitative data about your customers and visitors, via surveys and questionnaires, to gain a greater insight into what they really want, so you can help and serve them better.

▲ It gives you the opportunity to test your marketing ideas. For example, you can optimise your return on investment (ROI) by testing the design and wording (the copy) of different landing pages. This is often referred to as "A/B Testing", where you send half of your visitors to one landing page and the other half to a different landing page to see which one works best. Once you have your fine-tuned marketing material, you can use it in other marketing channels, such as email, or in a good old-fashioned paper-based mail shot.

There are a couple of drawbacks you should also consider. For example, implementing and maintaining technology can be resource intensive — especially if you dig quite deeply into the analytics and use these insights to keep refining the design of your website to perfectly match your customers' needs. You also need to continually invest in driving traffic to your website which, again, can chew up both time and money. It is an important element of maximising the contribution your online presence makes to your "bottom line", as things can go stale very quickly if not updated. What you really want is for your visitors to keep coming back to find out what's new that might interest them. You want to encourage them to spend more time with you on your website, consuming your content, rather than visiting one of your competitors' websites.

Search Engine Marketing (SEM)

The buying decision journey has changed and we all now naturally turn to a search engine when looking for a new product, service, entertainment, or information. Being found at the "zero moment of truth" is vital for presenting relevant messages to prospects at the right time, to generate quality traffic to your website. Making sure Google (or any of the other search engines) present your value proposition at this crucial moment is where Search Engine Marketing (SEM) comes into play. There are two sides to the SEM coin: the first is Search Engine Optimisation (SEO) and the second is Paid Search (also known as "Pay-Per-Click" or PPC).

Search Engine Optimisation (SEO)

The search engine providers have one primary aim — and that's to deliver relevant content to users in the Search Engine Results Pages (SERPS) based on the search terms they enter. A while ago, there was a joke doing the rounds in Internet marketing circles that "the best place to hide a dead body is page 2 of Google search results" because, according to research by one of the online ad networks, 95% of users never look at the second page. You really want to appear on the first page of the SERPS listings for your preferred search terms.

As users and search algorithms become more sophisticated, the use of what's known as "long-tail search phrases" is increasing. This is where the user types in a short sentence or phrase to describe what they want to find, rather than just one or two indicative "key" words. In its continuous drive to deliver relevant content, Google frequently updates its algorithm, which makes it difficult to predict how it will behave in delivering results. Therefore, maintaining a high ranking in the SERPS requires continuous investment and technical capability as it is a complex and dynamic process. This is something you may want to get some specialist help with but, unfortunately, it is a bit of a minefield, because whoever you choose to help you optimise your SEO activity really does need to spend quite a bit of time understanding your business. And, of course, time costs money!

Google makes its money by providing relevant information at the "zero moment of truth", so the more relevant your content is to what your prospects and customers are looking for, the greater the chance you have of Google selecting your content to present at this crucial moment. Creating "remarkable content" naturally motivates others to link to relevant content, particularly via blogs. This is important because search engines favour sites that are relevant and updated more regularly. Hence, the quality of content is an essential element of SEO; however, this takes time to develop and to be indexed by the search engines, so the results of SEO are not immediately visible.

That just about sums up the "free" option. The other choice you have is to pay for your traffic. This is where "paid search" comes in.

Paid Search (Pay-Per-Click, or PPC)
Paid search is similar to conventional advertising and gives greater control over the appearance of adverts in the "sponsored links" section of the SERPS. It is subject to both the amount the advertiser is prepared to pay for the keywords and the relevance the advert has to the search request. Google terms this the "Quality Score" and assigns a score between one and ten to reflect the page's relevance to the search term entered. Generally speaking, the higher your Quality Score, the lower the cost, because a high Quality Score is Google's way of saying that your PPC advert meets your potential customers' needs pretty closely. The better you are at meeting the prospect's needs, the less Google will charge you for the advert click.

Paid search has several advantages:

▲ Adverts are highly targeted and only paid for when traffic is driven to the landing page
▲ ROI can be easily tracked with the right tools, such as Google Analytics
▲ It is more predictable than with SEO
▲ It is technically simpler than SEO and, hence, a good place for the novice Internet marketer to start
▲ It is quicker to achieve SERP listing results than SEO

▲ There are also benefits with branding, especially when launching a new product or campaign.

Drawbacks include the ongoing cost, in terms of the time required to manage PPC campaigns and the direct cost associated with bidding on (and buying) the most appropriate "keywords" to meet your objectives. Some industry commentators suggest that PPC offers limited benefit and a PPC campaign does not equate to guaranteed traffic. In terms of its credibility as an advertising medium, research suggests that many people are unaware of the difference between paid and organic search listings, with up to 40% of web users being unaware sponsored links were actually adverts. This means that for many who search on Google, the difference between what is and what is not an advert, is not immediately obvious. Regardless, Google is pretty happy that paid search is still growing, as it is a huge source of billions of dollars in revenue for them — as reflected in their corporate accounts.

Affiliate Marketing

Affiliates are effectively "commission only" salespeople and are a form of online partnerships. Affiliate marketing is a "pay-per-performance" commission-based arrangement, where you only pay an affiliate when a sale is made or lead generated. It can offer many benefits, such as increased SERPs visibility, as affiliates usually have advanced SEO & PPC skills, which can also have a positive effect on brand awareness. Research findings reveal the profile of UK affiliates to be mature, well-educated and with a wealth of online experience, with nearly a fifth of those surveyed having at least ten years' affiliate marketing experience. Extended reach is also a bonus as affiliates often have access to users and markets that would be cost prohibitive for many companies to develop.

However, you have virtually no control over what your affiliates do whilst the nature of the "commission only" business model dictates a product/sales rather than market orientation, because if they don't sell, they don't get paid. Affiliates are very "money driven" and some may not find "small ticket items" attractive unless you pay huge commissions. If you operate from a market orientation and building strong, lasting relationships with your end customers from day one is important to you, affiliate marketing may not be the way to go. You may also find the associated overheads of managing an affiliate network too costly and resource intensive and perhaps should direct your limited resources elsewhere — certainly in the early stages.

Display Advertising

Interactive display advertising (IDA) involves an advertiser paying for an advertising placement on a third-party website, where adverts are selected from an "ad server" using specialist software. The purpose of placing your advert on a third-party (originating) site is to drive traffic to your website, which is commonly referred to as the "destination site". Your adverts will typically be displayed adjacent to relevant content using algorithms, which the search engines use to determine which adverts to display, based on relating trigger keywords.

Interactive display advertising can be quite complex and part of the challenge is to understand how advanced techniques, such as "re-targeting" via content networks, supports paid search ROI. IDA can be costly, so advert targeting needs to be carefully considered and managed as part of the overall SEM strategy. The level of technical knowledge to implement and monitor IDA will be a barrier to many micro-businesses and focusing your limited resources on paid search, rather than IDA, may well be the best use of your hard-earned cash, at least to start with.

Email Marketing

Email marketing is the online equivalent of direct marketing. It can be used as an acquisition tool, but this relies on either working with someone who already has a mailing list on a joint venture basis, or renting a list from a list broker of the types of people you're interested in. Sending email to a "cold list" is risky, as your messages may be marked as spam and may not be delivered. Therefore, its relative merit as an acquisition tool is quite low.

It is far better to seek your prospects' permission before sending emails, so interrupting them at the "zero moment of truth" and asking them to agree to be contacted, results in a far higher email delivery and open rate.

The earlier comments on junk mail and direct mail also apply online, but the Internet does provide a platform for marketers to be much more creative than paper and ink allow. Plus, you can redirect your prospect to other web pages, to refine the content of interest and ensure it's highly targeted.

Once you have built your in-house list, email is a great tool to keep in contact with your prospects and customers at every step of their customer journey. This is because they have given you their consent to contact them by email, by providing their email address. This significantly increases the chance of your messages being opened and actually read. In short, email is an effective tool for building relationships with customers online and can still drive good response rates.

Key benefits of email include:

▲ Your messages can be easily personalised and delivered cheaply (compared to direct mail)

▲ It facilitates faster campaign deployment; for example, you can design an email campaign in the morning, send it out after lunch and have feedback before you go home

▲ It also provides rapid measurable results unavailable in traditional direct marketing.

Email does have a couple of drawbacks. For example, it can be difficult to cut through "noise" as the typical email subscriber may receive hundreds of permission-based messages per month. Declining subscriber engagement is also an issue, as email recipients are most responsive when they first subscribe and their interest tends to decline over time — so keeping them engaged is an ongoing challenge.

The other key challenge is getting your email delivered through ISPs and firewalls. Large email campaigns can be technically resource-intensive and often best served by employing a specialist email service provider — but, of course, there is a cost associated with this. As a micro-business owner, email is certainly something you should seriously consider; building your own in-house list will become a hugely valuable marketing asset to you and, hence, well worth the effort.

Online PR (E-PR)

PR is "the discipline which manages an organisation's reputation, with the aim of influencing opinion and behaviour between an organisation and its stakeholders". Online audiences are better informed than ever before and can easily share their views with the organisation and others. The speed news can disseminate is also a significant distinguishing factor of PR, delivering a high level of credibility and cost-effectiveness, which many of the other marketing tools fail to provide. Basically, PR is considered more credible and believable, because it's written by a third party who does not have a vested interest in the "story" itself; their interest is merely in delivering the "story" to their target audience.

E-PR can offer significant reach at minimal cost, with independent comment adding credibility and, hence, raising trust. Additionally, E-PR can have SEO benefits by generating favourable exposure for your brand and, when effectively combined with SEO, it can be a significant traffic driver to your website.

Forming relationships with online publishers is an effective way to extend reach, as more journalists rely on blogs for stories. Influential bloggers also need a continuous supply of material to write about and are constantly on the lookout for quality material to share with their audience. So contributing to influential blogs, as a guest blogger, is an effective way to build authority and credibility with your audience and, as a by-product, it can also help with SEO.

Webinars

A "webinar" is a presentation, lecture, workshop, or seminar that is transmitted over the Web using video conferencing software. The term "webinar" is short for "Web-based seminar" and a key feature of a webinar is its interactive elements, as it provides the ability to give, receive and discuss information in real time.

Using webinar software, the host can share audio, documents and applications with their webinar attendees. This is useful when the webinar host is conducting a lecture or information session, as the presenter can share their desktop application, such as PowerPoint slides, with the attendees whilst talking.

Attendees are usually invited by email — so sending invitations to your in-house list is one way to fill the "virtual room" — and, whilst most webinars are free, some webinar hosts charge to attend, particularly if they share specialist knowledge.

Typically, webinars are used as a lead and sales generation tool where a presenter will talk about their specialist subject to demonstrate their expertise in a particular area. They may then take questions and interact with the audience and quite often make a "pitch" to sell an online product or course they have developed around their specialist subject.

Unfortunately, some webinar hosts come from a sales orientation and spend most of their time trying to sell, which turns the webinar into an hour-long sales pitch (or even longer). In my opinion, this cheapens the opportunity webinars provide, because webinars are a great way to connect and interact with your audience. Personally, I think you should spend more time delivering value and building relationships before trying to sell. That doesn't mean you shouldn't use a webinar to sell your product or service — far from it! It just means you should be mindful of the entire relationship-building process described earlier in this book — and where webinars fit into that process — before using this platform as a sales tool.

Webinars are particularly good for informational-type products or consultancy-based services. They are not extensively used for practical trade-based businesses, such as plumbing; however, having said that, if you are a plumber and want to start building awareness for your business, there is no reason why you shouldn't use webinars to explain what you do and why it's important to your target audience.

As a micro-business owner, webinars can be a very cost-effective way of reaching your target audience, especially as a webinar can be recorded and replayed "on demand" after the event. All you need to host your webinar is a computer with a microphone (and possibly a camera), some presentation software, such as PowerPoint or Keynote, a good Internet connection, access to webinar hosting software, a quiet room and an interesting topic to talk about.

Webinars are a fantastic tool to educate your audience and explain why they need you and can be used to deliver your message in every step of AIDA and DRIP.

Mobile Marketing

For many users, mobile devices have become indispensable and have overtaken desktops as the first port of call for accessing the Internet. They are a good way to engage and retain customers because they are "always on". They command so much of their owners' attention and dominate their daily lives. Have you ever noticed the mobile phone taking priority when you're talking to someone and they get a text? For that reason, mobile can be considered a direct line and immediate connection with your target audience.

Changes in consumer behaviour also mean not having a mobile-friendly website is an area you cannot afford to ignore. Particularly as modern consumers have access to information at their fingertips twenty-four hours a day and they expect their mobile devices to make their lives easier. According to Google (2013), 45% of mobile searches are goal-oriented and are conducted to help make a decision, with 81% of mobile searches being driven by speed and convenience. All interesting statistics, but the key message here is that entrepreneurs and micro-business owners should at least optimise their website so it can be displayed and read on a small screen — otherwise, for many potential customers, they may as well not exist!

Therefore, as an entrepreneur and micro-business owner, it is worth investing the extra resources to ensure your website is "mobile friendly". Research by the Mobile Marketing Association shows that over 50% of smart phone users employ their mobile phones to determine if they need a product and increasingly use mobile as a tool to learn more about products and engage more deeply with brands — usually at the "zero moment of truth". The bottom line is lack of mobile optimisation delivers a poor user experience, resulting in frustrated users and this ultimately leads to brand damage.

There is an awful lot more to mobile marketing. For example, sending your prospects special offers if they walk past, but not into your store — this takes location tracking and location marketing to a completely different level, for which specialist skills and an industrial-sized budget are required. Mobile marketing is a specialist area in its own right and very resource intensive. As a micro-business owner, my advice would be to get the most out of all the other areas of your marketing first, and then, when you have a sizable chunk of cash to put the icing on your marketing cake, seek the services of a mobile marketing specialist.

This is a comprehensive list of the digital marketing tools available to you in 2017. If you can master these in your business context, you'll be well on the way to building an impressive digital marketing footprint.

What did my research show?

So, what are other entrepreneurs and micro-business owners doing online? That's probably best illustrated by the following list, which I used during my research and, again, I asked which of these digital marketing tools business owners used:

a) during start-up, and

b) when they were established.

Digital Marketing

Website	Online Partnerships
Build Website	Affiliate Marketing
Manage Website	Sponsorship
Mobile Responsive	Co-Branding
Landing Pages	Link Building
Analytics	**Display Advertising**
Domain Names	Banners/Skyscrapers/MPUs
Search Engine Marketing	Ad Servers/Networks
Paid Search — Pay Per Click (PPC)	**Email Marketing**
Search engine Optimisation (SEO)	
Content Marketing	**Online PR**
Blogs	
Articles/Special Reports	**Webinars & Podcasts**
Newsletters	
Video	**Mobile Marketing**
RSS Feeds	
	QR Codes/VCards

It will probably come as no surprise to you that every business owner I interviewed —without exception —said they considered having an online presence to be essential. Remember the guy I mentioned earlier, who said, "If you're not online, in my world, you don't even exist"? That, I'm sure you'll agree, is a pretty strong argument to create and maintain at least a minimal online presence. We know from our discussion on the "zero moment of truth" that, for many, Google or one of the other search engines is the first port of call and if you don't present your offering to your target audience at this critical point in the decision-making process, you don't stand a chance of getting their business. Therefore, you simply must have an online presence if the search engines are going to find you — it's as simple as that!

For most business owners, having an online presence meant having a website. For those who didn't, a social media presence, such as a Facebook page or LinkedIn profile, was considered sufficient. This is the absolute minimum if you're going to stand a remote chance of being found at the "zero moment of truth". I would strongly recommend that every business has its own dedicated website — even if it just acts as an online brochure. In fact, in the early days of the Internet, websites were just that —online brochures — and they can be just as useful and valuable today as they were back in the mid-late nineties. Of course, websites can be a lot more than online brochures. We see and use many examples every day where business transactions and other interactions happen online — eBay, Amazon, online banking, shopping, booking hotels and travel, to name just a few. You can even do your weekly shopping on your iPad or laptop, without getting out of your armchair.

At the point of start-up, all participants had either a website (the majority) and/or a presence on Facebook or LinkedIn. Several used PPC to drive traffic to their website and whilst many were conscious about SEO, it was not something they were able to invest in during the early stages of their business.

Once they were established, a few had started building an email list and took advantage of what email marketing had to offer. Maintaining their website was high on their agenda and several had blogs that they regularly updated and even used to drive traffic to specific landing pages. A search engine friendly website was certainly the topic of conversation and most website owners were trying to get to grips with this area of their marketing activity. Once they had mastered the basics, they were keen to take what they had learnt and redevelop or enhance their website, to make sure it was not just more search engine friendly but also mobile friendly. They were also keen that any redesign should improve usability, to keep their website visitors on their site as long as possible.

At this stage they were also looking into the benefits of SEO to try and increase traffic to their website and two were beginning to experiment with webinars. This seems a typical progression and certainly a path worth considering, as you build your online presence and develop your digital footprint. As for the timescale — that really depended on the individual, but most did have, at least, a basic site before they opened their doors and the more advanced, digitally capable micro-business owners employed the more sophisticated techniques within about twelve to eighteen months.

Website analysis tools, such as Google Analytics, can help interrogate the numbers behind the activity to find out how well your website performs. Several of the more established business owners I interviewed were beginning to get some interesting insights from this free Google tool. This helped them make changes and tweak their websites to convert as many visitors to customers as possible. However, this is yet another resource-intensive process and requires ongoing investment.

That's the overview of digital marketing, which needs to be integrated with the traditional marketing methods, and, of course, the newer and ever-changing scene of social media.

The Social Media Marketing Landscape

Social media includes any of the online social media platforms available and they play a very important part in the New Engagement Paradigm. With traditional and digital marketing channels, you have a little more control over how and when your message (or content) is consumed; however, with social media, you have absolutely no control whatsoever! This is because most of the conversations happen in the social space — and many of those conversations will happen whether or not you are actively involved in the discussion. As marketers, we cannot dictate what people do or say, or when they do it. In fact, you actually want your target audience to be having conversations about you without you actively taking part (as long as what they say is positive) because that's the ultimate in terms of marketing: other people generating positive word-of-mouth to promote your brand, product, or service without any prompting or undue pressure from you. But be warned — your target audience will "sniff out" an engineered or contrived conversation a mile away and spot if you're not being genuine. They will also tell others, which will create negative word-of-mouth and hence damage your brand. Fake or coerced five-star reviews are one example of this dodgy practice.

Your (genuine) conversations can be instigated by either the traditional or digital channels. For example, you may send an email containing a link to some content on YouTube which your target audience will find highly engaging. You hope they will then "like" and "share" this content with other like-minded individuals, which may very well lead to conversations on social media platforms such as Facebook, LinkedIn, or Twitter. You may even get a mention in someone's blog post, recommending their target audience also take a look at your content. This is great, as it really utilises the power of the influencer to influence others who you may not be able to reach directly yourself.

In "the good old days" if someone made a complaint against you or "badmouthed" your products or services, you could ignore them and hope they'd go away. Unless they got the attention of the press or some TV consumer protection programme, there was limited damage they could do to your brand or your business.

Fast forward twenty years and opinionated consumers in the social media space cannot be ignored. If they are, they often become more vocal and you end up with a real battle on your hands to keep the credibility you worked so hard to create. Social media has given your customers and your critics a voice — and an extremely powerful one. You enter the realms of social media marketing at your peril and, even if you don't want to invest time here, your customers will drag you in kicking and screaming, because that's where they want to have conversations about your product/service/

brand. If they say great things about what you have to offer, it will be your biggest marketing asset; if they don't, it could consume a lot of time and energy in "damage limitation". To move into the social media space, you must have a strategy to maximise its potential impact and a contingency plan if things go wrong.

The best strategy to manage your social media activity is be totally honest up front and don't try to pretend to be something you're not. Always live and act according to your core values and you won't go far wrong. Honesty is always the best policy and this most definitely applies in the social space. However, one thing it can also do, is show your human side and we, as human business owners, want to build mutually beneficial relationships with our human customers. Social media does provide the opportunity to build and strengthen relationships in a way that was impossible just a few short years ago.

As far as your contingency plan is concerned, you need to monitor and be aware of what people are saying about you in the social space. If they start badmouthing you, it's often best to first talk to them on the platform where they have posted their negative comments, so everybody who has seen their comment can also see your response. If that fails to resolve the issue, it's often far better to take the conversation/dispute offline and talk to them on the phone or in person. If they have a genuine complaint, you can get some valuable feedback and act accordingly to rectify or smooth over the situation. Either way, you prevent more negative comments being posted in the social space. Quite often people who have a gripe just want to have their voices heard and it's far better for this to happen in private. There are a number of social media sentiment monitoring tools, such as HootSuite, Social Mention and Google Alerts, that can help you "listen" to what's being said about you on social media. If you want to become really active with social media marketing, it's certainly worth checking out tools like these.

What Is "Social Media"?

Social media refers to a collection of websites and applications that enable you to create and share content. It also allows you to interact with other users pretty much any time of the day or night regardless of your physical location. As long as you have a device connected to the Internet, you can use one of the many social media platforms to stay connected to the "virtual world".

Generally speaking, social media can be split into seven broad categories:

▲ Social networking
▲ Blogs and micro-blogging
▲ Video sharing
▲ Online photo management and sharing
▲ Social curation
▲ Forums and online communities
▲ Review sites

Social Networks

Social networking is the physical activity associated with expanding the number of people in your social or business network by making new connections through other people. It is a well-established activity and has been around for many hundreds of years — certainly a very long time before the Web was even thought of. Creating these new connections previously relied on you being in the same room as those you may have wanted to connect with — business networking events being just one good example.

The Internet has removed this physical barrier. Now you can make new connections online by using one of the many online social networking sites. Largely based on the concept of the "six degrees of separation" (the idea that any two people on the planet could make contact through a chain of no more than five links, or intermediaries), the idea behind these online platforms is to create online communities that help you make contact with people you would have been unlikely to meet in the real (offline) world.

There are a whole array of online social networking sites, but the three main ones micro-business owners should consider are Facebook, LinkedIn, and Google+, if for no other reason than they are the biggest.

Facebook

Facebook is a popular free social networking website that allows registered users to create profiles, upload photos and video, send messages and keep in touch with friends, family and colleagues. The site is available in more than thirty-five languages and. by the end of 2016, had 1.86 billion registered users worldwide, which makes it the largest online social network. According to the Nielsen Group, US Internet users spend more time on Facebook than any other website.

Many users see Facebook as just that — a free online social networking site — and are quite happy to share a lot of their personal details in the public domain. Facebook loves (and encourages) this behaviour and, as a result, it knows an awful lot about its users. It has even been suggested that Facebook knows more about US citizens than the FBI! Facebook makes its money through advertising because it is able to place highly targeted adverts in front of very large numbers of its users.

It has several publicly available features, such as:

▲ Presence technology — this allows you to see which of your contacts are online and start chatting to them

▲ Pages — this allows you to create and promote a public page built around a specific topic or area of interest

▲ Events — a facility to publicise, invite guests and track who plans to attend your event

▲ Groups — allows you to find and interact with other members who have common interests

▲ Marketplace — a facility that allows you to post, read and respond to classified ads.

Your personal profile will give you access to a number of key networking tools. The most popular is what's known as the "Wall", which is effectively a virtual bulletin board. Your contacts (known as "friends") can leave messages on your Wall in many formats (text, photo, or video). Another popular feature is the virtual Photo Album; you can easily upload photos from your smart phone, tablet, or laptop and your friends can then comment on your photos and identify (tag) people in the photos.

Another really popular profile component is status updates, a micro-blogging feature that allows members to broadcast short SMS-type announcements to all their friends in a matter of seconds. All interactions are published in a news feed which is distributed in real time to your friends — and if they are online, they'll see your update instantly.

Facebook offers a range of privacy options. You can make all your communications visible to everyone, block specific contacts, or keep everything completely private from the prying eyes of the wider world. You can choose whether or not to be searchable, restrict parts of your profile to just your contacts rather than make them publicly available and limit who can see the posts on your Wall and news feeds. If you want to use Facebook to communicate with one of your friends privately, there is also a messaging feature that closely resembles email.

The bottom line is that Facebook offers a feature-rich online social networking platform with lots of users who use the platform for large portions of their day. Some argue this is a bad thing, claiming some users are addicted to Facebook. If that sounds a bit far-fetched, consider this: in 2012, researchers from the University of Bergen in Norway published the "Bergen Facebook Addiction Scale", which is the world's first psychological scale to measure Facebook addiction!

What this essentially means to you as a micro-business owner is that Facebook may well be a suitable platform to advertise your product or service at a relatively low cost compared to traditional media advertising — providing, of course, that your target audience actually are avid Facebook users.

LinkedIn

LinkedIn is an online social networking site designed specifically for the business community, which allows registered members to establish and document networks of people they know and trust professionally. Basic membership is free and members of your network are referred to as "connections". Unlike Facebook, LinkedIn requires you to have a pre-existing relationship with your connections. With the basic (free) membership you can only establish connections with past or present colleagues, those who know you professionally (online or offline), or someone you have gone to school or University with.

As a LinkedIn member, your profile page documents your professional experience, education and professional interests. LinkedIn was built for professionals who want to use their existing and future social networks to build their career, for companies that want to find qualified employees and for job hunters.

Connections up to three degrees away (based on the "six degrees of separation") are seen as part of your network, but you are not allowed to contact them through LinkedIn without an introduction. However, a premium subscription can be purchased on a monthly subscription basis and this allows you to send a small number of emails to people you would like to connect with but you do not yet know.

LinkedIn was co-founded by Reid Hoffman, a former executive vice-president in charge of business and corporate development for PayPal. The site was launched in May 2003 and by the end of 2016 had over 467 million members from over 200 countries, representing over 170 industries. Recent figures (in 2016) show there are more than 40 million students and college graduates, which makes them the site's fastest-growing demographic and fertile ground for recruiters. This group represents around 30% of LinkedIn subscribers.

However, it's not just for job seekers and recruiters. If you're looking for venture capital for your start-up, you can use LinkedIn to find experienced professionals for your "dream team" from the tens of millions of experienced professional members.

Plus, if you're an independent contractor, you can use LinkedIn to:

- ▲ List your business in the Service Providers directory
- ▲ Send business updates to your network
- ▲ Create a group or join an existing group related to your business
- ▲ Ask your clients on LinkedIn to recommend you
- ▲ Answer questions to establish your expertise
- ▲ Use specific keywords to search the people database and find potential clients.

There are also real benefits to using LinkedIn's "Groups" feature. You can use the power of Groups to boost your potential network, as the real opportunity is getting the chance to introduce yourself to new people in a familiar setting.

For the micro-business owner, LinkedIn could be an invaluable source of relevant and active contacts. For example, in early 2016, the UK's 20 million members put them in third place in terms of traffic generation (just over 6%), slightly behind India (6.65%) and way behind the US, whose 124 million subscribers generated about one-third of the total traffic on the site. The implication for the micro-business owner is that LinkedIn could provide a very fertile prospecting ground at a relatively low cost. Certainly worth thinking about, especially if you operate within one of the many professional fields.

Google+

Google+ (pronounced Google Plus) is Google's attempt at social networking. The Google+ design team sought to replicate the way people interact offline more closely than other social networking platforms such as Facebook. The project's slogan is, "Real-life sharing rethought for the web". Google claims their emphasis is on creating the kind of space that replicates casual ad-hoc gatherings in the real world.

Google+ was launched on June 28, 2011, as a bit of a latecomer to the online social networking platform party and struggled to gain traction against the mighty Facebook, despite Google having an estimated 2.2 billion user accounts across all its services. Estimates of the number of active Google+ users vary wildly and the best guess, somewhere around 1-2% of what Facebook boasts, is probably not far off.

The Google+ service delivers functionality and many features similar to those of Facebook, including "Posts", which are similar to Facebook "status updates"; "Circles" for sharing information with different groups of people (like Facebook Groups); and "Sparks" for offering videos and articles users might like. It also offers an option for video chat for several people at any given time since this technology is evolving quickly and new products are coming out all the time.

Additionally, "Huddle" is a group messaging app for Android, iPhone and SMS devices to keep groups in touch with each other. For example, if you're trying to get several people to meet for coffee for, say, a business meeting, a Huddle can turn the typical one-to-one conversation into a group chat so everyone is on the same page at the same time. One of the key benefits is that it can save time and prevent miscommunication.

Instant upload is an option to automatically send pictures and videos taken with a mobile device to a private photo album. Users can then decide whether to share them and which circles to share them with.

Google+ is unique because it functions as a micro-blogging, video conferencing and community-based forum all at once; consequently, it offers multiple ways to share your content with an interested audience. It is also a bit different to some of the other social networking platforms because it is integrated with other Google applications, such as Gmail, Google Maps, Google Books and Google Calendar.

For the micro-business owner, it may offer some benefits, providing your target audience are Google+ fans. In particular, some might find the "Hangouts" video chat/conferencing feature useful. However, some industry experts predict it will never catch up with the likes of Facebook or LinkedIn, so think carefully before you invest your limited resources in this direction. You may find the other platforms offer a better return on your investment, due to their sheer scale and active market penetration.

Blogging

What is a "blog"?

A blog is a frequently updated, online personal journal or diary. It is a place to share your thoughts and your passions and to express yourself to the world. Originally, blogs were primarily places for people to write about their day-to-day activities. Their mundane, everyday tasks became fodder for journal entries and somehow these writers gained a following and the hobby of blogging was born. Many people blog about their interests as a hobby and a few even end up making a full-time career of blogging, though that's very rare.

Terminology

The word "blog" is derived from the words "web log", which is an on online diary or journal. Just so we're clear on the terminology, someone who writes a "blog" is referred to as a "blogger" and the act of keeping a blog up-to-date is known as "blogging".

Why would you bother writing a blog?

Why would anyone want their own blog? The answer lies in the fact that every human has a voice and wants their voice to be heard. The Internet gives the ordinary person a platform that can potentially reach a huge audience with minimal effort. Bloggers have the opportunity to reach hundreds, or even thousands of people, each and every day.

What to blog about

Whilst there are still many people who like to share the mundane details of their days, such as what they ate for lunch and how many times the cat meowed during the latest reality show on TV, there are bloggers who give almost no detail about their lives and write instead about their hobby or something else they are passionate about. Blog topics can take many forms, from hair tips to celebrity scandal or political rumour. Blogs on cooking, health, gardening and sport are quite popular and some even encourage people to volunteer for charity work or other good causes.

A blog can be anything you want it to be, but in the micro-business marketing context, we'll define a blog as "a section of your website that you update and add to regularly with content your target audience find relevant and useful". The whole point of investing time and energy in a blog over an extended period of time (years) is to ultimately promote yourself and your business, keep in touch with your customers and target audience and continually reinforce the relationship, as it keeps your brand at the front of their minds.

It is possible to have a website that is 100% a blog and, if you're blogging as a hobby, this may be the most suitable way to design and deliver your blog. Many have mastered the technology of setting up their own blogs on platforms such as WordPress — which is actually quite simple, especially as there are lots of YouTube videos and other material to show you exactly how to do it. However, as a micro-business owner, you really want your blog to be part of your search engine friendly website. It is inevitable that a fair portion of your website will remain static, but by including a blog as part of your website (rather than having it as a separate unconnected site), every time you add a blog post, Google and the other search engines will notice there is something new. This will usually help encourage them to list you higher in the search engine results pages (SERPS), so there is also an SEO advantage to blogging on a regular basis.

When to blog

How often you blog will largely be dependent on your industry, your motivation to write and your resources. Make no mistake: blogging takes time and a lot of care and attention should be applied to even a relatively short blog post. If you search Google, you'll find many differing opinions on how regularly you should blog, but as a micro-business owner with plenty of other things to do, I'd initially suggest no more than once a week would be a sensible start. The best thing to do is test it and ask your customers what they want (via your blog) and then work out your publishing schedule accordingly.

As for the length of your posts, they do need to be reasonably short to match your reader's probable attention span. They also need to be packed with relevant information, not waffle. It's far better to post a decent piece of high-quality information once a month, rather than a bunch of drivel every other day. So around three to four hundred words would be a sensible guide — but if it's a lot shorter and says all it needs to, that's fine. The only way to really find out is to test it and ask for feedback. As always, relevance is the key!

Micro-Blogging

Micro-blogging is posting brief and often frequent updates online. Whilst you would probably host your blog on your custom website, micro-blogs are typically published on a social media platform and consume far less of your time than writing a full blog post.

Twitter

The most common micro-blogging platform is Twitter (which can be found at Twitter.com) and is free to use. It allows you to broadcast short posts known as "tweets" of 140 characters or less and may include "hashtags", which allow you to weave tweets into a conversation thread or connect them to a general topic. You can also include "mentions", which are links to other Twitter users or to online resources, such as web pages, images, or videos. When you post a micro-blog using Twitter, your updates are seen by all users who have chosen to "follow" you.

Unlike Facebook or LinkedIn, where members need to approve social connections, anyone can follow anyone on public Twitter.

Tweets can be delivered to followers in real time and might seem like instant messages to the novice user. But unlike instant messages that disappear when the user closes the application, tweets are also posted on the Twitter website. They are permanent, they are searchable and they are public. Anyone can search tweets on Twitter, whether they are a member or not.

Here is an example of how you, as a micro-business owner, might use Twitter. Let's say you are interested in learning more about email marketing. First, you could search Twitter to see if anyone is talking (tweeting) about "email marketing"; perhaps a quick search reveals that lots of Twitter members are talking about email marketing — which is great for you because you might learn something.

Now, you could do one of several things: you could simply keep tabs on email marketing by returning and searching Twitter each day (not very efficient, but effective), or you could join Twitter and follow people who have posted tweets that catch your interest. As a Twitter member, you can post your own tweets or you can just remain a follower and lurk in the background.

Tumblr

While Twitter is the dominant micro-blogging platform, there are several other options available. One popular service is Tumblr, which was launched in 2007 and acquired by technology giant Yahoo! Inc. in June 2013 for $1.1 billion. It had nearly 333 million users by the beginning of 2017 and allows you to easily insert photos, videos, quotes and links into your posts. It also includes a "reblog" feature for sharing other users' posts.

As they say themselves, "Tumblr lets you effortlessly share anything. Post text, photos, quotes, links, music and videos from your browser, phone, desktop, email, or wherever you happen to be." It is a cross between a social networking site and a blog. It is described as a "micro-blog", as users usually post short snippets of text and quick snaps (pictures) as opposed to longer diary-style entries found in more traditional blogs.

As a micro-business owner, you might consider micro-blogging, probably on Twitter given its dominant position. The objective is to keep in front of your target audience on a more regular basis and it involves a lot less effort than writing a full blog, each time you get a bright idea you want to share with the world.

Video Sharing
YouTube

If you've ever watched a video online, there's a good chance it was a YouTube video. YouTube was launched in April 2005 and purchased by Google in October 2006. It provides a forum for people to connect, inform, and inspire others across the globe and acts as a distribution platform for original video content creators and advertisers large and small. Essentially it is a free video-sharing website that makes it easy to watch online videos. You can also create and upload your own videos to share with others.

YouTube is now one of the most popular sites on the Web with visitors watching around 6 billion hours of video every month. One reason YouTube is so popular is the sheer number of videos you can find. On average, one hundred hours of video are uploaded to YouTube every minute, so there's always something new to find and watch. You'll also find all kinds of videos on YouTube, including adorable cats, quirky cooking demos, funny science lessons, quick fashion tips, and a whole lot more. Another reason YouTube is so popular is that it's all about user-generated content created by people just like you and me, rather than videos from major TV networks and movie studios.

As a micro-business owner, this provides you with a huge opportunity because you can create your own videos about your own products and services with just a smart phone and upload them to YouTube quickly and easily. It is also incredibly easy to embed them into your website. If you have the time and resources, you can make very professional-looking videos by editing them using even basic video editing software, and many YouTube-ers will add their logos and other branding to their video to create a greater presence.

YouTube is a great platform for demonstrating products or just putting a "face in front of the name" to increase you brand presence and build trust in your business. One key advantage is once you have uploaded a video you don't have to worry about it again; Google manage all the technical stuff for you, which removes a big headache for micro-business owners, as you don't have to worry about hosting huge video files on your own website.

Vimeo

Vimeo is a video-sharing platform that was launched in 2004 by a group of filmmakers. Since then, the platform has grown to over 14 million members who use Vimeo as a way to share, promote and showcase their work. Most members are artists in the film, animation and music industries. The main difference between Vimeo and YouTube is Vimeo has a smaller, niche community of film enthusiasts, but its modest size creates an intimate and fully engaged community. Vimeo is regarded as more of a professional network of artists who are genuinely interested in film quality: hence the community is much more appreciative of the content that gets shared there.

Aside from the difference in video genres, Vimeo offers a cleaner aesthetic interface than YouTube. Videos are larger and there's limited clutter around the frame, so it really feels like the primary focus of the website is on the video and nothing else.

Vimeo has a paid subscription model for the most active members who want more features. The fact that members are willing to pay money to showcase their work shows just how serious they are about art and content creation. The community is, therefore, quite friendly and supportive.

Vimeo offers several different options for members who want specific storage and feature needs, from "Vimeo Basic", the basic free version, to "Vimeo Pro", for professionals who require more storage, unlimited bandwidth and detailed analytical data.

Some of the cool features Vimeo offers to its content creators include: the ability to add a music track from its music catalogue to any of your videos, many of which are free to use; a section completely dedicated to showing tutorials and lessons on how to create the best videos; "tip jar", which allows artists to accept small cash payments from viewers who wish to tip them in appreciation for their work; and the ability to create a channel to showcase collections of videos centred around common themes.

The community on Vimeo is strong and genuine and "Vimeo Groups" help bring members even closer. You can chat with others about videos and common interests by creating your own group or joining existing ones.

One key differentiator between YouTube and Vimeo is that there are no distracting banners or thirty-second commercials before your video starts — a huge perk for the viewer. YouTube, on the other hand, relies on its lucrative advertising revenue and the site is literally littered with adverts.

As a micro-business owner, if you have a small number of videos and want to present a more professional image, Vimeo may be a better choice than YouTube. However, if you need more space and want to take advantage of some of the more advanced features, you will have to pay — but the costs are not excessive.

Online Photo Management & Sharing

Flickr

Many consider Flickr to be the best online photo management and sharing application in the world. Flickr has two main goals: making photos and videos easy to share and organising them more flexibly for later retrieval.

Photos and videos can be put into and retrieved from the system in many different ways: via the Web, from mobile devices, or from home computers, regardless of the software you are using to manage your content. Content can be made publicly available or restricted to a group, thereby allowing photos and videos to be shared with just close family and friends.

These days, people take a vast number of pictures and videos on a number of devices, such as smart phones, tablets and cameras, making it very easy to get overwhelmed with the sheer number of photos or videos you take. Organising photos and video can also be overwhelming and part of Flickr's solution is to make the process of organising photos or videos collaborative. With Flickr, you can give your friends, family and other contacts permission to organise your digital assets, as well as allowing them to add comments, notes and tags — all of which is searchable, which makes them much easier to find later on.

Instagram

Instagram is a free online photo sharing and micro-blogging platform and was acquired by Facebook in 2012 for $1 billion. At the beginning of 2017, it had a highly engaged user base of more than 600 million users. Instagram allows users to upload, edit and share photos with other users through the Instagram website, email and social media sites, such as Twitter, Facebook, Tumblr, and Flickr.

Instagram's editing features include various digital filters, one-click rotation and optional borders. Photos can be shared on one or several social media sites at once with a single click, making it very easy to push material to multiple platforms.

Instagram has quickly turned into the favourite social network for many brands, largely due to its appealing user experience. Another reason for its popularity is that it blends the creative and high-quality environment with the engaged audience that not only uses the platform as a source of inspiration, but also as the first step in their next purchasing decision, as it showcases products being used by customers, thereby creating peer approval appeal. Something for the micro-business owner to think about. if you're in the retail or fashion sector — or, for that matter, any industry where a high-quality picture is "worth a thousand words".

Social Curation & Bookmarking
Pinterest

Pinterest, derived from the words "pin" and "interest", is a social curation website for sharing and categorising images found online. The site is described as a "visual bookmarking site" and has a number of categories, including architecture, art, DIY and crafts, fashion, food and drink, home décor, and science and travel, among an almost endless list of other possibilities.

Users can add a "Pin it" button to their browser and then select and "pin" online images to virtual pin boards which are used to organise categories. Pinterest requires brief descriptions, but the main focus of the site is visual. Clicking on an image will take you to the original source, so, for example, if you click on a picture of a designer T-shirt, you might be taken to a site where you can purchase it. An image of a cake might take you to the recipe; a picture of a craft item might take you to the tutorials. Users can browse or search for image content and can follow the boards of other users and can "like" or "Repin" other users' pins.

TechCrunch selected Pinterest as the year's top start-up in 2011, just a year after it was launched and Time magazine named it one of the top fifty websites of 2011. In 2016 Alexa, the website ranking service, ranked Pinterest as the twelfth most visited site in the United States and thirty-first globally, making it one of the fastest-growing social media platforms in the world. As of January 2017, the site had over 150 million users on a monthly basis.

Forums

An Internet forum is an example of an online community and is usually a discussion area on a website. Website members can post discussions and read and respond to posts by other forum members. A forum can be focused on nearly any subject and a sense of camaraderie or community tends to develop among forum members. This type of forum may also be called a message board, discussion group, bulletin board, or web forum, but it differs from a blog, which is usually written by one user and only allows others to comment on a specific blog post. A forum, on the other hand, usually allows all members to make posts and start new discussion topics, which other members can contribute to, making it similar to a proper conversation.

Before a prospective member joins a group and makes posts to others, they are usually required to register. The prospective member must usually agree to follow certain online rules, sometimes called "netiquette", such as to respect other members and refrain from using profanity. When a member is approved by the administrator or moderator, the member usually chooses his or her own username and password. An avatar, or photograph or picture, supplied by the member might appear under the member's username in each post.

The separate conversations in a forum are called "threads", and they are made up of member-written posts. Members can usually edit their own posts, start new topics, post in their choice of threads and edit their profile. A profile usually lists optional information about each forum member, such as the city where they are located and their interests.

An Internet forum administrator or moderator may also participate in the forum. An administrator can usually modify threads as well as move or delete threads if necessary. Moderators often help the administrator and monitor and guide the discussion to make sure the forum rules are being followed.

In the micro-business context, creating a forum or online community can be quite a useful customer engagement tool. For example, if you have a technical product such as software, having a forum can facilitate discussion about various features or workarounds, which allows members (your customers) to support each other. Whilst it should not replace your official support service, it is a good place to encourage experienced members to help the less experienced, creating camaraderie amongst your tribe of loyal followers.

Review Sites

A "review site" is a website where visitors can post reviews about products, services, a business, the service they have received, or even individuals. Two popular review sites are TripAdvisor.com and RatedPeople.com.

TripAdvisor allow users to leave reviews and rate businesses such as hotels, restaurants and travel services, based on their personal experience.

RatedPeople allows customers to "rate" tradesmen they have engaged. It then makes it easier for other customers in need of similar services to find a reliable and professional tradesman by referring to publicly available feedback. Customers also have the ability to post jobs and tradesmen have the opportunity to bid for these jobs, in the hope they will be awarded the work. The site charges for matching the customer with the service provider and is a good example of online word-of-mouth marketing in action.

Studies by independent research groups like Forrester Research, comScore, The Kelsey Group and the Word-of-Mouth Marketing Association, show that rating and review sites influence consumer decision-making behaviour, particularly because they'll check them out at the "zero moment of truth".

The implication for the micro-business owner can be significant. If you're starting a new business, it can take time to generate word-of-mouth and get referrals from happy customers. Review sites can speed up this process significantly because the Internet is usually the first port of call when seeking information at the all-important "zero moment of truth". The key thing to remember is that what others say about your business has far greater influence than what you say yourself!

What Did My Research Show?

During my research, I asked business owners which social media marketing tools they used from the list below. Again, I asked which one they used at:

a) start-up, and

b) when they were established

Social Media Marketing

Facebook	YouTube	Instagram	Review Sites
LinkedIn	Vimeo	SnapChat	TripAdvisor
Twitter	Flickr	Forums	Which?
Google+	Pinterest	Guest Blogging	
Other Social Networks			

Not surprisingly, Facebook was top in the Business-To-Consumer (B2C) space and LinkedIn took prime place in the professional Business-To-Business (B2B) market. Video rated highly (both YouTube and Vimeo) and several of the more experienced marketers used a variety of other social media platforms for a diverse range of reasons. Two of them, I would say, had "cracked it" and were getting very impressive results from their social media activity. However, many were struggling to generate a positive impact for their business and it was no more than a money pit and time thief! The problem was that many of them were trying to use social media the same way as they use the traditional marketing tools — primarily to "tell" their audience what they wanted them to hear (broadcasting) rather than engaging with them and being an active part of the conversation.

The more successful ones created "remarkable" content which triggered positive conversations; these were then shared with friends and, subsequently, generated more positive conversations. These all serve to strengthen the bond between the business and the consumer, increase goodwill and automatically generate positive word-of-mouth.

Generally speaking, social media marketing should be used to primarily build and manage relationships, not as an interruption tool — although, of course, there are exceptions to every rule.

Revisiting the
New Engagement Paradigm

One thing that was absolutely clear from my research was that there is no one set way to use traditional, digital, or social media. This is in line with my personal experience and you need to find the best way to make a combination of these channels work for your business. The lines between each discipline are extremely blurred and very intertwined — especially between digital and social media! Getting them all to work together seamlessly is a huge challenge, even for the most highly qualified and seasoned marketers.

As I mentioned earlier, successful marketing is all about building strong and lasting relationships, by engaging your customer with relevant content. A series of relevant messages delivered via a combination of traditional, digital and social media is what you're aiming for, providing, of course, these messages support your customers' journey through your business to achieve your ultimate goal.

If we take another look at the New Engagement Paradigm and overlay some of these tools, as shown in figure 1.12, it should now make sense as to why content is at the core of the model and traditional, digital and social media are used to deliver your content and engage with your target audience.

Figure 1.12 The New Engagement Paradigm with the Tools

During my research, it became very clear that most of the business owners had no formal marketing training whatsoever. Many asked their friends or colleagues for advice and many of these also had no formal marketing training. It was very much a case of the blind leading the blind.

As you read this book, I hope you'll quickly see that you don't need to study marketing for years and years to become an efficient and effective marketer to market your own business. You certainly don't need a PhD to get started! With just a little of the right knowledge you can make a huge impact with your target audience and once you start to understand this, you will be the one giving advice! Remember, "in the land of the blind, the one-eyed man is king!" Better still, when you have finished reading this book and put some of the lessons into practice, you'll be head and shoulders above your competitors because you'll have both eyes wide open.

At the start of this book, I said the Internet has "levelled the playing field" allowing small businesses to compete on equal footing with the "big boys". There are two reasons for this. The first is that power is now in the hands of the consumer, because the process of influencing them starts at the "zero moment of truth". The second requires having the skills to take advantage of these changes and optimise your own marketing efforts to build, sustain and manage relationships — both online and offline. And that, my friends, is the revelation that took me several years to discover!

> Entrepreneurs and micro-business owners need a good understanding of modern marketing to survive and prosper in the twenty-first century. The global digital marketing skills gap is huge and the harsh reality is that they have to fend for themselves.

My research also led me to conclude that the digital marketing skills gap is so large and technology is advancing at such a rate of knots, that there's going to remain a digital marketing skills gap for a very long time. In short, there are not enough people with the digital marketing skills to meet the demand of the modern marketing environment. When new skilled people come onto the market, they are attracted to the companies that can pay eye-watering salaries and offer huge perks. Micro-businesses with tiny budgets are at the bottom of the food chain and rarely even get to meet the people who could help them.

The harsh reality is that, as a micro-business owner, in terms of marketing — and especially digital marketing — like it or not, you're pretty much on your own! It is, therefore, imperative you have at least an understanding of some of the basics of marketing theory and principles — if nothing else, to ensure you don't invest your hard-earned cash into marketing activities that are doomed to failure.

We've already taken a look at AIDA, DRIP, Maslow's Hierarchy of Needs and the Loyalty Ladder. We now need to explore some of the other marketing planning models and theories. By understanding just a few core marketing principles, along with the 21st Century Marketing System and the rest of the information shared in this book, you will be way ahead of the game. You'll be able to see things from a completely different perspective and even evaluate your competitors' marketing campaigns to see whether they are failing and then identify how you can do better. Armed with the knowledge in this book, you'll be a skilled modern marketer in no time.

In the next section, we'll extend and develop the New Engagement Paradigm with the final two outer rings: business and marketing strategy, together with the established marketing theory and principles. Along the way, you'll learn how to translate the whole thing into usable and profitable strategies and tactics you can easily use in your business on a daily basis. Plus, you'll have the whole thing solidly grounded in some of the most powerful, proven and well-established marketing principles known to man (and woman) which nearly every digital marketer and business owner overlooks — if they even knew them in the first place!

We're now going to raise the game and look at the five elements of the 21st Century Marketing System in detail.

Are you ready?

Good! Let's crack on.

WHAT it is

The System

The 21st Century Marketing System (see figure 1.1) has been designed to address the real business and marketing challenges of the twenty-first century. Its primary purpose is to give you a "helicopter view" and a solid grounding in all the things that actually matter in the micro-business marketing context. It has also been designed to give you a holistic and comprehensive picture of your business and, as mentioned in Section 1, there are five parts to the jigsaw. In this section, we'll examine each one in detail.

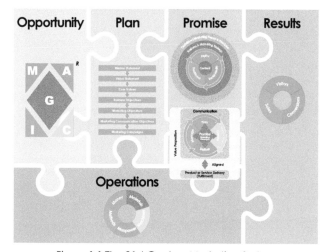

Figure 1.1 The 21st Century Marketing System

Crafting Opportunity:
The M.A.G.I.C. Marketing Matrix

 As entrepreneurs, we start by identifying opportunities. They need careful evaluation to determine if we can actually turn them into reality. If so, what will it take? How will we go about it? What help will we need? "Opportunity evaluation" is the first part of the 21st Century Marketing System and, amongst other things, it helps us identify the risks and rewards associated with any opportunity, as well as how we might tackle the challenges they inevitably present. We need some kind of "evaluation framework" to help us consider all angles and, if things look good, allow us to quickly and easily create a coherent plan of action.

The tool we've developed to help you achieve this is the "M.A.G.I.C. Marketing Matrix". It covers every element you need to consider when evaluating opportunities from a high-level strategic perspective. Once you have developed your strategy, it's something you can keep coming back to and update as your business evolves and grows. It becomes much more than "just another planning tool"; it is also a flexible, easy-to-use, strategic management tool and will become a welcome addition to your business management toolbox.

So what exactly is the "M.A.G.I.C. Marketing Matrix"?

Simply this: A straightforward, usable and practical tool to help you think strategically about the five most important parts of any business, from a customers' perspective, when you're evaluating new opportunities and designing a business to take advantage of them. It is the first part of the jigsaw puzzle and binds the whole system together.

The M.A.G.I.C. Marketing Matrix is depicted by the model shown in figure 2.1.

Figure 2.1 The M.A.G.I.C. Marketing Matrix

The M.A.G.I.C. Marketing Matrix has been specifically designed to help you focus on all the key elements and sub-elements, necessary to build a profitable, long-term sustainable business. If you are in the process of planning your next venture, it may help if you create your own version of the M.A.G.I.C. Marketing Matrix as we go through. If you're already in business, why not apply what you learn here to your existing business and use it to audit your current activities — you might be surprised what it reveals.

When designing and developing a strategy, we often need to look at the wider picture and construct what's known as a "Macro Level Analysis". The acronym we use for that is PESTLE.

A PESTLE analysis considers the:

▲ **Political**

▲ **Economic**

▲ **Social**

▲ **Technological**

▲ **Legal**

▲ **Environmental**

factors which impact an organisation's operating environment. These external macro-level pressures affect the way the business is designed, how it operates and, ultimately, how much profit it makes. They are the external constraints put on a business that dictate what is and what is not acceptable and directly contribute to the design of the resulting business model.

A PESTLE analysis will help you shape the boundaries you must operate within. For example, political considerations might dictate acceptable behaviour. In 2016, large corporations avoiding tax was a hot topic, as was the UK's referendum on whether it should remain in the EU. In terms of economic climate, if you're in the middle of a recession, you may make very different decisions than in a buoyant, fast-growing economy. Social pressures will also shape your business; for example, using low-paid child "slave" labour in Third World countries is considered unacceptable practice and can cause your potential customers to actively boycott your business. In the digital age, technology has a huge impact on how you run your business. The way consumers behave and how businesses need to respond, as we saw earlier in this book, is another consideration — and let's not forget the eco-friendly movement that (rightly) considers the impact of business on the planet. Finally, all of this may be wrapped up in some legal framework; for example, in the UK, the National Living Wage enshrined in employment law dictates the minimum amount you can pay your employees. You need to take all these macro-level considerations into account at the very start of the process, as they will inevitably present some challenges but, more often than not, they also present new opportunities — especially for creative entrepreneurs!

Having done your PESTLE analysis and evaluated your opportunities, the next step is to use the M.A.G.I.C. Marketing Matrix to work out how to take advantage of them. Let's pull it apart and examine each component in detail.

Market

The "M" in the M.A.G.I.C. Marketing Matrix stands for Market.

In this section, we'll consider all aspects of your potential market. Every successful entrepreneur and business owner really understands their marketplace; hence, this is the first part of the M.A.G.I.C. Marketing Matrix.

Your market is broken into its three sub-components, "The 3 Cs": Customers, Challenges and Competitors, as shown in figure 2.2.

Figure 2.2 The M.A.G.I.C. Marketing Matrix - Market

Customers

The first "C" stands for "Customers". It is absolutely imperative that you understand exactly what your "ideal" customer looks like. This will require some research and serious thinking. Don't be tempted to skip this step or assume you already know!

So, who are your ideal customers? You really need to describe them in detail and for this marketers create something called "personas", as we did with Brian and Mary in the previous section. It is quite conceivable that you could develop three or more separate personas, representing each different member of your target audience. The reason we do this is because it helps us focus all our energy on our ideal customers. Therefore, we really need to know who they are, what they look like, what their likes and dislikes are, how they prefer to communicate and everything else about them. Are they business customers, or are they end consumers? Are you in the B2B or B2C marketplace? Or both? The key thing is to clearly define their wants and needs (a.k.a. their problems) and create a persona for each group of your target audience who share a significant number of common attributes.

Let's take Brian as an example. He's fed up with being a car mechanic for the local Ford dealer and wants a change. He has a long-held ambition to work for himself and open a specialist coffee shop with Mary, as he thinks this is something his town sorely needs. In planning his new venture, he starts developing his M.A.G.I.C. Marketing Matrix and quickly realises that "everybody" is not his target market.

He has done his research and identified several "categories" of customers:

▲ The early morning coffee drinkers who want a coffee on the way to work

▲ The mothers who drop off their children at school and want to chat to their friends on the way home

▲ The lunchtime crowd who want a sandwich to go with their coffee

▲ Professionals who want to hold a business meeting away from the office

▲ The casual coffee drinker who just wants to enjoy a great coffee whilst taking a break from shopping.

These are all the logical groups, or categories, he can think of at the moment, but if things change, he can always define some more.

His next step is to create a detailed persona for each category and make it as "real" as possible. For example: Nigel, mid-thirties, married with children and has a managerial position at the local IT company which employs thirty staff. He earns around £40,000 per annum and has an estimated freely disposable income of £100 per week and spends on average £5 to £8 per day on coffee and/or sandwiches and snacks. He sees his morning trip to the coffee shop as a chance to sit down, collect his thoughts and plan the day before he gets to the office, where he's hit with problems and phone calls from the minute he arrives. Janice, on the other hand, is Nigel's colleague and is always in a rush to get to work after dropping her two kids off at her mother's. She barely has time to call into the coffee shop and wants a takeaway to enjoy at her desk as she reads her morning emails.

Now, you could argue that Nigel and Janice deserve their own individual personas and if you want to break your target audience down a little further, you'd be absolutely right. However, Brian is happy with the "Early Morning" category and summarises their core attributes as follows:

▲ Mid-thirties

▲ Local professional office workers

▲ Key attributes: Time poor

▲ Requirement: Just coffee

▲ Estimated spend per visit: £3

▲ Consumption: In house and takeout

▲ Appreciates: Quality and speed of service

▲ Primary motivation: Energy boost/self-time

▲ Time: Visits between 7:30 a.m. and 9:00 a.m.

If you can include a picture of the character you're talking about, that really brings your character to life. If you can take pictures of real members of your target audience, brilliant! If not, you can always find a picture of an appropriate individual on the Internet and put the photo next to your detailed description. The point is, to have an accurate description of the type of people you want to serve and all your energy when communicating with this section of your target audience, should give clear messages aimed at serving just their needs.

Challenges

The next "C" stands for "Challenges". It is important to realise that in both the B2B and B2C situation, every business and potential customer has some form of challenges, because most businesses continually strive not only for survival, but also to grow their market share and become more successful. Individuals also have challenges big and small and, regardless of the industry or sector you are in, you need to find out what challenges or problems your ideal customers face and how you can help solve them. What's stopping them from moving forward in their business? How would their lives be better if these problems were solved, either by you or somebody else? What challenges can you help your ideal customers overcome?

For Brian, in this example, it's quite simple: he solves Nigel and Janice's "need for a great coffee to make them feel better first thing in the morning on the way to work" challenge. In a B2B scenario, the challenges may be a little more complex, but the trick — particularly for micro-business owners — is to keep things as simple as possible. That way, it's easy to communicate your message to your target audience.

Competitors

The third "C" stands for "Competitors". It is vital that you understand who your competitors are and what they offer your ideal customers. Without this knowledge, you are merely guessing at how others may be serving your market and you'll make costly assumptions. If you're fortunate enough to be in an industry where there are few competitors, that's great, but the likelihood is you are not the only player in the market.

You should continually be conducting what's referred to in business as "Environmental Scanning". This basically involves keeping an eye on your market, to see what's happening in your marketplace that could affect your business. By keeping your finger "on the pulse", you'll soon know what others are doing more successfully than you (as well as watching their failures). When a competitor looks as if they are about to threaten your position, you can react quickly to protect your market share.

Let's consider the competition for a second. Some will be far better than you at some of the things you do. It is also quite conceivable that there is absolutely no way you could compete with some of your more professional competitors because they may be just too big or too well established. Their customers may well be very happy with the service or products they provide. However, it is highly likely in most marketplaces that there will be some dissatisfied customers or, indeed, some new customers that you can serve better than anybody else.

One of your primary goals should be to aim to be the best you can possibly be. You, therefore, become the natural choice for your ideal customers.

When thinking about competitors, you really need to know a couple of key things:

▲ Who are your closest competitors?

▲ How big are they?

▲ What are their challenges?

▲ What are their customers saying about them?

▲ What do they offer that you cannot?

▲ What can you offer that they cannot?

▲ Why would a customer come to you to buy your product or service rather than go to one of your competitors?

One key thing here is you must be ruthlessly honest with yourself. There is absolutely no point in kidding yourself that you're better than your closest competitor when they clearly have the advantage. What you must do is turn any negative into a positive — and an advantage. One often-quoted example is AVIS, who in the car rental market, are second to Hertz. Their "tag line" is "We try harder", which is a reflection of their acknowledgement that they are the "underdogs". By comparison, Hertz are much bigger and the chance of AVIS catching them up is remote. Therefore, they have to compete from a different "angle" or value proposition — by "trying harder" to satisfy their customers' needs better than Hertz.

What you're actually doing here, is what's referred to as a "micro-environmental analysis". There are five main factors that could affect your profitability and we use a model called "Porter's Five Forces" (see figure 2.3) to assess the immediate impact on our business model.

Once Brian has opened his doors, if one of the big chains sets up shop next door, there's no way he's going to compete on equal terms. He's going to have to try and find a weakness in their business model and exploit it. For example, the big chains typically charge a hefty price for sandwiches, so Brian might consider a range of cheap sandwiches or a giant sandwich, twice the size of what his competitors offer at the same price. That's just one simple example, but there are many things he could do; he just needs to be creative.

Is Brian in the "coffee shop market" or is he in the "hospitality trade"? You sometimes have to think outside the box to consider your competition from all angles. For example, if there is a department store nearby with a café on the top floor, are they competition? How about the local pub, which has just installed the latest coffee machine to better serve their evening diners? What if they start advertising lunches with coffee — are they competition? Or how about the fast-food restaurant just round the corner? Whilst there may not be another "coffee shop", there may be alternatives that could compete with and, hence, affect Brian's business model.

Porter's Five Forces

These are:

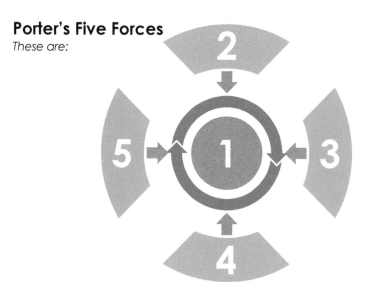

Figure 2.3 Porter's Five Forces

❶ Rivalry Among Existing Competitors
Existing competitors in the marketplace, who will be battling for the same customers in the marketplace at the same time

❷ Threat of New Entrants
The threat of any new players coming into the market, which means the existing pool of customers will need to be spread amongst more suppliers

❸ Bargaining Power of Buyers
If there are plenty of service providers in the area, then customers may start buying based on price; this increases their purchasing power and may start a "price war" — particularly in a crowded market

❹ Bargaining Power of Suppliers
The same could be said for your suppliers; if you use the same suppliers as your competitors and they pay more than you do for essential supplies, you may find the prices of your raw materials go up and hence squeeze your profit margin

❺ Threat of Substitute Products and/or Services
And finally, the threat of substitutes is always a tricky one to nail down. If your customers didn't buy your product or service, what could satisfy their needs equally as well? For example, Eurostar provides a train service from London to Paris under the English Channel. The alternatives or substitutes are airlines and ferry operators. Therefore, Eurostar is not in the "train business" but the "cross Channel transportation business".

The key thing is to find ways you can offer something of greater value to your ideal customers — something which your competitors could not match that gives you the "edge". Therefore, you really need to understand who all your competitors are and what they are doing, in order to satisfy your ideal customers' needs.

Don't be tempted to skip this step, because here's the reality: just as you are watching them and trying to work out how they serve the market, they are watching you to see how they can steal your ideal customers. That's the nature of business!

Action

The second letter of the M.A.G.I.C. Marketing Matrix is "A" which stands for Action. This is deliberately the second item in the process, because you must first understand your target market, before you decide what action you will take to serve this market and satisfy your customers' needs.

It is unlikely you will be able to serve everyone in your chosen market because it will be too broad, so you need to think about limiting the scope of your target market and focus on what you are really good at. Two good questions to answer are "What is the precise industry or sector my business is in?" and "Can I narrow this definition and be more specific?" For example, Brian is in the "coffee shop business" but, more specifically, he's in the "premium independent high street coffee shop retail sector".

Here, we have another three key elements to consider, "The 3 Rs": Results, Relevant and Rare, as shown in figure 2.4.

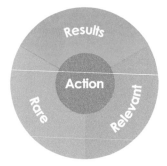

Figure 2.4 The M.A.G.I.C. Marketing Matrix - Action

Results

The first "R" refers to "Results". As we already know, every customer you serve will have a problem that needs to be solved. However, they may not specifically recognise that they are looking for a solution to their problem. What they are actually looking for is the outcome that solution will give them — i.e. the "result". They need to solve a problem in order to get the desired result, either for their business (in the B2B context) or in their personal lives (in the B2C context). How can you help them achieve the results they desire?

We have already examined the market in the previous section and your results should relate very closely to your customers and the challenges they face. If you show you can produce the results that your ideal customers desire, you stand a great chance of building a successful business.

Relevant

The second "R" refers to "Relevant" which means, whatever you do, must be relevant to your target audience and the problems they face. Now, bear in mind that your customers will have many problems over a long period of time, many of which you cannot solve for one of two reasons. The first is that you are not capable of solving all their problems, so you need to pick the problems that you can solve and solve well. The second reason is that the timing may just not be right and you have absolutely no control over that!

It could well be, that the solution you have which solves your ideal customers' problem, is not yet on their radar. Your business plan has to be relevant to solving the problems or challenges your ideal customers face — at the time they face them. This implies that you need to know when your ideal customers will be facing the challenges you can help them solve and achieve the results they're looking for. You must be aware of the journey they are taking and where your solution fits in during their voyage of discovery. In a world of information overload, the correct timing of presenting your solution is becoming even more important. The "zero moment of truth" is usually a pretty good start!

Rare

The final element is "Rare" — this is where you can differentiate yourself from your competitors. If you provide a service or product that is rare, you will naturally eliminate a huge portion of all your potential competition. If you can make your offering so unique, so rare, that you are the only one who can provide the ultimate solution to your ideal customers, you become the natural choice to help them achieve their goals — or, in Brian's case, just service their wants and needs. That's a very powerful position to be in and dominating your particular niche is one way to achieve this.

Here's a quick summary of the sorts of questions you should be asking yourself when considering what actions you will take to serve your market:

Results
▲ What problems do your customers have and what results are they looking for?
▲ Why are these results important to them?
▲ How will their lives change if you achieve these results?

Relevant
▲ How is what you offer relevant to solving their problems?
▲ Is the relevance of your solution time-sensitive?
▲ What alternative solutions are available in the marketplace that can achieve similar results?
▲ Where are these alternatives and how can they reach your customers?

Rare
▲ How is what you can offer different to your competitors offer?
▲ What is special about your solution that makes it difficult to copy?
▲ How can you communicate your "uniqueness"?

To be successful in business, you need to align your actions with the market needs. By focusing on what results your customers want, understanding their challenges and why what you are offering is relevant to meeting those challenges and offering something that's rare — i.e. different to what your competitors offer — you place yourself in a very strong position to take advantage of your opportunities, because you place the customer at the core of everything you do. This is summarised in figure 2.5.

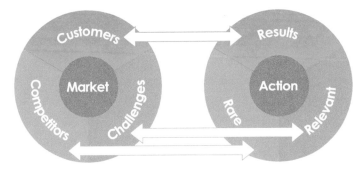

Figure 2.5 The M.A.G.I.C. Marketing Matrix – Mapping Market to Action

There are three well-established pieces of marketing theory that can help you achieve this: the SWOT analysis, Ansoff's Matrix and the GAP analysis.

Figure 2.6 SWOT Analysis

SWOT Analysis

A SWOT Analysis (see figure 2.6) is used in many business disciplines, not just marketing. The "S" stands for "Strengths and the "W" stands for "Weaknesses"; they help you identify what you're good at and where your weaknesses lie. These are both internal factors because you have some control over them. For example, if you decide digital marketing is one of your weaknesses, you can do something about it, such as hire in some new skills or get some training. If one of your strengths is a wonderful product you've developed that your customers love, you need to note this here too. By listing your strengths and weaknesses (honestly), you can quickly develop a strategy to exploit your strengths and minimise the impact of your weaknesses — for example, by buying in help or consultancy, or training staff in missing skills to build your internal capability.

The "O" stands for "Opportunities" and the "T" stands for "Threats". These are external factors you have no control over and they shape the environment in which you have to operate. You have to continually scan your environment to keep abreast of what is really going on. If you spot an opportunity, such as a gap in the market, you need to align your internal resources reflected by your strengths and weaknesses to take advantage of it. If you identify a threat, such as a new entrant to the market or competitors targeting your customers, again, you need to align and utilise your resources accordingly to protect your market share.

A SWOT Analysis forces you to think about everything that's really important to the success of your business. It's been used for years and is a piece of very useful theory that's certainly here to stay!

Conducting a SWOT Analysis complements the "A" stage of the M.A.G.I.C. Marketing Matrix and it's often best to do it with the help of a few people who know you and your business. If you are a "one-man band" perhaps a couple of friends, a friendly customer (or members of your target audience, if you're a start-up), or a couple of your suppliers may offer some unique and powerful insight in exchange for a couple of glasses of wine.

When Brian completed his SWOT Analysis, it looked like this:

Internal Factors

Strengths

▲ Mary has a reasonable income and the family expenses are low after Brian received a modest inheritance from his uncle; he does not need to take an income from the business for at least a year and has enough capital to take a risk.

▲ Brian and Mary are very pragmatic and have an exit strategy if it all goes wrong.

▲ Brian is a very popular, sociable guy and is well known in his local community. He has a bubbly personality and people are drawn to him. He has a few friends who have offered to help out now and then if he gets really stuck, so at least he has a backup plan.

▲ Brian has some management experience as he is a senior mechanic at the garage and is in charge of a team of four other members of staff, all of whom like and respect him.

▲ Marketing is something Brian has been interested in since school and he is quite creative. He likes reading business-related books and has been learning marketing in his spare time.

Weaknesses

▲ No retail experience, has never run a coffee shop before and no amount of enthusiasm can totally compensate for experience and knowledge.

▲ Will need to employ an experienced barista and make sure they are capable and willing to train other members of staff, including Brian and Mary.

▲ Brian is not especially good with computers and has no experience of accounting. However, his sister Gemma is an experienced bookkeeper, works for a small local accountant and has offered to look after the business finances for him.

External Factors

Opportunities

▲ There is a vacant shop unit on the corner of a busy street near the town centre. It is also not too far from the local school. The vacant property is in a good location and presents a good opportunity.

▲ The footfall in this area is five times greater than the best alternative outside the town centre.

▲ There are no other retail units available in this area, so the threat of a new competitor arriving is low.

▲ Unemployment in the town is low; hence most passers-by should have money in their pocket.

Threats

▲ Given its prime position, the rent is nearly double that of the closest alternative outside the town centre.

▲ With near full occupancy, landlords of commercial property in the town centre can command a premium and rent reviews may be high.

▲ Unemployment in the town is low and getting suitable staff might pose a problem.

▲ No parking nearby, so heavily reliant on foot traffic — but so is every other business in the vicinity and this remains a popular area.

The purpose of a SWOT Analysis, like many of the tools and models discussed in this book, is to help you make a well-informed decision. In this example, Brian thinks he's in a pretty strong position to have a go and is prepared to take the risk, so he decides to take the plunge.

Ansoff's Matrix

Like many other models that have stood the test of time, the beauty of Ansoff's Matrix (see figure 2.7) is in its simplicity.

Used when you're evaluating new opportunities or considering threats to help evaluate risk, resource requirements and, potentially, direction. What Ansoff said way back in 1957, is that businesses only ever have four options when growing:

1. *Market Penetration: Selling more existing products to existing customers (i.e. increase purchase frequency or purchase quantity)*

2. *Market Development: Start selling existing products to new customers (i.e. increase market share)*

3. *Product Development: Sell new products to existing customers (i.e. maximise the lifetime value)*

4. *Diversification: Sell new products to new customers (i.e. diversify into the realms of the unknown — which is the most risky option).*

Your business and marketing strategy will be determined by which of these four boxes you fall into. This will heavily influence your communication strategy and, ultimately, shape your marketing messages and, hence, your marketing material. For example, you'll talk very differently to an existing customer about an existing product, compared to a new customer about a new product.

If you are going into a new market with a new product, you'll probably be marketing to innovators who are motivated by the latest new, cool thing and probably revel in the risk associated with "getting there first". Conversely, a late adopter for a tried and tested product will want to be told it's a proven solution, risk-free and safe. Both scenarios will have very different marketing messages to be relevant to their intended recipients.

Ansoff's Matrix is one of my favourites because it makes it very quick and easy to assess risk and gives clear guidance on where to spend your marketing budget. Any new venture will naturally end up in the "diversification" box, because you're selling new things to new customers.

When Brian starts up, he has to convince his new customers, who don't yet know him that his new products are worth a try. Once he becomes

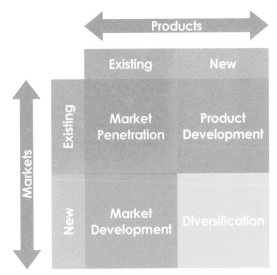

Figure 2.7 Ansoff's Matrix

established and has a regular flow of customers, he can identify other types of customers who might enjoy his friendly coffee experience. He's already defined five groups of people who he wants to target and if he subsequently decides he wants to stay open until 8 p.m. on a Thursday night to cater for the "late-night shoppers", he'd be well advised to create a new persona for this new segment. This is an example of "market development".

Once Brian's running at full capacity, he may adopt a "product development" approach and try to sell more cakes and sandwiches with every coffee. His other option is "market penetration" which is selling more of the same stuff to the same customers, i.e. getting them to come more regularly, for example three times a week, instead of two. But if he's at full capacity, this strategy might actually harm his business, if the coffee shop becomes overcrowded and people give up waiting for a table and leave before they get served. If that's the case, it might be better to consider opening a second coffee shop when he knows people really like his products, in which case a "market development" strategy is back on the table.

Gap Analysis

A Gap Analysis (see figure 2.8) is a strategic tool to help you identify where you are, define where you want to be and decide how you're going to get there.

It is often used in conjunction with a SWOT Analysis and is also another well-established tool to help set your strategic direction. It can be used at the beginning of your business life (i.e. start-up), as well as during regular (monthly) strategic and performance reviews in an established business.

Do not underestimate its simplicity; used correctly it is a very powerful and effective tool that will help you manage and grow your business with minimal overhead.

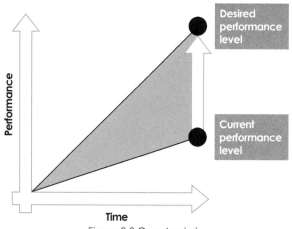

Figure 2.8 Gap Analysis

Brian should use the Gap Analysis every month when he reviews the management accounts with Gemma. Here's what happened during the monthly review at the end of month 7: According to the financial forecasts in his original business plan, he wanted to be making a profit by the end of month six, but at the end of month seven, he's still making a loss. Gemma has been looking at the occupancy rates (the number of customers sat at tables throughout the day) compared to capacity and he's struggling to reach an average daily occupancy of 15%, despite being full most lunchtimes between 12:30 and 2:00 p.m. This data comes from the till transactions, Brian's manual notes of relevant observations during the day and an increasing awareness of what's actually happening in the business as Brian gains experience. The Gap Analysis simply tells him the difference between where he wants to be and where he currently is; basically, it puts a number on the size of the problem. Brian can then consider his options and act accordingly.

He decides there is no point in trying to increase the lunchtime trade because he couldn't cope with any more business during this peak period. However, the early morning trade is pretty disappointing and Gemma advises him to ask his lunchtime customers (after they have paid) if they would like to try his "morning special". When he gives the customer their change and receipt, he also gives them a promotional business card with a voucher for a free bacon sandwich with each large coffee purchased before 9 a.m. He's now leveraging the success of his lunchtime trade with a market penetration strategy to increase the frequency of visit. When he goes through the figures with Gemma at the end of the next month, things are looking up and, although he's not reaching his original target yet, he is making a small profit.

It's time to revisit the Gap Analysis and come up with another strategy to develop his business further. He notices the lunchtime trade has dropped off a little, presumably because some customers will have transferred their custom from lunchtime to morning. Perhaps it's time to run an advertising campaign to promote both the early morning bacon treat and the lunchtime menu and, hopefully, attract new customers and optimise these time slots.

Group

Now we come to the centre of the M.A.G.I.C. Marketing Matrix, the "G", which stands for "Group. This is where we break down our target market into smaller groups, or segments, where all members of that group/segment share similar attributes. For example, a similar group of prospects or customers who are attracted by the same elements of your value proposition.

One of the biggest challenges many business owners face is understanding who their ideal customers are and what they look like. Many business owners I speak to regard "everybody" as their target market — and if, like Brian, you're selling a widely consumed commodity, like coffee, then you do indeed have a very wide target audience. However, not everybody will respond to the same message. In Brian's example, not everyone drinks coffee, so talking to non-coffee drinkers about coffee falls on deaf ears. Talking to non-coffee drinkers about exquisite offerings in the hot chocolate line, or speciality teas, may appeal to those who want to join their coffee-drinking friends in the social environment of a coffee shop. Surely that's better than ignoring or alienating them and could even lead to a boost in profits. It's an opportunity worth considering if you're in the coffee shop business and another segment Brian may consider promoting at some stage in the future.

Not everyone is in a business where they have wide appeal. In fact, the majority of us operate in quite tight niches. Therefore, the golden rule is simply this: "If you talk to 'everybody,' you talk to nobody".

It is important to understand you cannot be all things, to all people, all the time. You must — and I repeat must — focus your attention on meeting the needs of one very highly targeted group of your ideal customers, at any one point in time.

Segmenting your ideal customers into tightly defined target groups is a fundamental marketing principle and the first part of the segmentation, targeting, positioning (STP) framework. I cannot over-emphasise the importance of careful segmentation, when it comes to achieving your ultimate goal of generating positive word-of-mouth. This is because with a smaller, tightly defined group you can have a much deeper, much more relevant conversation than with a larger, more diverse audience. The wider you make your target audience, the more diluted (and ineffective) your message becomes.

Segmentation, Targeting and *Positioning* is often referred to as STP. These three elements are important when thinking about your target audience because they help you define the precise "group" you want to communicate with. The more tightly defined your "group" (or segment) is, the easier it is to "target" them efficiently and effectively and "position" your offering in their minds as the best choice to help them meet their needs. You can then lay claim to that vital part of your target audience's brain that associates their needs/wants with your product/ service/brand. In short, it is easier to communicate with small audiences who have very similar interests, than with larger groups with diverse interests and needs.

It is always better to take a rifle approach rather than a shotgun approach. This means you have to aim at a specific target and focus all your attention on hitting the "bull's-eye", not spraying the whole target and everything around it.

Separate segments of your target audience will have different wants and needs. Each segment will have its own set of communication needs and, as a marketer, it is your job to ensure your messages are appropriate for your target market. The clearer and more relevant your message is, the greater the impact of your communication. It's as simple as that. The STP model can help you create a set of highly targeted relevant messages your target audience will find irresistible and deliver significant return on your marketing investment.

If there was one lesson I could give you in this area, it would be this: the smaller (and more precisely defined) you make your ideal target group, the more successful you will be. Why? Because you are speaking to them precisely the way that fully engages them — in fact, they will feel like you are talking to them personally! Personalised communication in the digital age is becoming more and more important in helping you stand out from the crowd. This is why the personas discussed earlier are so important.

Your ideal group will take a journey; they will first become aware of your existence, gradually get to know you and hopefully buy from you, time and time again. They will not just appear in front of you as if by magic. You have to understand the process and work at it, to convert them from enquirers to customers and from customers to long-term "friends".

Customer Journey

The customer journey is the complete sum of experiences that customers go through when interacting with your business and brand. Instead of looking at just a part of a transaction or experience, the customer journey documents the full experience of being a customer and spans a variety of touchpoints, by which the customer moves from awareness to engagement and purchase. Successful brands focus on developing a seamless experience that ensures each touchpoint interconnects and contributes to the overall journey.

This is represented by the centre of the M.A.G.I.C. Marketing Matrix as shown in figure 2.9.

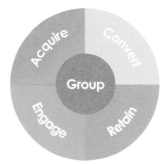

Figure 2.9 The M.A.G.I.C. Marketing Matrix - Group

We've said the Group category is made up of four sub-categories. These comprise the four stages customers typically go through. You must first "acquire" them (making your prospects aware you exist and what you're offering). You then need to "convert" them from prospects to paying customers. Once they have experienced your offering, you want them to come back for more and to "retain" them. Finally, you need to keep them "engaged" with your brand between transactions, so they think of you first, whenever they need more of what you have to offer.

Acquire

The first step is to "Acquire". Key questions to ask are:

▲ How will you acquire your ideal customers?

▲ How do you let them know what you have to offer and that they can trust you to solve their problems?

▲ How do your competitors acquire their ideal customers?

▲ What can you do that is different to your competitors in acquiring your ideal customers?

These are all great questions to consider when thinking about the group you are targeting and the AIDA model can serve as a useful prompt. To start with, prospects must be aware a business exists and, as mentioned earlier, advertising and PR are good ways to interrupt your prospects' attention. Presenting your offer at the "zero moment of truth" is incredibly effective and for that, of course, a search engine friendly website is a pretty useful tool, as discussed in Section 1.

So what can Brian do to raise awareness of his new coffee shop business and acquire new customers? Traditional advertising in the local media and some PR are an option, but they won't reach Andy, a new recruit at the local IT company, who at twenty-three years old is straight from university and the youngest member of the team.

Andy has taken a shine to Charlotte who joined the company at the same time and she seems to like him too. Andy has a dilemma because he's just asked Charlotte to join him for a coffee and she's agreed. Trouble is, they're both new in town and he doesn't know where to take her. He could ask Nigel, his boss, who would no doubt be happy to recommend Brian's coffee shop (word-of-mouth), but that wouldn't be a cool thing to do and Andy wants to keep his interest in Charlotte quiet in the office — at least for the time being. There's no way he's going to see Brian's ads in the local paper and the local printed copy of "Yellow Pages" doesn't even register on Andy's radar. Therefore, all of Brian's traditional print ads will miss Andy completely.

Andy does a quick search on Google for "coffee shops" in their town on his smart phone and Brian's mobile-friendly website pops up at the "zero moment of truth". Within thirty seconds, Andy knows where it is, how to get there, the fact that's it's a ten-minute walk from the office (courtesy of Google Maps), what he can expect on the menu and, according to the reviews, that it's a great environment run by a bloke called Brian, who's a bit of a character and treats everyone like his best mate. Fortunately, there's a cash machine next door to Brian's coffee shop, which could be pretty handy too.

Convert
Once you have acquired your ideal customers' interest, the next step is to "Convert" them into paying customers. That is, of course, if "conversion" for you means collecting cash or making a sale. It may be perfectly acceptable for the conversion process to be something different, such as acquiring a name for your database. So you need to think about what exactly the word "conversion" means in your business context. You may have several different definitions at various parts of the customer journey. Once you've defined exactly what "conversion" means, you can then decide how you will convert these prospects (or leads) into customers. I think it's fair to say that "conversion", for most business owners, will mean some form of exchange and it is highly likely that that exchange will involve money for either a product or service.

Lunchtime arrives and Charlotte asks Andy where he's taking her. Fully prepared, Andy slips into his James Bond routine and tells her about this great little place just a ten-minute walk away, run by his mate Brian, who's always the life and soul of the party. Fortunately, things go well and they have a great time — great service and great coffee ("first moment of truth").

Retain
When you have acquired your ideal customer and converted them, they become a valuable asset to your business. You must make every effort to retain them, so they keep coming back. The third element of the Group category is "Retain". There are several things you need to know and have

clearly defined as part of your business, including:

▲ What is the lifetime value of your typical customer?

▲ Will they only buy from you once, or do you have the opportunity for them to come back time and time again?

▲ Once they've bought from you, how can you retain them, or nurture the relationship, so they add value to your business in the future?

In some businesses, it is perfectly feasible the customer will only buy from you once. If this is the case, it is important to realise that the relationship does not stop there; you want them to continue talking about your business long after their initial purchase and, hence, keep generating word-of-mouth.

Think back to the luxury hotel on that "once-in-a-lifetime" holiday: the customer will visit once, but you want them to keep talking about their (wonderful) experience to all their friends and anyone else who will listen, for as long as they have breath in their body. Reminding them of their experience once in a while can evoke the original feelings of pleasure, which they will then share. That's the power of sending retention messages to past customers.

Customer retention is one of the most under-resourced areas in most businesses. Many businesses spend a huge amount of their budget on acquiring customers, but they often forget the value of retaining customers. This is just crazy, particularly when you consider the lifelong value of the customer.

I strongly encourage you to seriously think about having a customer retention programme of some description because, as mentioned earlier, it can cost up to twenty times the amount to acquire a customer than retain them. Having a decent customer retention strategy can really help maximise your return on your marketing investment. If nothing else, remember this: "Repeat business is cheap business" and the DRIP framework is a useful model to help develop your retention strategy.

Brian hands Andy two bacon sandwich vouchers with his change and Andy is now in line for a second date with Charlotte, Friday morning on the way to the office. The experience is equally pleasant and pretty soon they are regulars at Brian's coffee shop. Charlotte leaves a positive review on TripAdvisor ("second moment of truth"), lets the whole world know she and Andy are now dating and starts telling their friends and colleagues about this great little coffee shop ten minutes from the office — you get the picture!

Engage
The final element is "Engage". In an information-rich, instant gratification society, it is imperative that you engage your customers rather than try and continually bamboozle them with the "hard sell".

Again, there are several things to consider:

- ▲ Over what period of time will you engage with your customers?
- ▲ Obviously, this will have some impact on their lifelong value, so how will you engage with them?
- ▲ Which tools or techniques will you use?
- ▲ What stage of the journey are they at as customers of your business?
- ▲ How can you move them on to the next stage to maximise their value to your business?
- ▲ If you serve business customers in the B2B market where does your business touch their business during that journey?
- ▲ How does that apply to end consumers in the B2C market, if that's where you operate?
- ▲ Are you trying to build a relationship for the foreseeable future?
- ▲ How long is that relationship likely to last and can you sell them a range of similar products over an extended period of time?

These are some questions that need to be considered as part of your engagement strategy. And here's a key point: you must engage your ideal customers at all stages of their journey: Acquisition, Conversion and Retention. It is not just something you do once and forget about! Think of engagement as the "glue between transactions" or major events on the customer's journey with your business — and you won't go far wrong.

Brian is now getting the hang of the 21st Century Marketing System and has started blogging and tweeting when the coffee shop is quiet. Nothing heavy, just a few observations about his day and a couple of funny stories he's heard from customers in the past week — just enough to keep his regular customers, who follow him on social media, smiling. If he's got too many cakes left over at 4:30 p.m. and trade is dead, he'll occasionally tweet that he'll stay open for an extra hour, so if any of his followers are interested they can pop in on the way home to "buy one and get one free".

Influence

The fourth element, the "I" of the M.A.G.I.C Marketing Matrix refers to "Influence". What can you do, or say, to help your prospects and customers change their behaviour in a positive way to a mutually beneficial outcome? This naturally follows on from having segmented your target market into various groups. For maximum influence, you should focus your marketing communications on one single, tightly defined group at a time. Again, we can break this down into three separate elements, "The 3Ts": Target Audience, Tale (or Story) and Tools as shown in figure 2.10.

Figure 2.10 The M.A.G.I.C. Marketing Matrix - Influence

Target Audience

The first "T" stands for "Target Audience" — i.e. which subsection of your group will you be talking to, using a particular piece of communication or message?

> **Tip:** When talking about influencing members of our target audience, we are highly focused on one single group. We are "talking" to just one persona.

So, which target group are you talking to? If you're talking to, for example, thirty-five to thirty-eight-year-olds, are they male or female? Will you talk to the male subsection of the group in a slightly different tone of voice to the female group?

Other things to consider with the target group are:

▲ How will you break your customers down into specific target groups, or segments, or sub-segments?

▲ How do these target groups differ from each other?

▲ What unique characteristics do these target groups have?

Think back to the coffee drinkers example earlier. You may want to deliver a different message to the early morning customers who want a boost on the way to work, than you do to the late afternoon coffee customers who meet their friends or colleagues for social or business-related encounters. In this example, the same product will have different attractions (benefits) at different times of the day, for groups with different interests or needs.

It's really important to have your target group very clearly and tightly defined when it comes to creating marketing and sales material, because it will ultimately influence whether or not they will buy your product or service.

Brian may well talk to his different personas in a slightly different way and, certainly, has different messages he wants to convey to different members of his target audience, to ensure his coffee shop is full for as much of the day as possible. From 7:30 a.m. to 9:00 a.m. he'll focus on his early morning drinkers; from 9:30 a.m. to 11:30 a.m. the mums and tots take priority, but he'll need the space clean and tidy before his 12:30 p.m. to 2:00 p.m. prime lunchtime trade arrives which makes up the majority of his daily sales. Different messages and offers will be needed to maximise his revenue from each group (segment) and each will have slightly different needs.

Tale

The second "T" in this section is "Tale". The tale — or story — is a great way to influence your target audience and it is widely recognised that telling a story is one of the most effective ways of getting your point across. Rather than bore your target audience with facts and figures, if you tell a story showing how someone has benefited from your product or service and then, perhaps, include a few figures at the end, it's far more effective than the traditional (and some would claim outdated) "hard sell sales copy".

Personally, I think the days of the hard sell are (thankfully) long gone and marketers need to find new ways to influence their target audience, by engaging with them and entertaining them.

Here are the sorts of things you should be asking yourself:

- ▲ What stories can you tell to influence each target group?
- ▲ What tales or stories are relevant to each target group?
- ▲ Why are these stories relevant?
- ▲ Why do they care?
- ▲ Is there a point to the story that can help them make a decision?

These are all important questions and I'm sure you can think of several more!

A good example is when Brian tells his little tales on his blog about what happened in his coffee shop, rather than keep talking about how wonderful his coffee is and how fair his prices are. This creates a sense of belonging, because if you'd been there yourself, you may have seen the characters he's talking about with your own eyes. You now belong to the "in crowd" that knows the jokes and stories about Brian's coffee shop, so you'd better keep going; something amusing is always happening and you might miss it!

This simple technique of telling stories (or tales) can have a huge impact on consumer behaviour because "belonging" is one of our core human needs — see the third level on Maslow's "Hierarchy of Needs" in figure 1.10, discussed earlier.

Tools

The third "T" of Influence is "Tools". The tools in marketing are the methods and means at your disposal to help deliver your message or tell your tale.

You'll be well aware by now that there are many traditional, digital and social media marketing tools available to you, but not all of them will be appropriate with all specific target groups in your context. It is your responsibility to identify which tools your ideal customers will use and will prefer to use, rather than just make assumptions that everybody uses, for example, Facebook — because not everybody does!

▲ What marketing tools are relevant to each target group?

▲ Do you have the skills and resources to use all these tools?

▲ Which tools have the greatest chance of influencing each group?

Your choice of tools is a key part of how you will influence your target market.

The process of influencing your target audience starts with deciding who you are going to talk to first, then what you'll tell them, then finally how you'll deliver your message to get the greatest impact and influence the largest number of people in your target audience. You may need to use several tools to achieve this; for example, for Brian's early morning drinkers, he may use a combination of radio, flyers, website, blog, Facebook and Twitter to attract their attention, reinforce his brand message and to keep them up to date. But for young mothers, Facebook, a street sign and the community magazine may work best.

Control

The fifth and final element of the M.A.G.I.C. Marketing Matrix is depicted by the letter "C" which stands for "Control".

There is absolutely no point in doing all the other steps, if you do not monitor your progress. You need to exercise some form of control over your marketing and if you don't act on the feedback you're getting, you'll never maximise the return on your marketing investment. One of the great things about digital marketing is that it is measurable and you can change things very quickly if you find out they are not working. To help you think about Control, we use the "The 3Ms" — Measure, Monitor and Manage — as shown in figure 2.11.

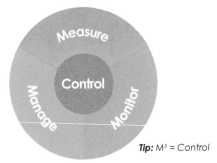

Tip: M^3 = Control

Figure 2.11 The M.A.G.I.C. Marketing Matrix - Control

Measure

The first "M" stands for "Measure". Here you need to think about what we term the "Key Performance Indicators" (KPIs). These are the numbers that will be naturally produced, as you go through your day-to-day business activities. These are numbers you really need to understand, because they give you insights into how well, or how badly, you are doing. To define them, you need to decide what things are important to helping you manage your business. This will depend on your objectives, which we'll talk about in more detail a little later.

The problem we face in the technology-driven information age is that we have far more information than we know what to do with! The trick is to pick a few things that will make a big difference and measure and monitor those. Here, the Pareto Rule (80/20) is the key to avoiding information overload and analysis paralysis: 20% of the things you could measure will give you 80% of everything you need to know in order to manage your business and marketing effectively.

What you're looking for are the "headline numbers":

▲ What KPIs will tell you the most about your business?
▲ How will you measure them?

▲ What do these numbers mean to your business? Is ten good? Is it bad? How does it compare to the numbers one or twenty-five on whatever scale of meaning you're using?

If your objective is to gain one hundred new customers per week and this KPI shows you're achieving just fifty-five to sixty, you could argue this is a good thing. However, if a metric of fifty-five to sixty relates to the number of customers who were leaving you every day, this could be a disaster. It's important to define exactly what your KPIs mean in your business context and what they are telling you.

How many you pick is up to you and will ultimately depend on your business. However, I'd advise, at least initially, that about half a dozen KPIs should be enough to handle. With a small number, you can monitor them easily and ensure the data they produce is meaningful in helping you run and manage your business.

Not sure what to measure? List twenty to thirty things you could measure, then pick the top 20% that you think will make the most difference to your business at a particular point in time. Don't worry too much if you're not 100% sure what these top items should be; you can always change them later if they turn out to be less helpful than you imagined. You'll soon work out what the most important numbers are, what they mean and how you can use this feedback to improve and build your business.

For Brian, two important KPIs in the early days are the number of lunchtime customers versus the early morning trade. Knowing what these two KPIs were and, more importantly, what they meant, allowed Brian and Gemma to do a Gap Analysis and work out a strategy to increase the business's performance.

Monitor

After you have decided what you're going to measure, the next step is to determine how you're going to "Monitor" these key measurements and how often.

It's okay having these key performance indicators, but you really need to think about how you are going to monitor them, too. Key considerations are:

▲ What software tools or other measurement technique are you going to use to monitor your KPIs on a regular basis?

▲ How will you collect the data?

▲ How will you subsequently analyse this data?

▲ How often will this analysis occur?

▲ Do you have the resources to both collect and analyse the data so you can do something meaningful with it?

▲ What will you do with the data once you have it?

▲ How will you keep it safe?

Monitoring your KPIs is something you must do on a continuous basis. It is, therefore, important you don't overload yourself with measuring and monitoring things that don't add value to supporting your primary business objectives.

As your business grows, you will naturally want to measure and monitor more things and, perhaps, you'll drop some of the original KPIs that no longer seem important. You should change this process and adapt it, to keep you informed of what you really need to know as your business develops and grows.

Two key tools at Brian's disposal in the very early days were the numbers from the cash register reports, as well as Brian's own observations recorded on his notepad. It is obviously a very simple example, but sufficient and, most certainly, fit for purpose at the time. Later on, the number of cakes left over on certain days, or the number of bacon sandwich vouchers redeemed, can serve as other measures of success. In terms of his marketing, the number of visitors to his website, the number of people who looked at the menu, how long people spent reading his blog posts, the number of social media "shares" and how many Twitter followers he has, could all be measures of engagement with Brian's brand.

Management

The final "M" stands for "Management" and helps you make informed decisions and justify why you are doing what you are doing. Remember, the whole point of collecting data is to help you manage your business and make informed decisions. You can then decide where your limited resources can be best deployed, to optimise your chance of success.

The key things you need to consider here are:

▲ Once you have the data, how will you "report" it?

▲ How long will you keep it for?

▲ What will you do with these insights and what does this mean for your business?

▲ How can you act on the information and insights gleaned from this data?

▲ What can you change as a result of having these insights?

▲ How will you know if these changes have improved things, or made them worse?

▲ How much time can you dedicate to managing this whole process?

▲ When and how often will you "look at the numbers"? Every day? Every week? Once a month?

You do not want to fall into the trap of "analysis paralysis". KPIs are only worthwhile if they add value to managing your business. For example, is your conversion process as successful as you'd like it to be? What do your results tell you? What can you change if they're not what you want? How could you do this? How will you know if it's worked?

As Brian's business grows and becomes more successful, Gemma is able to provide him with more detailed information during their monthly management account review meetings. As he begins to understand the numbers more, he can start seeing deeper into his business and spot trends, which means he can plan for highly probable future events, such as a dip in trade during the summer or directly after Christmas. This gives him the opportunity to plan future marketing campaigns to acquire new customers, or to re-engage old ones during these low periods and keep his turnover stable.

The key point when it comes to "The 3 M's" is that you first decide what's most important to measure, then you monitor these numbers consistently, making time to analyse and examine the results. Finally, you use these insights to manage your business, make decisions and change things as necessary.

Your KPIs can give deep and powerful insights into the way your business is performing and this feedback should not be overlooked. It never ceases to amaze me the number of companies that collect huge amounts of data and then do absolutely nothing with it! Acting on a small insight can lead to just one better decision, which, in turn, can reap huge rewards.

Never underestimate the power of your data, but do only measure, monitor and manage what you can handle. A small amount of actionable insights is far better than a mountain of data you find confusing and can't make head nor tale of.

Summary

To summarise: We navigate the M.A.G.I.C. Marketing Matrix in a Z format and then return to the beginning and repeat. Just because you've gone through the process once, doesn't mean you can stop. If you're going to be successful in your business, you must continually check to see if you are still meeting your customers' needs. It could be argued, therefore, that repeating the process is the most important part.

> **Key point:** Marketing is a continual process, not a series of random events!

Think about it for a second. Your business is your income — and you want a steady stream of income, right? Therefore, your business needs to be continuous and your marketing also needs to be continuous to support your business.

It never ceases to amaze me the number of businesses, large and small, that cut back on marketing budget when times are tough. This is exactly the time when they need to spend more, to increase their presence in the marketplace, to generate more business and, hence, more income.

So, how much of your time should you spend on marketing as an entrepreneur or micro-business owner? From my personal first-hand research, the business owners I spoke to all agreed marketing was a vital part of their business. The more successful ones spent anywhere between 25% to 40% of their time marketing their business on a continual basis — certainly in the early days. Some actually spent a lot more! It really depends on the business and resources available to you. As a (very basic) rule of thumb, I suggest you spend at least two days a week marketing your business when you start up and, when you have sufficient business, think about dropping back to no less than one day a week. Yes! A minimum of 40% to start with and no less than 20% when things are going well. Also, bear in mind, that during your early stages you may well spend 100% of your time on marketing, as several of my research interviewees did. So it's worth investing the time up front, to make sure you are doing what is necessary to bring you the best results in the long term.

The time these micro-business owners were prepared to invest in marketing their fledgling businesses really shows the importance of marketing in their ultimate success. Whatever the size of your business, its survival and ongoing success can be directly correlated to the level of commitment you make (and actively demonstrate) in marketing your business over the long term. That's a huge amount of time — right? Sure it is! But, remember this: no one is going to promote your business better than you, the business owner. Therefore, the role of marketing manager falls squarely on your shoulders. By the time you have worked your way through the M.A.G.I.C. Marketing Matrix and the rest of the 21st Century Marketing System, you should be crystal clear on your strategy and what you actually need to do to achieve your business goals.

What This Means to the Micro-Business Owner

As an entrepreneur and micro-business owner, evaluating opportunities from the customers' perspective puts you in a very strong position to turn an opportunity into reality.

The M.A.G.I.C. Marketing Matrix is a strategically focused tool to help entrepreneurs and micro-business owners consider all aspects of their potential or existing business — and how it might become a viable, profitable and sustainable venture. Once the business is established, elements of the M.A.G.I.C. Marketing Matrix can be used to monitor performance, identify new opportunities and keep highly focused on your ideal customers and their associated needs. All this can be done within a structured framework, with marketing at its core. Successful marketing is all about getting the right message in front of the right audience, at the right time, using the right tools. Marketing is a continuous process and, as an entrepreneur and micro-business owner, you should commit and invest sufficient resources into constantly marketing your business.

Ultimately, marketing should be viewed as a core business discipline and something that happens all the time, not something that's just done now and then. Marketing in the twenty-first century is a complex business process, with so many things to consider both offline and online. As an entrepreneur and micro-business owner, you must regularly take a step back and see the "helicopter view" to ensure your marketing activities contribute to your overall business objectives. The M.A.G.I.C. Marketing Matrix is the first piece of the puzzle and underpins the entire 21st Century Marketing System, so it's worth making sure you understand it before we move on.

The next step is to turn your strategy into a workable plan of action — because its action that gets results!

Turning Opportunity into Reality:
The Seven Point Plan

 "If you fail to plan, you plan to fail". I imagine, by now, you're getting used to the idea that planning is an important factor in the success of your business. Sad but true and, for some, it may feel like a real "ball ache". To ease some of the pain, let me introduce you to the Seven Point Plan, the second part of the 21st Century Marketing System. Here, we break down the high level strategy created in the previous chapter and turn it into a plan of action, to achieve your goals.

The good news is that, having completed your M.A.G.I.C. Marketing Matrix, you will have already thought through many of the steps. You need to go a little deeper in several areas before you are tempted to play with Facebook or build a "pretty" website — that comes a lot further down the line.

The purpose of the Seven Point Plan is to help you build your 21st Century Marketing Blueprint. It guides you through each step you need to take to develop your marketing capability, so when you start doing your marketing "for real" you'll know precisely "what" you need to do and "why" you are doing it. This is a very powerful position to be in and it will stand you in good stead for a very long time, especially if you review your plan regularly. This could take as little as an hour a month — so no excuses!

The Seven Point Plan to building your 21st Century Marketing Blueprint is shown in figure 2.12.

Figure 2.12 The Seven Point Plan

It is designed to help you build your marketing capability quickly and easily, without missing any of the essential components. You want to attract your ideal customers, people who will naturally gravitate towards you because they recognise you can help them get the results they are looking for. They are also far easier to convert into paying customers. Let's examine each point in turn.

Mission Statement

If you search the Web for definitions on mission statements (and several of the other concepts discussed in this chapter), you'll get a variety of definitions and explanations. This just adds to the confusion around this topic, so I'm going to start by putting a "stake in the ground" with what I believe these should be. The reason we expend the effort to develop them is to give clarity and become highly focused on our true purpose or cause — our mission, our dream — because this is what you want to communicate to your customers.

> **Mission Statement:** The reason your business exists. It is your purpose or cause and is timeless. For as long as the business exists, it is the only thing you will do.

Your mission statement should be made up of three parts and clearly articulate:

1. The reason your business exists (its purpose)
2. How your business contributes to making the world a better place
3. The evidence you will look for, that demonstrates you are achieving your mission.

It is the reason why you set up your business in the first place and should be written in a short, concise paragraph to convey your primary message — quickly and memorably. Think of it as the start of your "elevator pitch". Imagine you have just got into the elevator (lift) at a hotel with a stranger and they ask you what you do. The answer should be your mission statement. It is a hugely powerful form of communication and, if you get it right, it can be the opening for some very beneficial conversations. A crisp, well-prepared and delivered mission statement can act as a great icebreaker and often leads to the exchange of business cards and an invitation to extend an initial conversation.

For example, a friend of mine runs a small accountancy practice and his mission statement is *"To provide a friendly and affordable bookkeeping and accountancy service to small business owners with limited financial knowledge, and help them understand what the numbers actually mean so they can make the right decisions to grow their business."*

Let's break this down. The reason his business exists is *"to provide a friendly and affordable bookkeeping and accountancy service to small business owners with limited financial knowledge"*. Immediately, we know what he does and who his target market is. The contribution he makes to society is helping small business owners *"understand what the numbers actually mean so they can make the right decisions"* — again, we are in no doubt about what value he adds. Not only that, he has articulated in just a few words how his business is different to his competitors and conveyed the primary benefit he offers to his target audience. I know from personal experience that many accountants are just content to do "their thing", produce a set of accounts that fulfil the legal obligations for the tax man, submit a bill and wait for a cheque to arrive in the post. Whether or not the client actually understands what they have done for them and how this adds value to their business is far too often overlooked. Finally, the trail of evidence we should see over time is a happy band of small business owners who have been able to *"grow their business"*, rather than end up contributing to the government failure rate statistics.

It works an absolute treat for him and often sparks a whole series of secondary questions:

- ▲ What's the difference between bookkeeping and accounting?
- ▲ How much do you charge?
- ▲ How much knowledge do your clients typically have/need?
- ▲ What kind of decisions do they need to make?
- ▲ How do you know if these are the right decisions?
- ▲ Do you provide training?
- ▲ How does that help them grow their business?

And the one he absolutely loves:

- ▲ Can you help me with my business?

Quite often, micro-business owners associate themselves so closely with their business it becomes an extension of themselves — after all, it's their "baby". That's not a problem, just an observation and it may result in a different style of mission statement to some of the larger companies, who may have a more commercially focused original grounding and, hence, a more formal-sounding mission statement. If that's your position, that's fine, but you may want to just change the tone of your mission statement a little as you develop it. What really matters is to define something that works for you; make sure it's something that you like and can live with for a very long time. And, of course, something that accurately reflects what you want to achieve and your true purpose.

Guess what's on the back of my friend's business card? You got it! His company's mission statement. Why? Because it reinforces his message, long after the initial encounter; every time the recipient sees his card, it reminds them what he does, where they met and how he can help them. It serves as a "psychological anchor".

Many companies have such bland, boring mission statements about objectives and social responsibility and a whole bunch of other things, it ends up being a mish-mash of meaningless waffle. These types of mission statements only turn people off and no one ever believes them anyway. Here's a bad example — do not be tempted copy, edit and fill in the blanks!

"Our mission at < please don't insert your company name here > is to protect and increase our shareholders' investment in the business whilst delivering quality products and services to our customers. We also aim to keep our employees happy and develop their full potential whilst doing our best to ensure we do not damage the environment by developing an eco-friendly approach to everything we do."

Would a mission statement like this encourage you to invest your life savings into a bland, faceless organisation with no clearly defined purpose? Any idea why an organisation like this might exist? What could their clearly defined mission be?

I hope you get the idea!

To close this section, let me give you a couple of good examples of corporate mission statements that hit the mark.

Virgin: To embrace the human spirit and let it fly.

EasyJet: To provide our customers with safe, good value, point-to-point air services. To effect and to offer a consistent and reliable product and fares appealing to leisure and business markets on a range of European routes. To achieve this, we will develop our people and establish lasting relationships with our suppliers.

Google: To organize the world's information and make it universally accessible and useful.

eBay: To provide a global trading platform where practically anyone can trade practically anything.

Amazon: To build a place where people can come to find and discover anything they might want to buy online.

Which of these do you like? Which resonate with you? After reading them, do you know why these organisations exist? Are you intrigued to find out more?

Before you go any further, stop and think about your own mission statement. Why does your business exist? How are you going to communicate your primary message and capture my attention in just a few seconds?

It is actually quite thought-provoking to do this correctly. You may have to come back to it several times as you clarify and develop your thoughts. In addition to the reason/contribution/evidence mentioned above, here are a few key points to help you focus on what's important.

Your mission statement should be:

1. Short and sweet
2. Clearly state why you exist (as a business)

3. Timeless (i.e. no deadline) stating why you exist now and in five, ten, twenty, or even twenty-five years' time

4. Intriguing and raise questions

5. Focused on how you expect to serve your target audience

6. Identify how your target audience will benefit if you achieve your mission

7. Purposeful and help you focus on what you want to become as you achieve your mission.

Please do take the time to complete this exercise before continuing as it will make the next section a lot easier to understand.

Vision Statement

There is often quite a bit of confusion between mission and vision statements. I would argue that whilst your mission statement defines your purpose or cause and articulates your dream, your vision statement is a vivid mental image of what you want your business to become at some point in the future, based on your goals and aspirations and how you're going to get there — the journey. Collectively, these give you clarity of purpose and a crystal-clear idea of the path you intend to take. They are parts of your marketing arsenal and directly contribute to building your own 21st Century Marketing Blueprint, so please don't gloss over this section or only make a half-hearted attempt. What you do here will have an impact on your later success.

> **Vision Statement:** A vivid mental image of what you want your business to become at some point in the future based on your goals and aspirations.

My accountant friend has a vision for his business: "To become the leading accountancy practice and training provider for small business owners in need of bookkeeping and accountancy services, and foundational accountancy-based training in my local area."

Mission and vision statements are key tools to help you keep on track when faced with a decision on the direction of your business. In particular, they should be regularly referred to when evaluating new opportunities, to make sure you don't go off on a tangent. One question I really like when faced with making this type of decision is: "Is this <whatever decision it may be> going to take me closer to or further from my primary goal?" And, of course, your primary goal is clearly defined in your mission and vision statements. If you spend the time and effort to clearly define your mission and vision statements, it becomes pretty easy to answer this question, which can contribute greatly to your continued and future success.

Brian's mission statement is: "To serve great coffee and other hot drinks and quality snacks that people enjoy, savour and look forward to, in a relaxed, friendly environment where they feel cheerful, appreciated and at home."

This has the three components discussed earlier:

Purpose:	To serve great coffee and other beverages and snacks
Contribution:	Service people enjoy, savour, and look forward to, in a relaxed, friendly environment
Evidence:	Cheerful, happy customers who feel relaxed and at home

Brian's vision statement is: "To become the leading independent chain of coffee shops and first choice for regular local customers in <His Town> who want to enjoy quality, hot drinks and supplementary products in an environment they consider an extension of their home."

By their very nature, mission and vision statements will be quite close because they support each other. They both give Brian clarity of purpose and direction and, when he's presented with a new opportunity, he can lean on these two statements to help make his decision. For example, if he's offered another premises in a noisy location, he may decide it does not meet his "relaxed, friendly environment" criteria. Likewise, if a friend approaches him to go into partnership to open a wine bar, bakery, or newsagent, he can quickly see that none of these would contribute to his primary goal — in fact, they'll all take him further away and he should refuse. Unless, of course, his current business does not need him full time and he can work with his friend to start an entirely new business — which will have its own independent mission and vision statements and, of course, its own completely separate 21st Century Marketing Blueprint.

Core Values

Now that you know why you exist and how you plan to achieve your mission, the next step is to define your core values. These are the things that will ultimately determine how you behave whilst you achieve your quest. Your core values are a fundamental part of the DNA of your business. They will be communicated every time anyone deals with, or comes into contact with, your business and are crucial to building your brand.

> **Core Values:** Your core value and belief system which determines what behaviour is and is not acceptable to you and in your business.

Yes! We are discussing brand at the strategic level, not the product level — which is where far too many people start to think about developing their brand. It may be different for multi-nationals that have several brands to manage but, in the context of a micro-business, your brand should be considered at the strategic level, not the product level. This is because you want to convey a clear and consistent message in everything you do.

The main purpose of your brand is to communicate your core values which, in turn, will build recognition, trust and an emotional connection with your target audience. Building trust must be one of your fundamental objectives because trust leads to positive word-of-mouth. And generating positive word-of-mouth is your primary objective.

Basically, it works like this:

your core values = your business's DNA = who you really are = the basis on which people (your customers) decide whether or not they like and trust you = word-of-mouth (good or bad).

Let me give you an example.

In my own experience, many tradesmen have a bit of a reputation for being just a little unreliable, especially when it comes to timekeeping. Now, I'm not saying all tradesmen are like this, but when they say they will be there by 9 a.m. and you're still waiting for them at noon, you understandably feel a little annoyed. It really does not matter why they are late; the mere fact that they are late generally gives a bad impression. You subsequently find it hard to totally trust them and, when a friend asks for a recommendation, you feel obliged to reflect their timekeeping qualities as part of your conversation (word-of-mouth). Which, you may also reflect, is sad because they did a really good job — but you always remember the time they messed you around and made you late for work. Of course, one of the reasons you picked them was because they claimed to be "your local, reliable friendly tradesman" — but they did not live up to their promise.

One of your core values (as a customer) may be that punctuality is important — after all, you are always in the office by 9 a.m. and haven't been late in years — so you want to work with others who share this core value. When a tradesman claims (either on the side of their van or on their business card) that they are "reliable", you assume (not unreasonably) that they will turn up when they say they will. After all, they have made a promise.

In this example, from a marketing perspective, there is a mismatch of core values. This leads to expectations not being met and, hence, lack of trust, resulting in negative word-of-mouth. Do you see how this works?

So what exactly are "core values" and how do you define them?

Core values define what you, as either a person or a business, stand for. They highlight an acceptable level of behaviour and, ultimately, determine what is and isn't important to you and help determine how you or your company spends time and money. In terms of a company's culture, values are the core. Obviously, for a micro-business, the owner is often "the business", especially if they are a "one-man band"; therefore, their core values and the business's core values will be the same.

The best way to define them is to think about what's really — and I mean really — important to you. What level of behaviour do you consider to be acceptable? What really makes you angry? How would you change things for the better? Basically, it boils down to this: how do you like to be treated? And, of course, you should treat others as you would like to be treated yourself.

Why is defining your core values so important?

Because core values are the standard operating principles that guide you and your business's culture, which includes your behaviours, attitudes, language and focus. Ultimately, you attract and retain people (customers, employees, suppliers and other associates) who share your core values — it's one of the "laws of the universe". When there's synergy at the core level, it works easily; when there's not, it's hard work or even destructive.

Your core values are reflected in the way you communicate with the outside world. In business, your core values are communicated through your brand. Branding (the process of creating a brand) should be considered at the strategic level, to make sure you communicate your core values effectively to your target audience. That way, you attract the right kind of customers who also share your core values and doing business becomes a pleasure, not a chore.

Branding is another huge subject, but for the purpose of our marketing journey in this book, we will define your "brand" as: "The perceptions you create about your business that serve to differentiate you from your competitors". Your brand communicates what you stand for, engenders trust and creates an emotional connection with your target audience". "Branding", on the other hand, is "the deliberate process of creating positive perceptions about your brand in the minds of your target audience". Branding, therefore, is a process you have some control over and forms part of your marketing activities.

If you are absolutely clear on your core values, it makes it much easier to identify the core values of other people and organisations you may choose to sell to or work with. This is because you have a baseline and framework to evaluate them against. It's a bit like having a measuring stick (your core values) you can use to judge whether or not you share common values, which will help you determine whether or not you can trust them and want to spend time, or do business with them. If you identify a "core value mismatch" with a customer or supplier, you may feel reluctant, or even refuse, to enter into any form of relationship with them. However, if you feel you have a close "core value match" then the whole thing feels far more comfortable and the relationship has every chance of working out well. There may be some instances where there is a close match between several of your really important core values, but you differ on one or two which may be a little less important to you. In these situations, you can at least enter into the relationship from a position of knowledge and with a realistic expectation of how the relationship may pan out.

I like working with organisations where there is a very close "core values match" as it makes everything so much easier and more pleasurable; it feels like doing business with friends who really understand me. Some companies freely publish and talk about their core values openly on their website. If you choose to do this, make sure you live up to your claims and "walk your talk". There are numerous examples of large organisations that claim to be ethically motivated and spend a large portion of their marketing budget trying to paint a whiter than white image to convince the public they are "goody two-shoes", then get slammed by the press for complex tax avoidance schemes or using child labour in Third World countries.

On a personal level, when I reflect on my previous experiences where conflict has arisen, it's usually down to incongruence or mismatch of core values. To me, honesty and integrity are fundamental and form a very important part of my "belief system". I can recall one encounter with a "specialist" training company who created a huge razzamatazz about a live training seminar they were running in London. I kept getting emails saying they only had something like "one hundred places available and they were filling fast" so I needed to "book my place before it was too late". I wanted to hear what they had to say, so I hit the credit card and booked my place.

A key benefit plastered all over their marketing material was the "opportunity to network with like-minded entrepreneurs" and I was really looking forward to the day. When I got there, disappointment quickly set in and deepened throughout the day. Less than a dozen people turned up and I'd done all the networking possible before the end of the first coffee break. The "Gala Networking Buffet Lunch" (for which I'd paid what I considered to be a handsome price) was nothing short of pathetic and they'd almost ran out of food by the time I got to the front of the queue. I even ended up nipping out to the nearest McDonald's before the afternoon session started.

The content wasn't much better either. Most of the day was either self-congratulatory waffle about how wonderful they were, or an overt sales pitch for other highly priced products and services containing content "they didn't have time to go into today". Well, I'm sorry, guys, but that's exactly what I expected you "to go into today" and why I parted with my cash. If you didn't spend so much time trying to sell yourself to the people who already came to your event, you would actually have had time to talk about the things I thought I'd paid to hear. Incidentally, I wasn't the only one who felt lied to and cheated. They certainly didn't make me trust them and now, I'm afraid, they serve as a good example of how not to behave and subsequently created negative word-of-mouth for themselves.

The key message here is that you must live up to your promises. When your promises are based around living up to your core values, you stand a very good chance of delivering and, hence, satisfying your customers and generating positive word-of-mouth. These core values represent your belief system — which is an acceptable and expected level of behaviour that you, your employees and your partners must embrace, demonstrate and live by. Whether you're a large company or a micro-business owner, the same principles apply. Before you start, it really is worth thinking about defining and articulating what your core values are and what they mean. This can then be expressed through your brand and all your branding-related activities. Ultimately, if you keep your promises and delight your customers, they will talk about you, generate that all important positive word-of-mouth and become your advocates. "Walking your talk" is ultimately the way you build trust in your business and your brand — and it's all based on living up to your core values.

They are typically summarised by single words and explained in short sentences, for example:

Honesty: Always tell the truth, or

Integrity: Always do the right thing (even if it's not profitable, like fixing a mistake).

They are your "guiding lights" you follow without question; they shape your thinking and, hence, dictate your natural behaviour.

Brian considers himself to be reliable, honest, fun-loving, motivated, optimistic, passionate and respectful and has defined his core values as follows:

Reliable	If Brian makes a promise, or says he's going to do something, he'll do it to the best of his ability. He more often than not achieves what he sets out to achieve, no matter how mundane and, if Mary asks him to pick something up from the grocery store, he often promptly obliges without complaint. Mary knows she can rely on Brian.
Honest	Brian was brought up in a household with strong moral values. Honesty and integrity are very important to him. He hates being lied to and can't help taking it personally. He admits it's probably the fastest way to get on the wrong side of him.
Fun-loving	According to his friends, having a laugh and seeing the funny side of things is one of his greatest qualities. Although he doesn't exactly consider himself the "life and soul of the party", he does like people and is always smiling.
Motivated	Being a "self-starter" he finds it pretty easy to get up in the morning and get on with things. He hates lazy people and "doesn't suffer fools gladly". One of the worst things his girls can say to him is "I can't be bothered".
Punctual	Timekeeping is high on his list and, if people don't turn up on time, he feels they don't respect him. One of his lifelong work habits is turning up for work ten minutes before he's due and leaving at least ten minutes after the end of his shift. This goes hand-in-hand with "reliability" noted above.
Passionate	He's a firm believer in "If a job's worth doing, it's worth doing properly" and just cannot bring himself round to doing "half a job". This probably comes from his father, who spent some time in the Army, but it's a quality Brian feels has always stood him in good stead.
Respectful	"Treat others as you would wish to be treated yourself" is another favourite motto and, like most men, Brian likes to feel respected. He always had great respect for his late grandfather and his father and he's also a great advocate of "manners don't cost anything". These are values he and Mary are drumming into their two daughters.

Brian's pretty much a "happy-go-lucky" kind of a guy and, whilst he knows he has some solid character traits, he also recognises he has a few weaknesses. Being passionate about what he does, means he's not the most efficient character on earth and, whilst he can motivate himself and his family and a few guys at the garage, he's not really an inspiring leader. This probably accounts for his lack of interest in planning and general management-related activities, so it's a good job Mary likes planning the family holidays — although he does like to be included in the final decisions.

When defining your own core values, it is very important to be totally honest with yourself, otherwise there's absolutely no point — it's a complete waste of your time and effort. If you say you share Brian's views on timekeeping, but are forever five minutes late, you're kidding yourself and, if you make punctuality-related promises which you don't keep, you'll end up disappointing your customers and damaging your brand. It's far better not to make a promise, rather than make one and then immediately break it!

When you know what your core values are, it makes it easier to define and find the people/businesses like you, because you have common core values and these become shared values. You then build relationships with these people (customers, suppliers, joint venture partners) to turn your vision into reality.

In summary: Your core values are your beliefs, which define your values. Values are demonstrated through behaviour and behaviour reinforces beliefs. It's a never-ending process, as shown in figure 2.13, which essentially "plays out" how you live according to your core values.

Figure 2.13 The Belief | Values | Behaviour Cycle

The MVCV Grid:
The Foundation of Your Brand

It is important to understand how all this fits together, because it forms the foundation of your brand which, in turn, influences how you communicate with your target audience and what you will ultimately say. You may see many variations of these concepts on the Internet and it can all become quite confusing. However, we've summarised it in the MVCV Grid (Mission/Vision/Core Values Grid), shown in figure 2.14, to help you get to grips with each element and piece the jigsaw together.

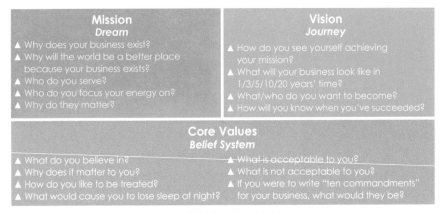

Figure 2.14 The MVCV Grid

The MVCV Grid is essentially the DNA of your business. Once you understand it, it allows you to clearly articulate and stay tightly aligned and focused on what you want to achieve, to turn your opportunities into reality.

It allows you to say:

"We believe in < core values > and do things this way < behaviours >. We see ourselves as < vision > in order to fulfil our < mission >. That is what makes us different from everybody else and forms the DNA of our business. This is reflected in our brand and communicated through our branding."

For example, Brian is a stickler for timekeeping, so if he says on his advertising, "Fresh coffee available from 7:30 a.m." his customers know they can call in at 7:31 for their morning brew, come rain or shine. After all, they can rely on Brian, because he lives up to his core value of reliability. It also means that if he takes on staff who are always late and have a plethora of excuses, they'll probably not get on, as he cannot rely on them and they don't share his core values of timekeeping and respect. He'd be better off finding someone else, because this will cause less friction and, ultimately, conflict — which will impact other areas of his business.

Business Objectives

All the work you have done so far starts to get pulled together with your objectives and, if you've done your homework properly, your business objectives should be fairly easy to define.

When defining business and marketing objectives, we often use the popular acronym SMART.

SMART Objectives:
▲ S = Specific
▲ M = Measurable
▲ A = Achievable
▲ R = Realistic
▲ T = Time-bound

SMART stands for:

Specific: Your objectives need to be specific, they must be crystal clear and not have any ambiguities or vagueness. They should state precisely what you aim to achieve.

Measurable: Your objectives should be measurable, otherwise how will you know if you've achieved them? This also helps you measure your progress to ensure you keep on track.

Achievable: There is no point setting completely unrealistic goals, such as "Build Rome in a day!" because neither you, nor anyone else on your team, will believe them. If they are so far out of reach, or too simple, they will be meaningless and you'll be wasting your time.

Realistic: A short dose of realism goes a long way in believing you can achieve your objectives. You should take into account all of your available resources, including the limits of your time, knowledge and money. For example, there's no point kidding yourself you're going to "build the website within twenty-four hours and have it up and running by Friday evening" if you've never done it before, especially when your friends, who have more experience, are telling you it will take a couple of weeks. The key thing to remember here is that if your objectives are not realistic, you won't believe them and they will fall by the wayside.

Time-bound: Committing to a target date keeps you focused and also allows you to monitor your progress. It also instils a sense of urgency which helps keep you motivated and working toward your desired objective.

Napoleon Hill, in *Talk and Grow Rich*, defined a goal as "a dream with a deadline". That's the best definition I've ever heard. Your business objectives should be your tightly defined goals, complete with deadlines and must be as precise as possible. How complex your business is will determine the nature and time frame of your business objectives.

I suggest you define two or three "big-picture" goals/business objectives that reflect your mission and vision statements and then break them down further into long-, medium- and short-term objectives, in order to actually achieve them. The trick here is not to have woolly high-level objectives, but precisely defined goals with target deadlines that can easily be measured.

In writing/defining your business objectives, you should refer to your mission and vision statements because the business objectives will be the first step in achieving your mission and vision.

Brian's vision is to ultimately end up with a chain of coffee shops. In order to achieve that, he should have a specific business objective of developing and refining his business model, so it is replicable. For example, his first objective could be: "To refine and document the business model for the first coffee shop, by reviewing accurate monthly management accounts with a professional advisor (Gemma)". This will also involve keeping a diary on at least a weekly basis which will record all operational activity, challenges, decisions and changes to the model as it evolves — in addition to keeping the 21st Century Marketing Blueprint and M.A.G.I.C. Marketing Matrix updated at least once a quarter.

OK. Brian is now off to a good start and, as long as he does what he's set out to do, he should have a very clear picture of what works, why it works (or an explanation of things that failed), the problems and challenges he experienced and what he had to change to make it work — as well as a whole bunch of other things that document his progress. This will be an invaluable set of resources, if and when he's ready to open his second coffee shop and will save him trying to remember what he did and "reinvent the wheel". This forms part of the Control element of the M.A.G.I.C. Marketing Matrix and contributes to the Results element of the 21st Century Marketing Blueprint. Incidentally, keeping a business journal, or reflective business diary, is a very valuable tool, because you will inevitably forget things over time as you focus on solving your next challenge or problem. It does not have to take long; recording your thoughts in just a few paragraphs for five minutes at the end of each day, will soon build into a wealth of carefully documented knowledge you can reflect on and use again later.

Brian's second business objective is "to break even within six months" — which is a pretty tall order by any stretch of the imagination! But he thinks he can do it, if he keeps his overheads low and doesn't take a salary during this period. This, at least, gives him something concrete to aim for and, most importantly, it's a measurable event (SMART objective) that is on the right path to achieving his mission.

The third objective is: "To be at 50% capacity for both the early morning and lunchtime peak periods (7:30-9:00 a.m. and 12:30-2:00 p.m.) taking an average of £3 per transaction by the end of month three, increasing to 75% by the end of month six". Again, ambitious goals and something very specific to aim for. By breaking this goal into two parts (i.e. 50% at month three and 75% at month six), the three-month review point will serve as a timely reminder to update his other management documentation and adjust his projections accordingly. In larger organisations, there would be a formal strategic review and planning processes, but there's no way it's going to happen in a micro-business. Brian should make more detailed notes in his business journal during this period and, perhaps, make the effort to write a couple of pages rather than just a paragraph or two.

His fourth and final initial business objective for the first year is "to make sufficient profit by the end of the first year, to be able to take a net personal income equal to 50% of his previous net annual salary from the Ford dealership". If he achieves this in the first year, he'll be pretty happy, especially as he can replace some of his inheritance he sunk into the business at the outset. He may define other objectives as he refines his plan, but that's a pretty good start.

Your business objectives could define your goals for one, three, or even five years (or longer in large organisations). Most micro-business owners I spoke to, focus on a year, possibly two, but certainly no longer than three. This highlights the reluctance of entrepreneurs and micro-business owners to partake in regular formal planning practices and, hence, why a more flexible approach, such as the 21st Century Marketing System, is far more appropriate and useful. Your planning cycle should be no less than every twelve months and, ideally, every three to six months you should review your progress (preferably with an advisor). My personal recommendation would be to have a few detailed business objectives for the first year and just a couple more for years two and three, which you add to and flesh out as you progress.

For example, Brian has decided that he wants to achieve a net profit of 200% of his previous annual salary by the end of the second year and, by the end of year three, he wants to open a second coffee shop. Obviously, the business objectives he has set himself for the first year can be built on in the second year and all these will contribute to his third-year goal of expanding his "empire".

The purpose of these business objectives is to put a "stake in the ground" and have some real targets to aim for. They will also motivate you and your staff and dictate some of the support activities you'll need to consider. In Brian's case, recruiting and training (and retaining) sufficient staff, in order to achieve his occupancy and turnover targets.

Marketing Objectives

Your marketing objectives should define how you will achieve your business objectives. Not all of your business objectives will have associated marketing objectives, particularly if they are technical or product development related. Brian's first business objective of refining his business model is one example of a business objective that will not have an associated marketing objective. However, as your business becomes more established, your business objectives will be become heavily customer and, hence, sales focused and, therefore, will have associated marketing objectives.

But how do we define marketing objectives and what exactly are they?

The answer is: *"Any marketing-related activity that contributes to achieving your business objectives"*. This can include market research, marketing planning, developing campaigns, monitoring results and revising strategy, based on the effectiveness of the results. Marketing is such a huge area and covers many disciplines, so all of these can be considered marketing objectives.

One of Brian's business objectives is *"To be at 50% capacity for both the early morning and lunchtime peak periods (7:30 a.m. to 9:00 a.m. and 12:30 p.m. to 2:00 p.m.), taking an average of £3 per transaction by the end of month three, increasing to 75% capacity by the end of month six"*. To translate this into a concrete marketing objective, we need to first establish exactly what it means. At full capacity, his coffee shop can cater for sixty people (covers) on a combination of one, two and four-seat tables. Therefore, 50% capacity means thirty people. Assuming each person stays for twenty minutes, this equates to 3 "sittings" per hour x 30 customers = 90 customers per hour x 1.5 hours = 135 paying customers in total for the lunchtime period x £3 per transaction = £405 turnover.

That's his target, but how many people/prospects does he have to make aware his coffee shop exists to gain 135 paying customers? If he needs 135 customers per day for just the lunchtime period, multiplied by five days, that's 675 customers a week. Admittedly, some of these will be repeat customers and Brian estimated 175 will come more than once per week, which means he needs to attract about 500 new customers per week, from the time he first opens his doors. Over a month this is 500 x 4 = 2,000 new customers and the best estimate he can get from one of the sales guys from the local radio station is, that for ten people who hear the ad, one will "check him out", visit the coffee shop and spend at least £3. Therefore, based on this assumption, he needs to make 2,000 x 10 = 20,000 people aware his coffee shop has just opened.

This means he needs to communicate his message to 20,000 members of his target audience in the first month. Therefore, *"to make 20,000 members of the local community aware his coffee shop has opened and has a*

£3 lunchtime special between 12:30 p.m. and 2:00 p.m. within the first six months" becomes his first marketing objective.

He estimates that his early morning trade will be far more successful (because no one else is open that early in the morning and he has a captive audience) and. based on a "hit rate" of one in five rather than one in ten, he needs to "make 10,000 people aware his doors are open from 7:30 a.m. for a great cup of coffee on the way to work". This becomes his second marketing objective.

His initial marketing objective is to make these prospects aware he exists and what he has to offer, so using the AIDA framework, he needs to communicate Awareness messages — at least in the early days.

Your marketing objectives express what you want to achieve when promoting your product or service — for example, awareness amongst your target market or providing information about your products and reducing buying resistance.

Translating business objectives into marketing objectives using this "top-down" approach can really help you focus on how you can achieve your objectives and goals in the "real world". The point to remember is that marketing objectives express what you want to achieve, not how you are going to do it. This is done at the next level down, which is where you define your Marketing Communication Objectives.

Marketing Communication Objectives

Ah ha! At last we are getting very close to the tactics — not long now.

Marketing communication objectives specify how you are going to achieve your marketing objectives. Every marketing communications objective should support a clearly defined marketing objective; otherwise you run the risk of wasting time and money. Effective marketing communications is all about getting the right message in front of the right audience, at the right time, using the right tools. Here, you need to be very specific about what you say and to whom. Let's take the two marketing objectives defined in the last section:

> *Effective marketing communications is all about getting the right message in front of the right audience, at the right time, using the right tools.*

1. Brian's first marketing objective is to *"make 20,000 members of the local community aware his coffee shop has opened and has a £3 lunchtime special between 12:30 and 2 p.m. by the end of month six"*.

2. His second marketing objective is to *"make 10,000 people aware his doors are open from 7:30 a.m. for a great cup of coffee on the way to work by the end of month six"*.

The next step is to break each of these down further into a very specific set of marketing communication objectives, which will determine what precise actions you take in order to achieve your marketing objectives. For example, how do you make 20,000 people aware of your existence and what you offer within the first six months of opening your doors?

If you just said your target audience were "coffee drinkers" you'd now be struggling to work out how to best communicate your message to them. However, because Brian has followed the steps of the M.A.G.I.C. Marketing Matrix, he has segmented his target market into five distinct groups and knows what they look like, because he has developed personas for each group. As discussed earlier, segmentation is the first part of the STP (Segmentation/Targeting/Positioning) framework and, when we get down to our marketing communication objectives, we want to "target" just one segment. We also want to "position" our product/service/business/brand in the minds of our target audience, to help them link our solution to their problem.

Brian needs to communicate two very different messages to two separate segments of his target audience. His aim is to make each group (segment) think he is specifically talking to them. He also needs to attract their attention in the most appropriate way, which means he needs to consider which tools are most appropriate to deliver each message, at a specific point in the customer's journey.

For example, Brian's objective is to make people aware he exists, so direct marketing, email, or webinars would be inappropriate because, at this point, he does not know who they are. The "4Cs" framework, shown in figure 2.15, has its origins in the traditional marketing era and is helpful in identifying the most appropriate tools to deliver your message. This is often referred to as the "Promotional Mix".

	Advertising	Sales Promotion	Public Relations	Personal Selling	Direct Marketing
Communications					
Ability to deliver a personal message	Low	Low	Low	High	High
Ability to reach a large audience	High	Medium	Medium	Low	Medium
Level of interaction	Low	Low	Low	High	High
Credibility					
Given by the target audience	High	Medium	Low	High	Medium
Costs					
Absolute costs	High	Medium	Low	High	Medium
Costs per contact	Low	Medium	Low	High	High
Wastage	High	Medium	High	Low	Low
Size of investment	High	Medium	Low	High	Medium
Control					
Ability to target particular audiences	Medium	High	Low	Medium	High
Management's ability to adjust the deployment of the tool as circumstances change	Medium	High	Low	Medium	High

Ref: Fill (2006)

Figure 2.15 The 4Cs Framework

Promotional Mix: The blend of marketing tools used to deliver a message, or series of messages, during a campaign.

The challenge is to find the optimal mix of the different tools to achieve the best results and maximise return on investment (ROI). The tools used in the modern promotional mix vary but, typically, include the following:

▲ Advertising

▲ Personal selling

▲ Sales promotion

▲ Public relations or publicity

▲ Direct marketing

▲ Websites

▲ Search engine marketing (SEO/PPC)

▲ Email

▲ Online PR webinars

▲ Various social media platforms

Whilst this model focuses on the traditional communication tools, it can easily be extended to include the modern tools, because the 4Cs of Communications, Credibility, Costs and Control are just as relevant in digital and social media. The appropriateness of each tool can be evaluated against each of the qualifying statements in each of the 4C categories, to determine whether or not they are appropriate to achieving the campaign's objectives.

Brian's initial challenge is to create awareness of what he has to offer. He realises that not everyone will drop everything and rush to his coffee shop the very first time they hear his message. He's calculated that he needs to at least get his message heard by quite a lot of people, even though the majority are unlikely to become customers in the short term. He also wants to position himself as "the leading independent chain of coffee shops and first choice for regular local customers in <His Town>" so credibility is an important consideration and will influence his choice of tools. Looking at the tools available to him on the New Engagement Paradigm (see figure 2.16), he has selected six tools he thinks will achieve his marketing communication objectives.

Figure 2.16 The New Engagement Paradigm – Brian's Choice of Tools

The tools he has chosen at the point of start-up are consistent with the findings of my own research. Because the venture is unknown, there is a heavy emphasis on interruption marketing, to create that initial "splash". He also has a limited budget and doesn't really know how to do marketing online yet, so his primary focus is in using the traditional tools. He also knows from the first section of this book that he absolutely must have an online presence to be found at the "zero moment of truth" and has decided that having a website and Facebook page is all he can cope with, as he's got so many other things to think about. He knows he must do more here later, but any more right now and his "head will explode". Therefore, he's taking the advice in these pages and has committed himself to doing a few things well, rather than a lot of things badly.

Here's a summary of the tools Brian intends to use and what he's planning to do with them:

Advertising	Adverts in the local press and on the local radio station will be his main tools and he'll also advertise in the local community monthly magazines, but does not expect this to be as effective. Two separate ads will be run in each publication several pages apart and he'll have two separate radio ads, one specifically targeting each segment.
Printed Material	Flyers to deliver to the local offices and to hand out to passers-by. Posters to put in his shop window and a couple of other locations around town. Business cards with his contact details and lunchtime offer on one side and a grid of ten boxes on the other, which serves as a basic loyalty scheme. He'll give every customer a card, stamp the first visit and, when they have ten stamps they get a free coffee as a reward and a thank you. He'll also need the physical stamp to use on the cards at the till.
Public Relations	Getting the local paper to do a feature on him in the "new business" section is a golden opportunity. He could also be a special guest on one of the local radio shows, where he might just chat to the presenter about his business in general terms rather than making a hard sell. An example topic might be an educational discussion explaining where coffee comes from, what the different coffee beans are, which ones make a great cup of coffee first thing in the morning and how this differs from the best blend for a lunchtime boost. Which, of course, he'll happily provide if you call into his shop.
Personal Selling	This might seem a strange tool to include in an awareness campaign, but it is a very useful and extremely relevant tool to leverage current interest. For example, all he needs to do is talk to each of his customers and ask if they work in an office. If so, would they mind taking a couple of his posters and putting them on the company notice board? In return, he can give them an extra stamp on their loyalty card and get them one step closer to their free drink. A very simple win-win!
Website	In the early stages, he'll probably just have a simple brochure-style website that explains what he has to offer (sample menu and prices), where the coffee shop is located and what his opening hours are. This is probably all anyone will want to know, so a clean, simple website is appropriate. He can always redevelop it later.
Facebook	He was pretty adamant that a company page on Facebook, which says pretty much the same as the website, is all he has time for at the beginning. However, Gemma has persuaded him to write a short post once a week for the first six months, just to support his awareness activities. She explained that he doesn't have to sell anything, just tell a funny story about something that's happened during the week and ask people to "like" his posts and follow his business on Facebook.

Now that Brian knows what he wants to say, to whom and which tools he'll use, he can set some very specific SMART marketing communication objectives (MCOs). Note: Brian will need a separate set of objectives for each segment; here are the MCOs for the lunchtime segment.

Lunchtime Segment

Objective #	Tool/Channel	Marketing Communication Objective
MCO 1	Advertising	1) Place an advert in the local weekly newspaper with a coupon code for a free cookie, to accompany a cup of coffee when the coupon is presented at the till. Objective is to redeem at least fifty coupons per week for the period of the six-week campaign.
		2) Place an advert in the local community newspaper with a different coupon code for a free cookie, to accompany every cup of coffee when the coupon is presented at the till. Objective is to redeem at least forty coupons per month for the three months the campaign will run.
		Note the use of different coupon codes for each publication, even though the reward (free cookie) is the same. This helps Brian evaluate how effective each publication is in delivering his message to his target audience.
		3) Radio advertising instructing listeners to quote "Radio XYZ" at the till to claim their free Belgian waffle, with the objective being to redeem at least one hundred waffles per week for the ten-week radio campaign.
		Key point: Measurability is important to achieving objectives, so having a different "reward" for each medium (print vs. radio) can help easily monitor the success of each initiative. The number of free cookies vs. the number of free waffles recorded at the point of sale can give Brian instant management feedback on the performance of his advertising. Obviously, it won't be 100% accurate, because not everyone will remember to claim their free gift, but it can certainly give a quick indication of how print is performing compared to radio.
MCO 2	Printed Material	Personally distribute 240 flyers to local businesses during the first three months and speak to at least one person in each business.
		Hand out 1,000 flyers in the street every Saturday morning for the first month, with a 10% introductory discount code for purchases made that day on presentation of the flyer.
		Hand out 2,000 date-stamped loyalty cards in the first month to every new customer served and keep a record of cards redeemed for a free drink for further analysis.
		Note: If Brian prints 5,000 cards and, at the end of the first month he has 3,000 left, as long as he and his staff have been diligent in handing them out responsibly, he can estimate he has acquired 2,000 customers during that month. He can then compare this with other metrics, such as the 200 free waffles handed out during the same period, which would suggest he can attribute 10% of his customer acquisitions to radio advertising.

MCO 3	Public Relations	Achieve one free PR article in the local print media per month for the first three months.
MCO 4	Personal Selling	Hand out five posters per day (Monday through Friday) during the first six weeks to customers willing to display them in their offices, or other public places they have responsible access to, such as community centre, doctor's surgery, sports hall, etc. — definitely not "fly posting"!
MCO 5	Website	Achieve an average length of stay of sixty seconds for new visitors to the website, with 25% of visitors viewing more than one page per visit over the initial three-month campaign. Note: Brian has no real traffic generation strategy to start with and people will probably find his website either by typing in the URL advertised on his other marketing material, or by accident. What he is interested in, is that when they do arrive on his home page, they stay on his site for a while and visit a couple of pages rather than just leave straight away. This will give him the comfort of knowing what he has to say is actually of interest to his target audience.
MCO 6	Facebook	Create one post per week for the first three months and achieve an average of ten "likes" per post and build a following of one hundred by the end of three months.

Brian also needs to define a set of marketing communication objectives for the "early morning drinkers" segment, which may be very similar to the "lunchtime" drinkers. He can use the same codes to help him track where the customer came from and the only thing that will differentiate early morning drinkers from the lunchtime crowd is the time of day — which will be recorded on his till — and, hence, he can do some detailed analysis, based on time periods, to get some deeper insights about the performance of his business.

Marketing Campaigns

Research shows people (your prospects) must be exposed to marketing messages multiple times before the message "sinks in". How many times varies quite considerably and depends on a number of factors, including the industry you're in, the type of product (consumable/investment/long-term), the price, the number of competitors, familiarity of the problem and potential solutions in the prospect's mind (for example, we all know cars solve a transport problem, but the choice is huge). As a rule of thumb, it can typically take anywhere between five and twenty "exposures" before your target audience "gets it".

Brian needs to deliver a series of messages to each segment over a period of time, rather than just one message on just one occasion. Delivering a marketing message multiple times, using one or more tools, is referred to as a "marketing campaign".

> **Marketing Campaign:** A consistent message delivered to a segment of the target audience over a period of time, to achieve one or more marketing communication objectives.

The key point to remember is that each campaign will talk to a specific group (segment) of your target market and deliver a consistent (single) message via the most appropriate channels. Campaigns can also deliver a series of related messages over a period of time, but that becomes a lot more complex. In the micro-business context, it is far better to keep it simple and think one message equals one campaign. If the second group hears the messages designed for the first group, then that's a coincidental added bonus, not an objective. Never be tempted to use one set of messages to talk to all your target audiences in order to try and save money; you will inevitably dilute your message to the point it talks to no one and completely misses the mark. By having a set of SMART marketing communication objectives for each campaign, you can keep highly focused on delivering the right message, to the right audience, at the right time, using the right tools. This should help you build and execute a well-coordinated measurable marketing campaign (note the use of the word "measurable") and achieve your marketing and overall business goals.

A campaign should be well executed and, for that, you need a campaign plan that details what you will do and when. A simple project plan represented by a Gantt chart is all you really need. Brain's initial twelve week campaign plan is shown in figure 2.17.

Brian should use this marketing campaign plan in conjunction with his marketing communication objectives, as a management tool to help him execute his campaign. This serves a couple of purposes. First, it makes you

Brian's Marketing Campaign Plan for the First 12 Weeks

	Week 1	Week 2	Week 3	Week 4	Week 5	Week 6	Week 7	Week 8	Week 9	Week 10	Week 11	Week 12
Advertising												
Weekly Newspaper												
Monthly Magazine												
Radio												
Printed Material												
Flyers & Personal Visits												
Street Flyers												
Loyalty Cards												
Public Relations												
PR Articles												
Personal Selling												
Posters												
Website												
Facebook												
Posts												

Figure 2.17 Brian's Initial 12 Week Campaign Plan

think through the entire campaign in a logical manner from start to finish. One thing Brian didn't appreciate was that his local paper needed the PR articles two weeks before going to print and had to change his plan to complete them in the middle of the month, not at the end. These dates are referred to in the trade as the "copy deadline" — the latest date you can get the copy (words of your article and any associated pictures) to the editor of the publication. They usually have strict deadlines and the sooner you get your piece to them, the greater the chance you have of being included in the next edition.

There are some things in Brian's plan which are "front-loaded", such as the adverts in the weekly newspaper. These are expensive and, initially, he only wants to try them for the first six weeks. If it works well and, when he stops if he notices his trade starts dropping off, he can always start another series of adverts. He hopes that after an initial "splash" he'll start generating word-of-mouth and his logic with running the radio ads for a little longer, is to keep the sound bites fresh in the listener's mind. With printed material, there is a longer "advertising lag" than with radio, because newspapers can hang around for several weeks before being thrown out and, hence, some ads may be seen after the initial "splash". The same cannot be said for radio. Keeping the radio ads going for longer also supports the other channels through a different sense (i.e. sound rather than sight).

With regard to personally distributing flyers, his plan is to visit local companies and introduce himself to the receptionist, or any senior member of staff who will give him the time of day. He anticipates each visit will take two to three minutes, just to have a quick chat and ask them to put up the flyers on their notice board. He hopes to visit ten companies in about an hour on Tuesday and Thursday afternoons, whilst Mary can spare a few hours to serve at the coffee shop. If he can visit twenty companies a week, he'll reach his target of 240 by the end of the twelve-week campaign.

Gemma has drummed into him the importance of posting regularly on Facebook. He anticipates Monday afternoon will be a good time to share his thoughts with his followers, because it will remind them to pay a visit to the shop after the weekend. Had he posted on a Friday, they may have forgotten about him by Monday morning — and his message will have fallen on deaf ears.

The key to a good micro-business marketing campaign is to keep it clear, simple and concise. It doesn't have to be complicated, but it does have to be well-designed, to make sure specific marketing communication objectives are met and measured. Taking the "top–down" approach forces you to think about the whole thing in a structured manner, from beginning to end. The problem a lot of entrepreneurs and micro-business owners encounter with lacklustre marketing performance can be attributed to doing things reactively and in an ad hoc manner. During my research, the least successful businesses fell into this trap, whilst the more successful had some kind of coordinated plan — even if it was very basic.

Summary of the Top-Down Approach

Thinking about your business, marketing and marketing communication objectives in this "top-down" manner, as shown in figure 2.18, really helps you focus on what's most important to achieve your business goals and turn opportunity into reality. Far too many entrepreneurs and business owners start by "stabbing" at the marketing communication objectives, without giving much thought to what they want to say, to whom, or how they might deliver their message.

Figure 2.18 The Top Down Approach

It then becomes a series of "hit and miss" reactive experiments, as you try to find out what works; it's a real gamble. If you go down this route, you're rolling the dice on your future business success, using your hard-earned cash — and marketing budget — to place your bets.

This "top-down" approach may take a little more effort up front, but it is a proven way to generate measurable results in a controlled environment by taking a strategic approach. Best of all, it really does limit your risk!

Extending the New Engagement Paradigm

The biggest challenge facing marketers these days, in such a complex and diverse environment, is delivering consistent messages across all platforms. It is critical, therefore, to plan and create all your content from a strategic perspective, rather than creating ad hoc content that does not serve a strategic purpose or contribute to a strategic business or marketing objective.

If we take another look at the New Engagement Paradigm and add the business and marketing and strategy outer layer, as shown in figure 2.19, it should now make more sense why all marketing messages should be defined from a strategic perspective. Reading from the inside out, we can say that "all content we create should be designed to engage our target audience and delivered by a number of traditional, digital and social media tools and channels, to meet specific business and marketing objectives".

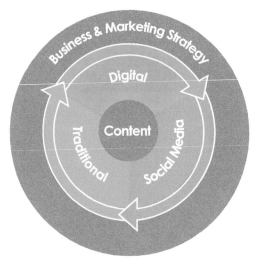

Figure 2.19 The New Engagement Paradigm (Enhanced)

The model helps us really clarify what we want to achieve with our limited resources and helps keep us focused. There is a lot of research around this topic and also a lot of evidence to suggest that many micro-business owners waste a lot of time, money and energy trying things out at the tactical level, without even considering their strategic implications. Many business owners don't have any formal marketing training and cannot afford to employ marketing professionals; they often resort to "just trying things out" to see if they work. All too often, they fall prey to the latest fad after being bombarded with emails or other marketing messages, proclaiming that "Product X" or "System Y" is the ultimate solution to all their problems. The problem is that "Product X" or "System Y" is all too often just another minor tool way down the list of things that really need to be considered to make the whole process work. It may be one element of, say, six needed to get from beginning to end.

A simple example may be a series of emails I received a while ago, extolling the virtues of some new hip WordPress templates. WordPress is software that allows you to build websites, templates give you a pre-conceived design with a lot of the standard programming already done for you. And Yes! You can build a cool-looking website with a number of great features really eloquently and easily (if you know what you're doing). However, it doesn't take into account the specific needs of your target audience, or help you write the website "copy" (the words) you will need to put on the website, that ultimately communicate with your target audience. That's another course or product, probably offered by someone else. A well-designed search engine friendly website is certainly going to help, but it's not the '"be all and end all". It's just one part of the jigsaw puzzle and, without all the other elements or components, it's going to have a very limited effect.

Making A Promise
The Art of Effective Communication

The Customer Journey

Marketing is all about communicating messages to your target audience. The previous section discussed marketing campaigns, whereby a series of related messages are directed at just one segment of your target audience and designed to influence your prospect, or customer, to move further along their customer journey, toward a desired outcome. But what exactly is a "customer journey" and why does it matter?

To help answer that question, we can use the Loyalty Ladder discussed in the Relationship Marketing chapter in Section 1 (see figure 1.11) to help us understand some of the steps our prospects and customers will go through. We can also use some of the communication models, such as AIDA and DRIP, to help us craft the appropriate type of messages, to encourage them to move along the desired path. In a perfect world, it would be very nice if just one message encouraged them to take one clear step and everything happened in a perfect linear fashion. For example, if we want to ultimately sell a product to a new customer, it would be nice to be able to send the first message, which raises awareness, the second message to generate interest, the third message to generate desire and the fourth message to encourage them to take the desired action — which is to buy the product we are offering. However, sending four messages in this way takes time and sending four messages is four times as expensive as sending a single message. Also, some prospects may not need all four messages to reach the point of decision.

The Loyalty Ladder is a very useful framework to help us think in terms of the type of relationship a prospect, or customer, has with our business and is reflected by the stage of their journey. It also gives a clear indication of the types of messages we need to send and helps us focus on the next step of their journey. However, as always, the devil is in detail and we need to look a little deeper to fully appreciate how this works, because it is highly dependent on both the context and the prospect's state of mind.

With regard to the context, there are a couple of factors we need to consider: the type of product, the cost or investment required, the purchase cycle and the purchase frequency. As far as the prospect or customer's state of mind is concerned, they will either be at the point of inspiration, the point of decision, the point of action, or the point of reflection. The points of inspiration and decision relate to the "zero moment of truth"; the point of decision relates to the "first moment of truth"; and the point of reflection relates to the "second moment of truth".

Regarding the factors that affect context, such as the purchase cycle, it rather depends on the type of product you're selling and what it will do for the consumer. With fast-moving consumer goods (FMCG), such as the items we purchase regularly from the supermarket, the frequency is high, the decision process is short (even subconscious) and the price (and, hence, risk) is usually extremely low. By comparison, purchasing a new TV typically has a longer buying cycle. It involves a greater amount of money (and, therefore, has higher risk) and is a more involved process. It is quite conceivable that you may spend several months doing your research and considering many options, before spending a large amount of money on the latest TV which will be sat in your lounge for the next five years.

The buying cycle and, hence, the amount of rational consideration and emotional involvement when purchasing a new car will be similar and you will require an awful lot more information before making your final decision. Where the buying cycle is long, there are many interim informational needs that need to be satisfied, to progress toward the final decision. Your prospect will need to receive a larger number of information-based marketing messages, to move them to the next stage in their customer journey. These are typically not impulse decisions and, as marketers, we need to craft appropriate messages, to help our prospects make a decision (hopefully in our favour) that ultimately moves them toward our desired conclusion.

By comparison, for items that are a lot lower risk and have a much shorter purchasing cycle, your marketing messages may be designed to move your prospect through several stages at once and as quickly as possible. For example, Brian sells a low-cost, low-risk consumable item (coffee). He will want to take members of his wider target audience from being suspects to prospects and to paying customers, as fast as possible and, preferably, in a single "hit".

When he places an advert in the local paper he wants to:

1. Raise awareness that his coffee shop exists
2. Create sufficient interest in his prospects' minds, which leads to
3. Generating a desire to try the product, and
4. The decision to at least visit his coffee shop (action).

He may also include some kind of incentive (promotion), such as *"Present this voucher and get your free cookie with your first delicious cup of coffee from Brian's coffee shop on the High Street"*.

One of the concepts we have to contend with as modern marketers is what's referred to as "media fragmentation". This is where members of our target audience consume our marketing information via different channels. It also means that to respond to their informational needs, we need to adopt a multichannel marketing strategy and deliver the same set of messages using a range of appropriate tools. Some of Brian's customers will see his messages in the local newspapers; others will hear his adverts on the radio; his posters and flyers he hopes will attract local office workers; and his website or Facebook page may be how his digitally orientated prospects hear about his coffee shop.

When he first starts his business, his first major task is to acquire customers and he needs to give a consistent message containing key elements of information, such as his location, what he sells and his opening hours. This whole combination of communication activity could be described as his "initial customer acquisition campaign" and should be designed to meet one or more of his marketing objectives e.g. "making 20,000 members of the local community aware his coffee shop has opened". This, in turn, contributes to achieving a specific business objective, e.g. "To be at 50% capacity for both the early morning and lunchtime peak periods". All his marketing activity should be designed to communicate what he has to offer (i.e. his "value proposition") to his target audience and encourage them to start, or maintain, a relationship with his business.

> **Value Proposition:** What an organisation has to offer to a prospect or customer, that will solve a particular problem or fulfil a want or need.

The art of successful marketing is all about communicating your value proposition to your target audience. You are, in effect, making a promise to your target audience and you want to encourage them to make a decision to start, maintain, or deepen a relationship with you and your business. Your marketing campaigns should be carefully planned and executed, but first you need to develop your messages and your content. This leads us to the "real guts" of this chapter: the process of creating and delivering a series of relevant messages that will engage your target audience and lead them through each step of their customer journey.

This is the third element of the 21st Century Marketing System and the tool we've developed to help you here is the "Value Proposition Communicator".

Value Proposition Communicator

The Value Proposition Communicator, shown in figure 2.20, is made up of two parts: communications and delivery. The first part focuses on making the promise to your target audience and the second part is all about keeping (or delivering on) that promise. These two must be perfectly aligned if you want to generate consistent, positive word-of-mouth.

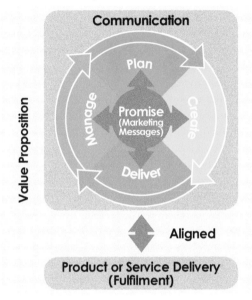

Figure 2.20 The Value Proposition Communicator

Think back to the earlier example of a plumber (or any other tradesmen) who said they will turn up at nine o'clock sharp and you're still wondering where they are at noon. All you remember is how they messed you around and you share your frustration with your friends, thereby creating negative word-of-mouth. If, however, they turned up at 8:55 a.m., you remember this and will probably sing their praises, thus generating positive word-of-mouth.

The "communications" bit is the marketer's job. The products or service delivery is the job of the "operations" side of your business which is responsible for delivering on your promises. In this section, we'll focus on the top part — the communication — because this is all about making promises you can keep and deliver. We'll talk about the operations side of the business in the next chapter.

Ideally, all businesses need to:

▲ Plan what they want to say

▲ Develop a message, or series of messages, that communicate this

▲ Deliver those messages in a way that is meaningful to the prospect/ customer

▲ Manage the whole messaging process to make sure they "hit the spot".

Campaign Plan

Marketing messages must be carefully planned, constructed and delivered to ensure they are not wasted; if no one hears (or "consumes") them, your efforts are all in vain.

Before you start, you must have a clear idea of your marketing objectives and how they support your business objectives. All the work you have done so far now starts to pay dividends, as you know who your specific target audience is (i.e. your personas), what their problems are and how you can solve them. You also fully understand how your value proposition can achieve this and you have a clear idea of what their journey will be through your business, to achieve your desired goals and satisfy their wants and needs.

As a marketer, your task is to create messages that communicate your value proposition to your target audience and engage them, to take whatever action is appropriate, to achieve your desired outcomes.

However, the reality is that very, very rarely do prospects walk through your front door and demand to buy "one of those, please". If they did, all our lives would be so much easier and we'd all be very rich!

Google did some research and estimated that in 2006, on average, it took six exposures to a message before awareness resulted in some kind of action. By 2011, that number had increased to eleven interactions and, by 2014, this number had risen to seventeen. This means your prospects need to be exposed to your message seventeen times before they "get it" and actually do something that will advance their customer journey with your business. That's a lot of messages, which take a lot of time, a lot of effort and, of course, a lot of money. There's no way of knowing exactly how many times any particular customer was exposed to your message before they took action. For some customers, it may be five and for others it may be as many as twenty or even thirty; therefore, these numbers represent a best estimate of the average number of messages it takes to initiate action along the customer journey.

Additionally, I'd suggest that these quoted numbers are different in different industries. For example, for a restaurant it may be nine or ten, but for the latest high-tech, high-spec TV stuffed full of the latest technology, it may be thirty or more.

What you can do is notice the trend; it would be reasonable to assume that this trend is reflective of most, if not all, of your buyers' behaviour. It makes perfect sense that in a modern, digitally driven society, drowning in an ocean of information, it takes more effort to get our message heard over and above our competitors. You should, therefore, take Google's figures as a guide and define your task as a marketer to "create a series of (seventeen?) consistent, informative, engaging and relevant messages that communicate your value proposition to your target audience, to take whatever action is appropriate to achieve your desired outcome".

That changes things a bit, doesn't it?

Given that we don't actually know (at least when we start out) precisely how many messages we need to reach our goal, we have to make a "best guess" for our given situation and refine it over time. It's certainly more than one and, most likely, to be in double figures for most businesses. For the sake of this discussion, let's assume Google are right and it's seventeen.

Pretty much anyone can place a single advert in one paper, but as explained by Google's figures above, that's unlikely to gain much new business. We need to build a series of messages (a campaign) to "drive home" our offering and communicate our value proposition to our target audience. Not every prospect in our target audience will be ready to hear what we have to say at the start of our campaign, so running a campaign just once is going to produce limited results, i.e. it will be limited to those who are ready right now. To maximise any chance of success, we need to run a campaign over several weeks or months and, when it is finished, we'll run it again and again and again. This is because we need to capture as many members of our target audience as possible when they are ready to hear the message, not when we want to deliver it.

Each message should be designed to move members of your target audience to the next stage of the customer journey. By defining clear objectives of what "success" looks like, you can focus on creating the appropriate messages to meet your SMART objectives.

Start by planning your campaign; you can make this as simple or as complex as you like, but I recommend keeping it as simple as possible, at least at the beginning. There are only two things you really want to think about once you have defined your objectives: your budget and your timeline.

As far as your budget is concerned, how much do you want to spend overall? How much are you prepared to invest at each stage of your campaign? You also need to have all your campaign material prepared before you press the "go" button. This will take time and probably some money, if you have to "buy in" help from outside.

Do not — I repeat, do not — be tempted to start Step One until you have all the follow-up marketing material ready (or you are at least 100% convinced you have the capability to create it super-fast) because you do not know how fast your prospects want to progress along their customer journey. If they have to wait, you will lose them and your investment will be wasted. Other prospects may take considerably longer, but the point remains and the lesson is: be prepared. You don't want to lose a prospect because you're not ready to escort them to the next stage of their journey. Never forget, they are in charge of the pace, not you!

Now we've got a plan and know what we're doing, let's take a closer look at the nuts and bolts of message development.

Developing and Managing Messages: The TAPAS Framework

The **TAPAS** framework is a useful model for message development. It stands for:

TA—Target Audience
P—Purpose
A—Action
S—Sequence

Target audience: Who are you talking to?

We discussed our target audience and the reasons for breaking it down into small segments earlier. We want to talk to a single sub-segment of our target audience and we develop personas to help us laser in on just them. Remember that a persona is a detailed description of a single member of your segment of interest. Brian created five personas and his "early morning coffee drinkers, who want a coffee on the way to work" segment, is represented by Nigel and Janice.

Nigel and Janice: Early Morning Coffee Drinkers

- ▲ Mid-thirties
- ▲ Local professional office workers
- ▲ Key attributes: Time poor/very busy lives
- ▲ Requirement: Just coffee
- ▲ Estimated spend per visit: £3
- ▲ Consumption: In house and takeout
- ▲ Appreciates: Quality and speed of service
- ▲ Primary motivation: Energy boost/self-time
- ▲ Time: Visits between 7:30 a.m. and 9:00 a.m.

Purpose: Why are you talking to them?

Every message should have a purpose, and one of the models we use to focus on purpose is **AIDA** — **A**wareness | **I**nterest | **D**esire | **A**ction. We also discussed the **DRIP** model — **D**ifferentiate | **R**emind | **I**nform | **P**ersuade.

Both these models have been around for many years and are rooted in the Old Broadcast Paradigm. Whilst they are still very useful today, they do not cover everything we need in the modern marketing landscape because, as we've seen, not all marketing is about selling. Therefore, we need to expand this section and go a little **DEEPER** to include the key elements of engagement.

DEEPER stands for **D**ecision | **E**ducate | **E**ntertain | **P**osition | **E**xpectation | **R**elationship. These six elements probably cover 95% of everything you're likely to do when it comes to creating content and developing messages.

Let's take each one in turn and explain them in a little more detail, along with when you might use them and how they differ from AIDA and DRIP.

Decision

AIDA and DRIP come from the sales orientation which limits their scope. There will be times when you want to engage your target audience, but not sell to them or persuade them to do something. Remember, we want to build relationships, so sometimes all we need at a certain stage is permission to develop a relationship.

For example, when I did my research, I needed to contact members of my target audience (entrepreneurs and micro-business owners) to ask if they would agree to be interviewed. University research is strictly controlled and governed by an "ethics board" — meaning I had to comply with ethical considerations while doing my research, which also meant I was not allowed to sell anything, or persuade or cajole in any way. It had to be a decision the interviewee took after merely being presented with the facts. All I wanted from my letter of introduction was a simple "yes" or "no" answer.

There are many occasions when a similar situation may arise when building relationships. Not all relationships last a lifetime and, certainly in the early stages, it's quite appropriate for both parties to decide if they want to proceed and how the relationship should develop. It is quite possible all you want your message or content to do is ask for a decision.

Educate

There are many occasions when you may need to educate your target audience about some aspect of your product or service. It could be argued that this is the same as the "Informed" step of DRIP, but I think it runs a little deeper than that. "Informing" is telling, whereas "Educating" is learning, the latter potentially having more intrinsic value and requiring a different type of content/message.

Free reports or white papers are common examples that can be downloaded from websites, but training may also include videos on YouTube or online quizzes to test knowledge and recommend solutions. Educating your audience so they understand what your product or service can do for them, or showing them how to use it, are excellent ways to build relationships whilst positioning you as an expert in your field.

Entertain

You may choose to create messages or content to build your brand and the goodwill toward you. Again, this element is not covered in the AIDA or DRIP models, but can be a very effective way to build brand equity. A good example that springs to mind is the Cadbury's gorilla playing the drums; if you haven't seen it, you can check it out by typing 'Cadbury gorilla playing drums' into your favourite search engine and follow the link. Entertainment content that definitely does not sell or cajole — i.e. they are created for pure enjoyment and amusement — are fantastic ways to increase engagement and "pay the rent" on the part of your target audience's brain that associates your solution with their problem. Of course, this is not restricted to videos; the written word and audio can be just as effective. But just one word of warning: use humour with care, because what you find funny, others may not — they may even find it offensive, which can only damage your brand.

Position

Some content may be designed to position your business or a product, for example, as a reassuringly expensive brand, or perhaps as a cut-price discount offering, at the other end of the scale. Positioning-focused content is another way to help build your brand and communicate your core values. For example, Avis Car Rental position themselves as the "number two" in the car rental market, claiming that makes them "try even harder" to delight their customers. It also gives them an advantage because no one else can claim to be "number two".

Expectation

Your marketing messages are intended to make a promise to your target audience and another good way to use content is to manage expectations. Budget airlines do this well; when you book with Ryanair or easyJet, you are under no illusion that there is one set of rules and no room for manoeuvre or negotiation. Managing expectations as relationships develop is an essential part of communicating your value proposition, because it creates a baseline level of service or expectation, against which your prospects and customers can judge you. This is very important to generating word-of-mouth because if your customers don't know what to expect from your business, how are you going to manage the promises you make? I said earlier, a good strategy is to under-promise and slightly over-deliver, but without a baseline expectation, how will you stop the exceptional from becoming the norm? The last thing you want to do is to set the expectation that you consistently over-deliver by 75%!

Relationship

An adaptation of a quote I mentioned earlier is "Every relationship exists for a reason, a season, or a lifetime". We all need to maximise our customers' lifetime value (LTV), but if your product or service is a "one-hit wonder" then your content should reflect that. An example might be the hotel you will only go to once in your lifetime. As described earlier, even though your customers may only go there once, you want them to talk about your hotel for as long as possible. The "maintenance of your old clients" campaign will be a very different to your "customer acquisition" campaign.

These three models (AIDA, DRIP, and DEEPER) should cover pretty much any content you are likely to need to create. When you create new content, you must have its purpose firmly in your mind and make sure you don't stray from it. One final tip: every piece of content should have one — and only one — primary purpose, but may have a few secondary purposes embedded within the message. Don't make your messages too complex, otherwise you will create confusion in the eyes of your target audience and your carefully crafted content will be wasted.

> **Key point:** When selling, it is imperative to keep your message clear and simple to avoid confusion — because the confused do not buy!

Action:
What action do you want them to take?

After consuming your message or content you will probably want your target audience to do something. As part of an integrated campaign, you may well want your audience to do several things, perhaps in a particular order to move them through their customer journey. Make sure you are clear on what you want to achieve in terms of the actions you want them to take, link them back to your objectives, and set KPIs so you can measure your success (or lack of it).

Sequence:
What happens next?

Your campaigns may contain several messages and you may have several pieces of content. Whilst you may be able to control the initial release of your content, you have no control over the sequence in which it is consumed. When you develop a series of messages or content, it's a good idea to inform your target audience of the existence of other pieces of content and the order in which they should be consumed. For example, it is quite acceptable if you to say something like, "This is the second in a series of four on the subject of X — if you haven't read part one yet, you can do so by clicking here". It is up to you to tell your target audience that your content is part of a sequence and that you have other content they might find useful. At the end of an article or web page which educates them around a particular topic, you could include a link to a YouTube training video or White Paper they can download to "round it off".

If you have your customer journey clearly mapped out, it's pretty easy to attach the relevant content you'd like them to consume at each stage. It then becomes easy to include the links to other relevant content to complete the picture.

How to Craft Your Message:
An Introduction to Copywriting

Developing you message is not a five-minute job, in fact, crafting marketing messages takes a lot of time. Crafting the right words to effectively convey your message is the skill known as "copywriting" and is the responsibility of a "copywriter". Whilst this skill has its origins in the advertising industry, many of the techniques used to write a compelling sales letter also apply to many other forms of communication. If you can master the craft of writing a great sales letter, you're well on the way to being able to craft any message for any purpose.

In my opinion, copywriting is another misunderstood and much underrated marketing skill and one that takes time and practice to develop. A simple definition of copywriting is "the art and science of crafting words that engage, educate and inspire people to make decisions". Obviously one decision you want to encourage is the decision to buy your product or service, but as we saw with the AIDA, DRIP and DEEPER models discussed above, there is a lot more to it these days than just pitching to make a sale!

There will inevitably come a point in time when you need to write a powerful message that inspires your target audience to make a decision, be it on a website landing page or in a letter. After all, businesses need cash to survive. Many sales-letter writing techniques that have been around for many years are still very appropriate today and, with a little creative adaption, can be used in pretty much any context.

There are nine components to a typical sales letter and a model we've developed to teach copywriting (and actually use ourselves) is the "Message Development Matrix" shown in figure 2.21.

Figure 2.21 The Message Development Matrix

This is a really useful model to help you apply the "rules" of copywriting to any message you need to create, as each component has a specific purpose. Once you know each of these elements and how you can apply them, you can mix and match — like swapping the bits in the jigsaw puzzle to create different pictures. I learnt these rules and techniques over twenty-five years ago and the core concepts still apply today, so it's worth your while investing the time to learn and apply them sooner rather than later. If you know how and when to use each element of the Message Development Matrix, you'll have a great framework to create powerful messages online, offline and in social media.

An important point to raise at the start is, regardless of the purpose of your message, the flow of any individual piece of content follows pretty much the same pattern.

So, what do each of the letters stand for?

The Headline

We see headlines on the newsstands every day. Their purpose is to try and entice us to buy the paper. In sales "copy" terms, the headline has a similar single purpose: to try to grab our attention and get the target audience to start reading the message. When it comes to headlines and sales copy, there are three basic "rules".

1. The first is its length. The experts will tell you a headline should be seventeen words or less and there's a good reason for this. Tests have shown headlines with more than seventeen words are less successful (on average) than those with seventeen words or less. Pretty conclusive, so it's worth obeying what the data tells us!

2. It should answer the reader's question, 'What's in it for me?' It should therefore focus on the reader, not the writer. I cringe when I see headlines that say things like, "We are company X and we are experts in solving problem Y..." This can so easily be rewritten to focus on the reader — for example, "If you want to solve (problem Y), look no further! The answer could already be in your hands..."

3. Great headlines should be positive and solution-focused and grab the reader's attention—by interrupting them—and then draw them into the text. There are many ways to do this. Here are just two quick examples:

   ▲ "How to solve (problem X) in three easy steps..."
   ▲ "Revealed! The secrets to solving (problem X)!"

People love to find out "how to" solve their problems, or being privy to little-known secrets. In both cases, these headlines work because the reader feels empowered or special — after all, they have some new information to share and discuss with their friends!

The Sub-Headline

The sub-headline can be a little longer and is used to add clarity or create intrigue around what was claimed in the headline. Its purpose is to draw the reader in if they are interested and filter out those who are not. Many people who write copy think its focus should be on getting and keeping every reader's attention; however, I disagree. Why would you want someone who is not really interested responding, being added to your database and then never buying anything? They just contaminate your list. Also, why would you want to encourage anyone who is not really part of your target audience to talk about your business? After all, they are more likely to say bad things about you and spread negative word-of-mouth. The sub-headline is the tool for filtering your readers. Using one of the example headlines above, here's an example of how a sub-headline might look:

Headline: "Revealed! The secrets of solving (problem X)!"

Sub-headline: "After years of research, Dr XYZ reveals the secrets to solving (problem X) and explains what it means for you in this fascinating new book..."

If your prospect is interested in the headline, they will almost certainly read the sub-headline. The majority of people who read on will be relatively good prospects. If they are not that bothered about "what it means for them" they're probably not going to invest time and energy to actually read the book. The quicker they realise this and filter themselves out by not responding, the better.

The sub-headline should be a single sentence or two, possibly a little longer, but the key is to keep it concise and punchy. You need to say what you want to say in as few words as possible and make a powerful statement.

Salutation

How you initially address someone and how you continue to address them has a significant impact on the quality of the bond and, hence, relationship, that subsequently develops. When I was at school, the sports teacher called us all by our surnames, yet he wanted to be addressed as "Sir". That was clearly an authoritarian relationship, with the authority demanding respect, yet demonstrating (in my opinion) lack of respect to his charges by referring to us by our surnames. To him, we may as well have been numbers, not people. By comparison, the Maths and English teachers addressed us by our first names, yet we still addressed them as "Miss" or "Sir" or "Miss/Mrs X" or "Mr Y". This still engenders respect, but on a different level and formed a different type of relationship. I'm sure you can think of instances from your past where someone got your name right and it made you feel good, or where they couldn't remember it, or got it wrong and it made you at least a little bit annoyed.

So how are you going to address your target audience? That depends on the stage of the relationship and how well you know them. In an ideal world, we want to be on first-name terms with them because this implies closeness or intimacy. Getting "close" to a large number of prospects or a target audience relies on them telling you how they prefer to be addressed and you remembering to use it in every piece of communication.

A daunting task for even memory masters but, fortunately, there are customer relationship management (CRM), content management and marketing automation systems that can help you capture this data and personalise your messages. Having spent a lot of time working with these types of systems, it never ceases to amaze me when I get a wrongly addressed email using anything but my preferred first name. I'm pretty diligent when completing the request forms because I know the value of "clean" data, so when I get emails that start *"Dear (email address)"* or *"Hey (surname), how are you doing today?"* my immediate response is to think, *"What are you trying to sell me?"* swiftly followed by clicking "delete".

Here's how my thought process works: *"If you can't even get my name right, you obviously don't respect me. If you don't demonstrate respect, you are out to fulfil your needs, not mine. I don't want a relationship with you. Goodbye. < Delete >!"* I don't care if you're selling half-kilo gold bars for a penny; I'm not even going to read your message because you didn't get past my "respect" filter.

Of course, there will be times, especially during the acquisition phase and before you capture your prospect's details, when you won't be able to personalise your message. Don't be tempted to try and "harvest" their first name using some "clever" algorithm from their email address, because chances are you'll get it wrong and that's just as bad, if not worse, than using the whole email address in the salutation!

So what do you do? Your objective is to make a connection and to do that you need some kind of common ground. For example, if your target audience are BMW owners, that may be the only thing you have in common, so a salutation like "Dear fellow BMW owner" may create that initial connection. Another simple example could be just saying the things you say when you meet a stranger in person — like "Hello" or "Hi there". However, when a new contact tells you their name, make sure you use it from that point on — and make sure you get it right.

Identifying the Problem

Having got past the first filtering mechanisms with the headline, sub-headline and salutation, you now want to deepen the relationship by communicating that you really understand their situation and the problems they face. A good way to create this connection is to describe and discuss their problem in their terms. There are many ways to do this. Two techniques I use are to either paint a picture (with words) describing the problem, or tell a story to illustrate it.

> **Key point:** People love stories because stories connect people to people.

There's a huge amount of material on how to tell stories and this is another subject that could easily fill a whole book. In the process of creating a powerful sales message, the purpose of your story is to take them back to a point where they feel the pain of the problem you can help them solve.

One technique is to describe the problem, tell how it affected you and then ask them if they've felt the same. Imagine you're starting your new marketing consultancy business, an example might look something like this:

"I've just been on the phone to John, a friend of mine, who is having a really hard time. He's just started his new business, which has taken a huge chunk of his savings, but so far he can't seem to get many customers. He's taken out lots of expensive ads in the local newspaper, paid someone thousands to build a website and even started using Facebook. Whatever he tries, it just doesn't seem to work. I really feel sorry for him because he deserves to succeed, he works so hard. I remember when I was first started my business, I suffered the same pain and challenges and I'm sure when you started your business, you did, too..."

Your story could be as long or short as it needs to be, as long as it's not boring or irrelevant. Use emotional language to paint a picture and really connect with your reader. The reaction you want, if you could see them, is to have them nodding in agreement with what you're saying.

But don't "overcook it"! Once you've made that connection, you can move on to discussing the solution.

The Solution

If you started by telling a story about the problem, you can (and should) continue with that technique to describe the solution.

Key point: You are not selling the solution at this point, just describing what the solution looks like. To continue the story above, we might say something like:

"Learning how to market your business can be a steep learning curve, particularly if you've never done it before! You quickly learn that marketing in the Internet age is extremely complicated and confusing because there's just so much you can do. Fortunately, I have a little marketing knowledge and a few friends who worked in marketing who were able to help me. What they showed me was that I didn't need to do everything — in fact, that was half the problem. Like John, I was trying to do far too much and getting absolutely nowhere — and digging a huge hole in my bank balance with a pickaxe! The key lesson I learnt was it's far better to do a few things well rather than a lot of things badly."

Can you see how the story is beginning to develop?

So far, in the space of a few sentences, we've "set the scene" and described the problem, i.e. not knowing what to do or how to do it, as well as trying to do too much. We also described what the solution looks like: getting some expert help to show you how to do just a few things well.

The next step in our stories is to "marry", or "link", the solution to the problem and we do that by talking about...

The Benefits of the Solution

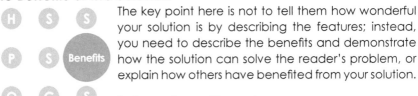

The key point here is not to tell them how wonderful your solution is by describing the features; instead, you need to describe the benefits and demonstrate how the solution can solve the reader's problem, or explain how others have benefited from your solution.

So to continue with our story:

> "When I started to get this right, I was spending far less time and money on marketing than I ever thought possible. I also started getting referrals — and quite quickly — which was a real surprise. But you know what? ~~The real thing my family and friends noticed was that I~~ was doing less and getting better results. Which meant I had more time for them. The icing on the cake was when they asked me about how my new business was going because I had so many positive stories to tell them that they actually wanted to talk about my business more often. Man! I must have been really negative and grumpy, when all I previously talked about was what my problems were and how bad I felt all the time! Luckily, all that's changed now..."

So far, you've grabbed your target audience's attention, connected with them, shown them you understand their problems and feel their pain. You've described the solution and how the world will look with that solution in place. They should now be excited, "champing at the bit" and ready for...

The Offer

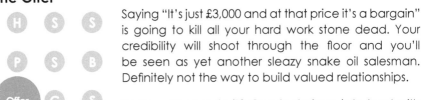

Saying "It's just £3,000 and at that price it's a bargain" is going to kill all your hard work stone dead. Your credibility will shoot through the floor and you'll be seen as yet another sleazy snake oil salesman. Definitely not the way to build valued relationships.

So how do you do it? One technique is to lead with and focus on the value, instead of the price. Once you present the price, it opens up possibilities for several techniques to close the deal and secure the sale. It's a technique I've used quite a lot because it can be quite conversational.

Let's continue with our example:

> "How would having more time to spend with your friends and family change your life — especially if you have plenty of money to enjoy it? What would you be prepared to pay to get as much new business as you wanted, whenever you want it, so you never have to worry about money ever again? £5K? £10k? £20K? With my help, you can get these benefits and more for far less than it cost me — and much quicker. I know the financial pressures when you're starting out and I'd like to offer to help you succeed. For the next month only, we are offering the full consultancy package for just £2,997, which includes < full details of the offer > To further assist, you can either pay up front and get a 10% discount or spread the cost over three equal payments of just £999."

By the way, that last bit is an example of an "either/or close". Effectively I said, do you want the red one with this benefit (less 10%) or the blue one with this different benefit (spread the cost)?

The whole story is developing, so we now need to ask for the order or get them to make a decision with the...

The Call-to-Action

The call-to-action is designed to close the deal or get a decision. If that decision is not to buy at this point in time, then you can nurture the relationship, to keep your brand/offer active in their mind (something in marketing terms we call "front of mind").

By "paying the rent" on the part of their brain that associates your solution with their problem, it just might pay off one day, when they are ready to buy and you'll be there waiting to take their order.

On the other hand, if they click the "Buy Now" button you can close the deal and bank the cash. However, the reality is that you'll more than likely to have to work hard to secure the deal and that's the purpose of the call-to-action. At this stage, you usually need to repeat your offer, espouse the benefits, summarise everything you've done before and offer an incentive for a quick decision in your favour.

You need to do this sensitively and personally. I hate long, drawn-out, repetitive call-to-actions that go on and on about the wonders of product X and its £6 million worth of "free bonuses" as long as I decide to buy in the next three nanoseconds. Personally, I think people are more intelligent and should be treated with a lot more respect. In our example, I might say something like:

> "I'd really like you to join the programme because I know you'll get < benefits one, two, three and four >. If cash flow is an issue right now, I hope the easy payment plan will help, so please fill in the order form and tick the "easy payment plan" box. If you prefer to get started right away and get measurable results in the next ten days, please tick the "pay now in full" box by < end of offer date > and receive your 10% discount. Submit your application form today, as places are limited..."

The call-to-action should leave your prospects in no doubt as to precisely what's expected of them and the specific steps they need to take to solve the problem you can clearly help them with.

Phew! So you finished, right? Not quite! There's just one more thing.

The Summary

Why would you want to summarise your offer when you've just spelt it all out in the call-to-action? A good question and, when it was explained to me, it was one of those "Aha!" moments. What if your prospect doesn't read all of your carefully crafted message/letter in the exact sequence you spent ages setting it out? The reality is your message is most likely going to be scanned by your readers quickly before they decide if they're actually going to read the whole thing. The summary is like an elevator pitch — it promotes your biggest benefits in thirty seconds or less, which helps your target audience decide whether or not they are going to get out of the lift (or elevator) with you to continue the conversation.

At the end of most good sales letters you will see a P.S., a P.P.S. and possibly a P.P.P.S. which summarises the key benefits of your offer in a paragraph or two (three at most).

My advice is to use the headline to answer the question, "What's in it for me?" then state the top few benefits in the P.S. peppered with elements of the offer and the call-to-action.

Using and Breaking the Rules

Now that you know the nine "golden rules", or elements, of a powerful message and why you should follow them, it's time to explore how they can be adapted to any given situation.

If everyone did everything exactly in sequence, it would be so much easier. Figure 2.22 shows how it would look if every message was consumed in the correct order according to the sequence of the nine elements.

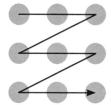

Figure 2.22 The Perfect Message Consumption Sequence

The problem is, your prospects will often try to join the dots in a different order and take a shortcut, so sometimes we need to think outside the box and anticipate what our target audience may do. For example, when I get one of these long sales letters or other long messages, either in the post, or in my inbox, my typical scanning sequence is: Headline/Sub-Headline/Salutation/Summary (P.S.)/Offer/Call-To-Action, as shown in figure 2.23.

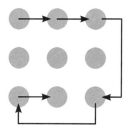

Figure 2.23 The Scanning Message Consumption Sequence

Like many people, I'm overloaded with information and time poor, so I need to filter marketing messages quickly and decide whether or not to discard them or invest the time to read them. If I decide it's relevant to me after my initial scan, I'll then go back to the beginning and read the whole letter in sequence, starting with the headline and finishing with P.S.

This is my information filtering system and most people will do something similar. What's yours?

Now you know what these nine elements are and how to define them, it's worth looking at how we can mix and match. We discussed all nine elements in sequence, but what if we don't want to do this, but still want to get our points across powerfully and quickly?

For example, if a sales message is 1,500 words and you want to create a shorter version with just 150 words, such as an email, postcard, or flyer, you would take some of the elements and summarise them, as shown in figure 2.24.

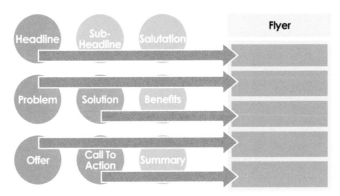

Figure 2.24 Creating A Brief Summary Message

You may need to cut them down a bit to make it fit the available space, but the main benefit is that you are, at least, delivering a consistent message across all forms of communication.

The same techniques can be used in PR articles, market research invitations and pretty much any form of written communication, using precisely these techniques. One client I worked with generated over £15,000 in revenue in just seven months (part time) from a single PR article that appeared in two local business magazines — for free! Yes, not a penny for a total of four colour pages that could have cost £1,500 each (£6,000 total). These techniques are powerful — very powerful — so please don't underestimate them! They are even more powerful if you supplement the text with pictures, to really get your point across both visually and emotionally.

You can also use some of these techniques in your own personal communication, such as emails. Your headline would be your subject line, to give your email a greater chance of being opened and your initial "lead-in" can be a quick story to engage the reader.

Creating remarkable content is a fantastic skill to master. Financially, it also makes sense, as the more you engage your customers, the deeper the relationship, the longer they last, the more you earn, the more profit you make — and of course, the more they talk about you, which gives you referrals and that elusive holy grail of marketing: word-of-mouth.

The stronger your relationships with your target audience and your customers, the harder it is for your competitors to steal them away from you. Words are at the heart of every message, so it's worth learning how to craft them for maximum impact!

Delivering Your Messages

There's not a lot of point in going to the trouble and expense of creating "remarkable" content if no one reads (or consumes) it. That's your next big challenge – because encouraging consumption of your material will depend on the format it's in.

Some content can be easily delivered, such as short text-based emails. However, other content can be so big in terms of the file size, such as videos, webinars, or highly graphical in-house newsletters containing many high-resolution pictures, that you simply cannot email it. There is a limit as to what you can physically "push" out via email, so you have to use other channels to store your larger content and then tell your target audience where they can "pull" it from i.e. "Click here to watch a YouTube video on..." or "Click here to download your free report".

This can actually cause a problem because, in order to make the "click here to take me somewhere else" bit work, you need to be connected to the Internet. Despite popular belief — especially by the digital natives — not everyone is connected to a high-speed broadband link 24/7! You should bear this in mind when you create your content and think how and when it will be consumed. For example, if you want your customers who commute to work by train to consume your content in the morning whilst travelling, maybe you should have two versions of the same report: one with the fancy layout and wonderful graphics as well as a text-only version, which is one-hundredth of the size and can be easily and quickly downloaded onto a mobile device in twenty seconds, whilst they are standing on the platform waiting for the train.

In the offline world, message and information delivery is very different: business cards will usually be delivered in person at networking events; brochures and leaflets may still be sent by mail, or collected from exhibition stands or shops. TV and radio ads will be consumed by the watching or listening public according to a schedule negotiated with the broadcasters. Outdoor advertising, such as billboards and bus ads, will be consumed by people on the move. PR articles and print ads will usually be consumed in "reading mode".

In the online world, things are very different. To start with, we need to raise awareness and get attention, so online advertising, search engine marketing, or online PR will be the main mechanisms to deliver your message. Once you have made contact and established a connection with your target audience, you can add emails to the list, which affords a more personalised approach. Email is a good mechanism to build your relationship, by keeping in regular contact and pointing your target audience in the direction of other content.

Your website will also be another major delivery mechanism. It will either immediately deliver content via web pages or give the facility to "pull" other content down, such as special reports and white papers, in addition to directing your visitors to content on other servers, such as YouTube, Facebook, LinkedIn, a webinar platform, or a blog post.

When you bring social media into the delivery mix, you really start to "muddy the waters". A blog post could point to a YouTube video or article on your website — as could a Facebook post, LinkedIn article, or Tweet. The links to your content can be shared by your followers, so they may also become the delivery mechanisms for your content. The combinations seem endless, but the key point is this: if you cannot — or choose not to — deliver your content directly, then you must tell as many of your target audience where they can "pull" it from and make your content easy to find and consume, to leverage all the channels available to you.

Brian thinks this all sounds great, but as a technically limited start-up micro-business owner, he's just going to stick with his website and Facebook page. The website will not be updated unless he gets new products. He knows this is not the best way of doing things, but to start with, that's all he wants to do. Gemma has persuaded him to invest properly in his website, so he's had it done professionally and put a short video on the home page that he hosts on YouTube. It's just a ninety-second video where he gives the viewer a short tour of his coffee shop and explains why he gave up his job as a car mechanic to start his own business. It gives him the chance to introduce himself to his target audience and he closes by asking them to pay a visit and explaining where he's located. The site has a downloadable PDF menu, a map and all the usual contact details. A simple brochure-style website is all it is and there is limited content, but it's still sharp, clean, informative and really gives a good impression of his brand.

Brian's Facebook page replicates some of the material on his website and he also intends to post a short story on Monday afternoons, which gives him the opportunity to create a little fresh content every week. In this example, he's using his Facebook page to engage with his target audience. His website contains more static information and is used to build his profile.

Marketing Automation

For the slightly more advanced, email is a critical tool for regularly and personally communicating with your target audience.

Customers these days expect information to be delivered "instantly" and if they have to press the refresh button twice and wait thirty seconds, they become impatient. If you have any more than a handful of customers to manage, you need a system to help you manage customer activity, respond to information requests, promote your products and services and send the next suitable message in sequence, at exactly the right time to keep your customers engaged. Remember, part of effective communication is getting the right message in front of the right target audience, at the right time and if they ask for it now, then "now" (i.e. immediately) is the right time.

Fortunately, there are some wonderful tools on the market that can help you and these fall into the "marketing automation" arena. You can set them up to send out a series of emails (even a complete campaign) in a predefined sequence and at specified intervals — for example, every three days. If your customer or prospect takes a specific action, such as responding to an invitation in a call-to-action, the more advanced systems can be configured to terminate the first sequence and start a new sequence with other highly relevant content, tailored to the next stage of their customer's journey. It is all rather clever, very effective if used correctly and a brilliant way to build and manage personalised relationships with a huge number of people in your target audience, in an extremely time-efficient manner.

> **Key point:** *Marketing automation systems will help you efficiently manage the delivery of your marketing messages and streamline the whole process, but they will not create your marketing messages for you!*

However, a word of warning: these systems will not do all your marketing for you. They simply automate the process and delivery of messages you have already defined. A computer cannot think for you (yet), but it can make the repetitive tasks of running a business a hell of a lot easier. This means that you must do all your thinking first and have defined your processes, customer journey and workflows, before you try to automate them. Once it's set up and running sweetly, all you have to do is monitor, measure and manage the process and leave it running on autopilot. Cool!

It'll be a long time before Brian starts sending out emails and getting this sophisticated. He currently estimates it might be worth looking at email marketing about eighteen months down the line and, if he does decide to give it a go, he's got six months for it to "settle in" before he thinks about opening his second coffee shop. If he can collect email addresses from his customers, he's then got the option of another communication channel and can start sending more personal communication to a large number of his customers on a regular basis.

Completing the New Engagement Paradigm

To complete the New Engagement Paradigm, we need to add the final outer layer: the Established Marketing Theory and Principles, as shown in figure 2.25.

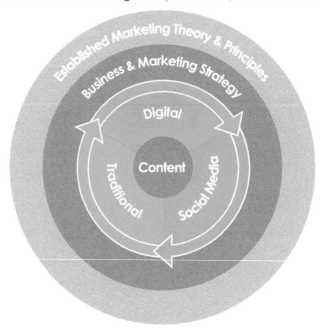

Figure 2.25 The Complete New Engagement Paradigm

This completes the picture and when you apply all elements of the New Engagement Paradigm, you have a very powerful formula for truly harnessing the full power of the modern marketing landscape, not to mention a rock-solid foundation on which to build and adapt your own 21st Century Marketing Blueprint. This can be tailored to suit your changing business needs and, once you've mastered the fundamentals, you'll quickly and easily be able to enhance your marketing activities, to take advantage of any opportunity that knocks on your door.

To conclude, let's examine the full version of the New Engagement Paradigm in a little more detail.

Reading from the outside in, we can say that *"all marketing messages should be based on established marketing theory and principles; they should be designed from a strategic perspective and delivered by the most appropriate tool and should contain engaging content the target audience find 'remarkable'"*. Applying just a small amount of proven theory and principles to your marketing activities, using the New Engagement Paradigm, can produce very impressive and satisfying results.

Conversely, reading from the inside out, we can say that *"all content we create should be designed to engage our target audience and be delivered by a number of traditional, digital and social media tools and channels, to meet specific business marketing objectives based on established marketing theory and principles"*.

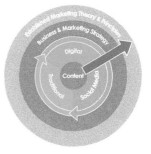

The New Engagement Paradigm helps us really clarify what we want to achieve with our limited resources and optimise the return on our marketing investment.

Resources are, indeed, limited and skills are in very short supply. The digital marketing skills gap is so large, partly fuelled by technology which is advancing at breakneck speed; the digital marketing skills gap will be haunting businesses for a very long time. Micro-businesses with tiny budgets are at the bottom of the food chain and can rarely attract new talent with highly refined modern marketing skills.

As an entrepreneur and micro-business owner, in terms of marketing — and especially digital marketing — you're pretty much on your own. It is imperative, therefore, that you have a good understanding of at least the basics of marketing theory and principles and how to use them in your business. The Seven Point Plan helps you achieve this, by ensuring you don't invest your valuable time and hard-earned cash into marketing activities that are doomed to failure from the start.

The Operations — Delivering On Your Promise

You might think it's a little strange to talk about the operational side of the business in a marketing book, but the operations are fundamental to the success of any business and how it's perceived by its customers. As marketers, we are primarily concerned with creating that all-important word-of-mouth and we expend an awful lot of time and energy aligning the company's communication activities to support its business objectives, as we've seen in the preceding sections. In the previous chapter, we looked at how we deliver our value proposition to our target audience. Communication is fundamentally about making a promise. Operations, on the other hand, is about delivering on that promise.

Here's a fundamental point many entrepreneurs and micro-business owners often don't fully appreciate and if there's just one thing you take from this book, let it be this: word-of-mouth is generated at the intersection of perception (i.e. the promise/communication) and experience (i.e. the delivery of that promise/operations), as shown in figure 2.26.

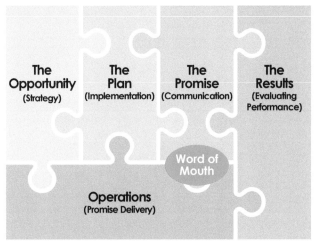

Figure 2.26 Generating Word-of-Mouth

For example, if you claim you're the best in your industry, state that you're reliable and offer good value, then you have made a promise to your target audience and, therefore, you have set a level of expectation when they deal with your business. If you do not deliver on your promise, you will generate negative word-of-mouth. On the other hand, if you meet or exceed your customers' expectations, you will generate positive word-of-mouth. It's as simple as that!

If we take a closer look at operations, it's all about the efficient management, allocation, utilisation and maintenance of resources required to deliver the product or service to the customer or end consumer. The role of the "Operations Manager" is to manage all the organisation's resources effectively and efficiently, in pursuance of the business's primary goals and objectives (its mission and vision).

There are many models we could use to help in this area and there are literally thousands of books on a whole range of subjects covering every aspect of operational management. The "Operations Productivity Optimiser" is the tool that focuses on the operational aspect of the 21st Century Marketing System and is based on the widely used "Lean philosophy".

Its origins can be traced to the mid-1930s, when Toyota led the way by developing and improving their manufacturing production systems. There has been a huge amount of research around "Lean" processes over the years, all aimed at achieving a highly efficient approach to managing an organisation's operations and creating highly efficient operating procedures, through a process of continuous improvement. In its simplest form, "Lean" focuses on the 5Ms of: materials, machines, manpower, methods and money, as shown in figure 2.27.

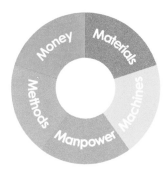

Figure 2.27 Operations Productivity Optimiser

Whilst there are many variations of this model we could use to help manage our key resources and develop an efficient operation, this version of the 5Ms model is very appropriate for micro-businesses, because it focuses on the five key elements applicable to any business. It is also easy to understand and can easily be aligned to your marketing activities, to help ensure you deliver on your promise.

Let's now take each one in turn and examine how they apply to the micro-business context.

Materials

In many businesses, the cost of raw materials can represent a significant proportion of its expenditure. Therefore, the careful management of materials is a critical factor in the smooth running and success of the business. Materials need to be purchased, stored, managed, consumed and disposed of in the most efficient manner, to ensure the business complies with any constraints of its operating environment ranging from conditions, such as being ethically sourced to the responsible disposal of by-products, waste and packaging.

In the manufacturing industry, the concept known as "just in time" sees the delivery of materials to the point they need to be consumed. A classic example is the motor industry, where components arrive at the location they are consumed on the production line and are immediately fitted to the vehicles, rather than being stored in a separate location prior to consumption. This is the epitome of manufacturing efficiency and requires extremely complex systems to manage the entire supply chain.

Entrepreneurs and micro-business owners will rarely have this luxury and will have to manage their materials through traditional, possibly manual, stock-keeping, allocation and reordering systems. Having too much stock costs money in terms of storage space and handling costs, whereas not having sufficient stock to meet demand will result in lost revenue, if customers cannot be served in a timely manner and, of course, reputation damage (negative word-of-mouth) if they are disappointed.

Materials are not just restricted to what's required to produce a product or supply service. Materials also include all the other consumables that are required by the business to run a complete operation. For example, in Brian's coffee shop, coffee beans, sugar, milk, food items, tea and other drinks, such as hot chocolate and a steady supply of water, are all required to meet his customers' expectations. He will also need a supply of infrastructure-related items, such as chairs and tables, cups, mugs, saucers, plates, spoons and anything else the customer may require to enjoy their experience and consume his products. He'll also need a supply of consumables, such as cleaning materials and associated equipment, which he must also manage to ensure the smooth running of his operation and, ultimately, the experience his customers expect — which is what it's all about.

Machines

Even the simplest businesses usually require machines or equipment. In the "good old days" we used to think of machines as being the large thumping pieces of equipment that were used to produce the final product sold to a customer. These are sometimes referred to as the "tangible machines" because they produce "tangible" results, i.e. goods or products. In the information age, it's highly likely you will have a laptop, computer system and other IT-related equipment to help manage some of the intangibles, such as information.

There are obviously many considerations around machines in any business, such as how they will be programmed to perform their function, how reliable they are, how durable they are, what their expected lifespan is, what training the operators of these machines will need and the cost and frequency of ongoing maintenance to keep them running efficiently.

Obviously, Brian's primary machine will be his commercial coffee machine, which produces anything from a latte to a double espresso and everything in between. This may require a commercial three phase electricity supply to operate efficiently and a continuous supply of water, in addition to being fed the precise amount of coffee to produce the perfect product the customer expects. It will also consume other materials during operation, such as filters and any cleaning products required to keep the machine in top shape.

If Brian cannot produce hot cups of coffee (and other drinks) on demand, that meet his customers' expectations, then his business is "dead in the water".

He'll also need other machines, such as a commercial dishwasher to efficiently wash his cutlery and crockery. A commercial fridge to keep his milk and other food products fresh will probably complete the bill as far as producing the product is concerned, but it doesn't stop there. Most customers will expect to be able to get online when they go for their coffee, so he also needs a machine (Wi-Fi router) to supply his customers with free Wi-Fi whilst they are in his coffee shop. There may be other things he needs to deliver the customer experience, but that probably covers the basics.

He will also require a computerised till and probably a laptop with Internet access to help manage his intangible, informational needs.

Finally, he may have some other equipment, such as a floor cleaning and polishing machine to keep his premises perfectly clean and present his establishment hygienically to his customers.

Machines on their own are not a lot of use without some kind of human interface. If his staff don't know how to use all these machines, or set them up correctly, all is in vain — which leads us on to the next resource.

Manpower

Manpower is arguably the most important 'M' of the Operations Performance Optimiser because without the right people, in the right positions, doing the right jobs efficiently and professionally, your business will suffer. Having the right people, with the right attitude, trained to perform their jobs correctly and motivated to perform to a high standard and keep your customers satisfied, are all critical success factors for your business. Your frontline customer-facing staff are the interface between your business and your customers. The more efficient your workforce, the more efficient your business.

Employing individuals who share your core values is particularly important in the micro-business context. It makes good sense to ensure that any staff you take on are as committed to your business outcomes as you are. This is one of the reasons why it's important to define exactly what your core values are during the strategic planning process. Not only are they vital to attracting the right type of customer, they also attract the right type of employees who want to become part of your team and willingly deliver on your brand promise.

Human Resource Management (HRM) is another huge subject. Getting the best out of people is one of the key tasks of any leader or manager. As far as the entrepreneur or micro-business owner is concerned, you should clearly define the functions that need to be performed, in order for your business to operate smoothly and efficiently. These functions should then be put into some kind of structure that defines the primary tasks for each function, or role, within the business. Each person you employ to perform a specific role will need a particular set of skills, in order to carry it out efficiently and effectively. Therefore, you should either recruit somebody with the right skills and experience, or train them so they acquire the skills you need. Finding the "perfect employee" with the "perfect skill set" is extremely rare and you'll probably recruit on the basis of staff having a number of skills (and possibly some relevant experience) before training them in the additional skills you need in your particular business.

In the micro-business environment, you'll expect quite a lot from your staff and you'll probably expect them to adapt to meet your business needs as the demands on your business change. As their leader, making sure you have the right members of your team and that each team member knows what they need to do in any situation, is a key part of communicating your performance expectations.

Let me give you a quick example. I live in the Isle of Man and every year we have the famous TT motorcycle road races. For several years, I was one of the many hundreds of volunteer marshals who were positioned around the course during the races, to help make sure everything went smoothly and according to plan. Motorcycle racing is very dangerous and, inevitably, there are accidents as riders try to break records. When an incident occurred, the teams of marshals positioned around the course had all been given specific jobs to do by their team leader: two people might be assigned to move the bike off of the race track, whilst two other people attended to the rider, whilst another marshal had the job of clearing up any debris and sweeping the road to make sure it was as safe as possible. Whilst all this is going on, the flag marshal would be waving a flag to warn oncoming riders to pass the incident scene with care. Everybody knows exactly what is expected of them and precisely what they need to do in the event of an accident.

Whilst nothing as dramatic as a motorcycle accident will happen in Brian's coffee shop, he will require at least a few staff to keep his operation running smoothly. He will need to utilise his previous management experience from the Ford dealership and apply it to the context of his coffee shop. For example, he's going to need at least one person whose primary role is to make the coffee (and other drinks), perhaps another member of staff to operate the till and maybe one or two more during busy periods, whose primary function is to clear the tables, collect the dishes, load the dishwasher and make sure the establishment is clean and tidy, to give that all-important good impression when customers come through the door.

To make sure your business runs smoothly, you must clearly define who does what and when, to ensure that your customers' experiences are as positive and enjoyable as possible which, in turn, will encourage positive word-of-mouth. It's often said that "it's not about the business, it's about the people" and that is very true — particularly in the service industry. You need to give sufficient attention to make sure your staff understand exactly what's expected of them and how they contribute to achieving your overall business goals.

Methods

"This is the way we do things around here". Your "methods" are the fourth element of the Operations Performance Optimiser and you need to really think about what has to happen, in order to give your customers the experience you've promised them. You also need to consider how you will react and what you will do, if things don't go quite according to plan. In business, these are often termed your *"standard operating procedures"*. In large organisations, these are often written down and presented in the employee handbook or communicated through an induction training process. In the micro-business context, this may be too much of an overhead, but you should at least have a clear idea of what has to happen in order to ensure that every function within your business is performed to the standard you expect.

Your guiding light will be the feedback you get from your customers (and others) and you should set yourself some key performance indicators to let you know how you're performing. This will help you optimise your processes (or methods) and keep the promise you have made to your target audience.

In the micro-business context, it will be useful to have at least two sets of procedures: the first defining what should happen during the normal course of business and the second defining what should happen if things go horribly wrong. For example, Brian has a short checklist that explains each of the steps his baristas must go through to make the perfect cup of coffee, from the range of drinks on his menu. Everybody who touches his coffee-making machine knows exactly what buttons to press, how much coffee to use, how to clean the machine and anything else to ensure things run smoothly.

Equally, he's devised a short set of instructions, explaining how the coffee shop should be kept immaculate at all times. It details how often the toilets should be checked, how quickly the tables should be cleaned when customers leave and what should be done at the end of the day, to ensure the coffee shop can be opened as quickly and smoothly as possible on the next working day.

He has also defined a set of procedures that should be followed when things don't go according to plan. For example, if the till breaks down, he has a calculator, a small cash tin with sufficient change in the right denominations and a notepad and pen which can be used to record each transaction. At least he can still function without a till. There are also clear instructions on the till to *"phone the maintenance engineer on < this number > quoting reference < xxxx >"* to get on-site technical assistance as fast as possible.

He has also thought about what will happen if his primary coffee-making machine fails during the working day. He's documented a simple procedure, which involves pulling out a couple of kettles and an industrial-sized tin of instant coffee from the storeroom, so he can at least give his customers a hot drink if he's in a position where he cannot deliver precisely what they asked for. This sheet is included in the file under the counter by the till which also states what to tell the customer i.e. that *"the coffee machine has gone down and will be fixed shortly"*. In the meantime, the only option the serving staff have, is to offer a cup of instant coffee. If Brian cannot meet his promise and can only offer an inferior product, his instructions are that these drinks should be free. This should at least satisfy his customers need for a hot drink — and buy some goodwill in the process.

Similarly, he has defined what the staff should do in the case of a fire alarm or power cut. All these procedures will form part of his staff induction training programme, so everybody knows what's expected of them both during normal operation and during any kind of emergency.

Obviously, every business will have different objectives and, hence, different ways of doing things. But the important point is to ensure the smooth operation of the business in any given situation. You should have the most common activities and procedures defined, so everybody knows exactly what to do if you're not there. It could be as simple as how to serve a customer, or how to deal with the complaint. Or it could be a lot more complicated, such as a set of instructions on how to use a sophisticated piece of equipment. Whatever it is that needs to happen in your business, whatever you need to do, if it's written down, there can be no ambiguity over what you expect of your staff — or even of yourself! These all contribute to "the way you do things around here" and, hence, how you will deliver on the promise you made to your target audience.

Money

The last element of the Operations Performance Optimiser is money — because money makes the world go round! Without money, no business can motivate their staff, acquire the machines they need to operate, or purchase the materials they need in order to provide the products or services they offer in their value proposition. Therefore, the successful management of money also means making the optimal use of the other 4Ms in pursuit of the business objectives and, ultimately, a profit.

But it's not all about making sales to pay the staff or purchase raw materials. When you're running a business, you also need to give serious consideration to the overall financial management of your enterprise. This will inevitably require keeping accurate accounts and reviewing them on a regular basis, to assess the performance of your business, often with the assistance of a professional.

Brian has enlisted Gemma to help him with his accounts. They will be using one of the many small business accounting packages available on the market, to keep track of the day-to-day activities and help them perform their weekly and monthly reviews. He will also have a series of methods, or procedures, to help him manage the financial aspects of his business. For example, at the end of the day, he will take the total sales from his till, prepare the cash ready for banking the following morning, adjust his "float" and enter the details of the day's takings into his computerised accounting system. At the end of each week, he will run his management reports and check a selection of numbers he has identified as being key performance indicators, to make sure they are what he expects them to be. He also has a "month end procedure" which he will perform with Gemma's help at the end of each month, to make sure all his records are up-to-date and that there is sufficient cash in the bank to pay his bills, the staff wages and any other liabilities he has to pay monthly, such as rent or finance charges on his equipment.

Careful financial management is another critical success factor to any business, large or small. Making sure you keep on top of all your regular financial transactions and recording them appropriately, will stand you in good stead when you need information on which to base your future decisions. If you do not have the skills, or inclination, to manage your business finances yourself, you must consider taking someone on to do this for you, as early as possible. Giving a carrier bag full of receipts and bank statements to your accountant at the end of the year, with no written record of what they mean or why you've collected them, is sure to give your accountant many sleepless nights — and result in an industrial-sized bill for their service. It is far better — and far more efficient — to prepare, record and manage all your financial transactions, on a regular basis.

If you run a high turnover business (i.e. one with many transactions to record), like Brian, then daily is the ideal time period. If you run a consultancy business where you have just one or two clients who take up the majority of your time, you may choose to record your transactions monthly. The bottom line is, the more frequently you update your financial information, the more accurate it will be when you rely on your financial records to make important decisions.

Linking the Operations Performance Optimiser to Marketing

Using the Operations Performance Optimiser to help you streamline your physical business activities and run an efficient operation, is an excellent way to ensure you deliver on the promises you've made to your target audience. It will help highlight any weaknesses or areas where you need to improve, as well as give you a lot of feedback on how your business is performing.

If things don't go well and you find it difficult to match the promise you've made to your target audience, you have two choices. You can either improve your operational efficiency and effectiveness to deliver on what you have promised, or you can change your value proposition to more closely fit what you are capable of delivering. Whatever you choose to do, you must ensure that what you promise is actually what you deliver, because the interface between operations and marketing is where the all-important word-of-mouth is generated.

As discussed earlier, one of your primary business objectives should be to generate positive word-of-mouth for your business and your brand. This can be achieved by slightly under-promising and slightly over-delivering, to ensure that you always "Wow" your customers within your standard operating capability. Remember, it's never what you think about yourself that matters; ultimately it is what your customers think and say about you that's the most important thing, because that will reflect how successful your business and, hence, your brand is perceived in the real world. A world made up of real people who (rightly) expect you to keep your promise!

Is It Working? The Results Are In!

The Dynamic Results Dashboard

The only way to find out whether what you're doing is actually working, is to measure and review your results on a regular basis. The "Control" section of the M.A.G.I.C. Marketing introduced the 3Ms of "Measure", "Monitor" and "Manage". You, therefore, must to decide exactly what you need to measure, monitor and manage to help achieve your business goals.

Whatever business you're in and however complex that business is, there will be numerous opportunities to receive and evaluate various kinds of feedback, which will help you keep your finger on the pulse of your business. The question is, what exactly should you measure, how often should you measure it and what will you do with the information once you have it? The rate at which data can be generated in the modern business environment is absolutely phenomenal and, if you're not careful, you'll end up with a huge amount of data that you struggle to do anything with.

Quite frankly, there is absolutely no point in doing everything up to this point if you don't monitor, measure and manage your progress toward achieving your objectives. Therefore, it is imperative that you have some kind of feedback and review system in place that helps you record and interrogate the important numbers. This is the purpose of the fifth element of the 21st Century Marketing System: the "Results". Essentially, there are three elements you need to consider: what you should measure, why it's important and how the data will be presented to help you make sense of it. Complex reports, with numbers buried in long columns of text, aren't exactly inspiring, so to avoid information overload, you need to have your data presented clearly and in a format you can actually use, to help you make your business decisions.

Large companies spend a huge amount of time collecting and presenting data to their decision-makers. This area of information management often involves the use of complex systems, such as data warehouses, business intelligence systems and a whole host of other analytical and modelling tools to help dig deep into the data. Senior management want a quick and accurate overview of the data and for it to be presented in a form they can quickly digest and understand. Quite often, this will be presented visually in the form of graphs and charts, which collectively form a management information "dashboard". Entrepreneurs and micro-business owners rarely have this luxury, but still need their critical numbers in order to make informed decisions.

> **Dynamic Results Dashboard:** The feedback mechanism of the 21st Century Marketing System designed to give the entrepreneur and micro-business owner an overview of their business in a simple and clear format based, on the most up-to-date data available, at a specific point in time.

This is where the "Dynamic Results Dashboard" (see figure 2.28) comes in. It can be as simple, or as complex as you require, depending on the type of information you need and your experience with setting up and using a formal feedback system. In its simplest form, it could just be a spreadsheet that highlights and records the key numbers. At the very least, the three KPIs you should watch are visitors, conversions and sales. At the other end of the spectrum, it could be a complex business intelligence system that interfaces with all other aspects of your business, to give you that one-page, high-level overview, but allows you to drill down and examine the details with the click of a mouse.

Figure 2.28 The Dynamic Results Dashboard

Quality feedback is essential to optimising your business and the three elements of a structured feedback system are questions, data sources and insights, as shown in figure 2.29. However you design and operate your Dynamic Results Dashboard, you will first need to decide what questions you want answered. You will have to identify the data sources that will provide the necessary information to answer those questions and, finally, you will have to work out how to interpret that data, to give you the insights you need to manage your business.

Figure 2.29 The Three Elements of a Structured Feedback System

Questions

What type of questions should you ask? That rather depends on the type of information you're looking for but the types of questions you should be asking typically relate to one of three areas: financial, critical success factors and key performance indicators.

Financials

The first looks at the bigger picture and how your business is performing from an overall management perspective. Management accounts will be a good place to start and, in particular, your income statement and balance sheet. It is good practice to update these at least on a monthly basis, as part of your standard financial operating procedures. If you are using one of the many accounting packages to manage your own accounts, after you have completed your month-end routines and have all the up-to-date information available, is the ideal time to run your management reports. Ideally, this should be no more than a couple of days into the following month.

Critical Success Factors

When you originally designed your business using the M.A.G.I.C. Marketing Matrix and the Seven Point Plan, you should have identified a number of what's referred to as "critical success factors" (CSFs). These are things that absolutely must happen in your business for it to succeed, such as finding the right premises, hiring suitable staff and ensuring you have any licenses or permits you need to legally trade.

You will also have a number of operationally focused critical success factors which are the things that must happen, in order for your business to trade effectively. For example, the success of your business will rely heavily on having sufficient customers coming through your door and buying sufficient goods or services from you, to ensure you can pay your business overheads. Another critical success factor may be the steady supply of your essential supplies. In this example, you could argue that paying your suppliers on time is essential for their businesses to survive and, if they go bust, it will have an immediate and devastating impact on your own business. Therefore, having an efficient procedure to simply pay your suppliers on time, could be considered one of your own critical success factors. As you create your 21st Century Marketing Blueprint, it's worth noting what your critical success factors are, so you can keep a close eye on them.

Key Performance Indicators

This will help you focus on what's referred to as "key performance indicators" (KPIs), which we discussed earlier in the "Control" section of the M.A.G.I.C. Marketing Matrix. A key performance indicator is a metric that can provide a very specific piece of information about your business that frequently changes. For example, the number of customers you acquire each month could be one KPI; the amount of cash that you take on a daily basis could be another, as could the cost of your raw materials. These will provide you with essential information on the health of your business. Your KPIs should be monitored on a very frequent basis. Depending on the type of your business, this could be hourly, daily, or weekly.

The top down approach, discussed earlier, also lays a clear foundation for the feedback system, as shown in figure 2.30. Half the battle in effectively and efficiently managing your business is knowing where to find the data you need, in order to make informed decisions to manage and grow your business. The philosophy behind the 21st Century Marketing System forces you to take a strategic approach to your business and marketing activities — and this really pays dividends when it comes to analysing your results.

Figure 2.30 The Foundation of the Feedback Cycle

If we look back to the top-down approach we took when defining our mission and vision statements, many of the business objectives will be reflected in the monthly management accounts. For example, if your business objective is to achieve a specific turnover figure, or acquire a certain number of new customers by a certain date, then your accounting system — and, hence, the management reports it produces — would be the first place to look. You can also check your progress to ensure that you are heading in the right direction, as defined by your vision statement.

Your marketing objectives will also identify a number of critical success factors you consider to be important to achieving your business objectives. It is very worthwhile to closely monitor whether you are achieving your overall marketing objectives.

Key performance indicators are typically "lower-level" metrics and would come from very specific and clearly defined SMART marketing communication objectives, with even more specific detail provided by individual marketing campaigns.

Now that you know what data you need to answer your questions, you need to decide where you'll get it from. That leads us on to data sources.

Data Sources

In our technology driven world, data can come from many sources. Typically, they fall into three areas: external data sources, internal data sources and using third party analytical tools to gain insights into other platforms we use to support our business, such as our website, Facebook, or Twitter.

External Data Sources

No business operates in a vacuum and there will always be external environmental factors which will impact your business. We talked about PESTEL, the macro-environmental analysis tool and Porter's Five Forces, the micro-environmental analysis tool, at the start of this section, along with other elements of established theory. Inevitably, there will be data outside of your business that you need to monitor, analyse and respond to in order to protect and grow your market share. The only way to capture this information is to continually be aware of what's going on in your industry, how it's changing and how you fit into it. Economic and political factors will also play a part and, keeping abreast of the latest changes in legislation and government plans announced in the budget, for example, will be just some of the factors you need to feed into your decision-making process.

The only realistic way for entrepreneurs and micro-business owner to keep informed of all of the external environmental factors is to keep abreast of current local and national news and other relevant developments. It may make sense to subscribe to various sources of pertinent information, such as a local Facebook business group, the local Chamber of Commerce, newsletters from relevant professionals, such as accountants and solicitors and any other suitable source that can deliver the latest news direct to your inbox. Then, of course, you need to allow sufficient time to scan these newsfeeds.

For example, if Brian sees an announcement in the local paper that a major coffee chain is seeking planning permission to open their first coffee shop just around the corner from where he is planning to open his next outlet, this may well cause him to re-evaluate his business plan. If he hadn't kept a close eye on the external factors that could affect his business, it could come as a real shock when customers at his new outlet start talking about the impending arrival of fierce competition with deep pockets just a stone's throw away.

Internal Support Systems

As you build your business and start trading, your data is likely to be spread over multiple sources or applications. For example, your financial data may be stored in your accounting system, your daily transactional data may be collected and stored in your electronic till whilst all marketing-related data may be stored in documents and spreadsheets. This makes managing your data — and, more importantly, reporting on a single view of that data — quite a complex task.

You need to spend time setting these systems up appropriately in the first place, so you can later get data out of your systems easily. It will save you a huge amount of time, effort and energy — and numerous headaches — particularly when you need information quickly.

It is also quite conceivable that you will have manual records to analyse; for example, Brian keeps his daily journal to help him reflect the daily activities within his business. It is highly likely that this journal will contain some real "nuggets" of information that can help him gain a deeper understanding of his business, but if he never looks back through his notes, they will remain hidden forever.

Online Analytics

In a small local business like Brian's, where he has a very limited online presence — certainly, at the point of start-up — there will not be a lot to analyse online. Furthermore, because the nature of his website is to merely inform his prospects and customers where he is and what he has to offer at the "zero moment of truth", any insights he could glean from website analytics tools wouldn't be very meaningful, because there's not a lot he could do with that information.

There are many hundreds, if not thousands, of metrics you could measure, but it doesn't necessarily mean that they will offer actionable insights. Paying any attention to them at all will just be a distraction and waste a lot of time. Once you have a stronger, more established digital and social media presence and you're investing a significant amount of your time, money and energy into these channels, using web analytics tools, such as Google Analytics and Facebook Insights, will be well worth the effort, to help you understand your target audience's online behaviour.

Google Analytics is a free tool that can track visitors' behaviour on your website. For example, it can identify where they came from, what pages on your website they looked at, how long they spent looking at various items of content and even the page they were on when they terminated their session. This can provide a wealth of information and, very quickly consume many hours, as you try to make sense of it all. There are a huge number of metrics available in Google Analytics, but it is important to understand what they mean in relation to your customers' journey. One metric referred to as the "bounce rate" is the percentage of sessions where the visitor left your site after viewing just one page. If you have a Pay-Per-Click campaign running and you have paid to get traffic to your website, a high bounce rate can be very disappointing if you expect them to click on various links and spend time consuming your "remarkable" content. In this context, a high bounce rate is a bad thing.

However, if they have found your customer support page through natural search, then a high bounce rate could be a good thing because it could indicate they've actually found the information they were looking for. Not only that, if they have found it without having to navigate to several other pages on your website, it would be safe to assume that their user experience is a positive one, because you have met their urgent informational needs.

Facebook Insights is a pretty powerful tool if you want to track user interaction on your Facebook Fan Page. It can help you track the number of active users to better understand the page's performance. Information provided by Facebook Insights can help you determine the best time of day and day of the week to post your thoughts as well as what type of content is most popular. LinkedIn provides a similar analytical tool and in all cases there is plenty of free advice on the respective platforms, to help you get the best out of their interrogation tools.

Another area you might consider in the social media space is referred to as "sentiment analysis". Measuring sentiment on your own can be quite time-consuming, especially if it turns into a large and active conversation. To record the sentiment, you would have to read each "mention" (or post), evaluate the tone and assign a score, such as positive, negative, or neutral. Fortunately, there are a few free sentiment-tracking automation tools, such as HootSuite Insights, that determine sentiment based on machine learning technology. For example, if a person tweeted about their experience with your business, the sentiment would be determined based on the descriptive words they use. "Another great coffee from Brian's Coffee Shop on the High Street!" would register as positive, whereas "Customer service at Brian's Coffee Shop on the High Street is the worst in town" would register as negative. With people being so eager to share their thoughts on just about anything, sentiment analysis can provide a real insight into what people really think about your business and your brand.

Insights

Having asked the questions and identified where to find your answers, the next thing to consider is what exactly the data can tell you. After all, you want meaningful answers to your questions and you want to turn all this data into useful and usable information. Having a pile of metrics on their own will not really do anything for you, unless you understand what they mean. If you can cross-reference several pieces of information to gain even deeper insights, you'll end up with a very powerful combination of business intelligence.

You do not necessarily need huge, complex systems and a team of analysts to get some very useful intelligence on your business. All you need is to be smart about the questions you ask and, then, based on the answers, ask more smart questions. For example, if Brian notices his takings are down by 25% on Wednesday lunchtimes compared to every other day of the week, he could look back over his last four to six weeks' diary entries, to see if anything could give some insights as to why trade is down at that particular time. It may be a good start to ask his customers on Thursday what's going on in the town Wednesday lunchtimes, as he didn't see them yesterday. It could be that the local weekly outdoor market has a couple of new stalls selling hot continental street food and this is affecting his Wednesday lunchtime trade.

If he hadn't dug a little deeper to find out why the takings were down, he could be forever guessing and, hence, making the wrong decisions — for example, unnecessarily increasing his advertising spend. In this example, a smart thing to do might be to visit the market himself (physical environmental scanning) and assess what's going on and why people like the street traders' offerings more than his. It may be that his usual customers just want something different and the market street traders have a novelty factor he can't compete with.

To boost his own trade, he may decide that it's better to try and attract a different type of customer on Wednesday lunchtime. For example, during his walkabout, he chatted to several elderly people carrying bags of shopping from the market and they told him street food didn't really appeal to them. This gives Brian an idea. He could advertise a "Market Day Pensioners Lunchtime Special" to try and attract the senior shoppers who are not interested in street food and prefer to enjoy their lunch in a more comfortable environment. That way he can support the small traders like himself, who rely on the market for their livelihood and, at the same time, also protect his own business by serving those who may appreciate something different that's not currently available at, but close to, the weekly market.

This is in line with his core values of supporting his local community and helps him achieve his business goals, without directly competing with the market traders. A win-win all round! He could even put a few flyers round the market stalls, to encourage the traders to pop in for a coffee when they get cold and need a break. A simple act of benevolence could create a lot of goodwill and positive word-of-mouth.

To address this "little hiccup" Brian decides to run a short campaign. Everything's going to be in line with his mission, vision and core values, so he doesn't need to change anything there. He reviews his business and quickly decides all he needs is a new marketing objective and a couple of marketing communication objectives to create a little campaign around. He knows the format by now and quickly updates his M.A.G.I.C. Marketing Matrix, by defining a new group (segment) of "Market Day Pensioners". His marketing objective is "to attract thirty extra people for the Market Day Pensioners Lunchtime Special within four weeks". Quite specific and, hence, SMART.

So, how's he going to do it? He drafts a rough persona based on what he knows about this target segment and decides traditional advertising is probably the best route, given the age and likely marketing consumption habits of his target audience and his current lack of digital marketing expertise. He doesn't want to spend much and decides a budget of £100 over the four-week promotional period is all he's prepared to risk, at least initially.

Not much, but sufficient to get some flyers printed. He also thinks some free PR wouldn't go amiss, so he contacts his local radio station and newspaper and asks them to do an article on him. He sets himself three marketing communications objectives:

1. To hand out 1,000 flyers over the four-week period promoting his market day offer
2. To get at least one five-minute radio interview with the local radio station during the campaign
3. To get at least two articles in the local press over the same period.

He estimates the flyers will cost about £30 and he'll pay Samantha, one of his part-time members of staff, to wander round the market for an hour or so on Wednesday mornings, handing them out to qualifying prospects.

With regards to the PR, his "angle" is "supporting the local traders" and all he wants is a five-minute slot on the Wednesday morning talk show, where he'll chat to the presenter about how it's important to "support the little guy". His idea is for the reporter interview him outside his coffee shop whilst the photographer takes a picture to supplement the story on the radio station's website. The story is that he's not just doing this for himself and he's extolling the virtues of the entrepreneurial market folk — basically, just telling the story of how he doesn't want to compete with them and show how they can coexist, by being just a little more entrepreneurial himself. The local media love the idea because it's a nice, selfless community story about a little guy trying to helping other little guys. All he needs to do is tell the story exactly as it is, i.e. how he discovered what was causing the drop in his market day trade and how he didn't want to compete with the traders, once he discovered they were "just like him".

Now, here's the clever bit. Because it's a PR piece, it's the media who are "writing" (or reporting) the story, so any heavy sell is a no-no! During the "story" he just says he saw all these poor pensioners wandering round the market in need of refreshment, so he thought he'd step in and offer a nice lunchtime coffee and snack for less than a fiver. After all, the weekly market is an important part of the local shopping scene and he wants to do all he can to support it. The reporter slips in a few comments about what he's offering the pensioners and, because it's from the media (not an advert), it has high credibility and can reach a large audience.

That's how easy it can be to initiate a short, cheap campaign when you know how to use the 21st Century Marketing System and how to effectively adapt them to your own business situation. Over the next few weeks, all Brian needs to do is keep an eye on his daily till reports on market day (metrics) to see if his £100 investment is producing results. If your target audience is active online and you want to do a similar type of campaign, you could create a Pay-Per-Click campaign, which would be the equivalent of Brian's flyers and write a couple of blog posts, which would be similar to the PR newspaper article. You could also create a short YouTube video, which could be the online equivalent of Brian's radio interview and share it with your following. The key message here is that for every offline activity, there is a corresponding online activity which can produce similar results — all of which should be tracked to monitor their effectiveness.

With so many potential metrics to measure, it's difficult to know where to start, so focusing on the key metrics of visitors, conversion and sales makes good sense, as shown in figure 2.31. These three simple metrics can provide a wealth of information to help you understand what's going on in the key areas of your business.

Figure 2.31 The Three Top Insights

"Visitors" could mean visitors to your website, your social media platforms, or in Brian's case, physical visitors who walk through his door. Whilst it is highly likely that every visitor to Brian's coffee shop will buy something, by contrast, in the online environment, getting a visitor does not necessarily mean creating a sale. However, without getting any visitors, there's no chance of anything happening!

Once visitors arrive on your website, for example, at each stage of their customer journey you must have a clear idea of what they will do next and what "conversion" means in that particular context. It could be that you want to turn a suspect into a prospect and merely collect their email address, in exchange for a PDF special report you can send them by email. In this example, "conversion" means "collecting email address to add a qualified lead to your list". If this meets one of your objectives, then that's absolutely fine. Equally, if the next stage of the customer's journey is to purchase an entry-level product, "conversion" could mean making a sale.

Sales are a vital part of every business. By measuring the three metrics of visitors, conversions and sales, you can also analyse the ratios and quickly make informed decisions to improve performance. For example, if you only convert one in every thousand prospects into customers, it could indicate your conversion process is not as effective as it might be. By understanding the metrics and the meaning behind them, you might decide to invest some time and money in improving your conversion rate. In this example, you may already be getting a significant amount of traffic to your website but the problem is in converting visitors into customers. Therefore, you would be ill advised to make any additional investments in generating more traffic, because 99.9% of it is wasted (or at least ineffective).

On the other hand, if you have a high conversion rate and, say, convert one in ten visitors into customers, there's probably not much more you can do to improve it. Therefore, the way you increase your sales is by attracting more visitors to your site, so an investment in generating traffic would be a wise decision.

Certainly, in the early days, focusing a good portion of your management attention around these three metrics can have a significant impact on the overall performance of your business. Thinking about these three metrics, in both the online and the offline context, can help ensure a coordinated approach to your core business activities, which leads to satisfying your most important critical success factors.

Business Intelligence

The ultimate goal regarding feedback, in whatever form, is to turn data into information and information into intelligence. The higher the quality of your information when it is cross-referenced and analysed in association with other high-quality information, the deeper your insights. Deep insights lead to a far better understanding of the business and how to improve it, for both survival and growth.

There are numerous business intelligence systems on the market with the capability of taking data from multiple sources and displaying them on a single dashboard, or set of dashboards, as shown in figure 2.32. The biggest challenge with these types of system is to integrate the multiple sources of data, so they can pull a plethora of information and provide a single view of the most important metrics. These systems can be incredibly complex and extremely expensive. They also require highly specialised skills, to take full advantage of them.

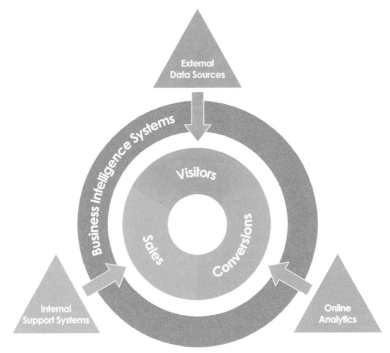

Figure 2.32 Business Intelligence Systems

At the other end of the scale, simple manual systems comprising spreadsheets can provide similar types of high-level information, but lack the ability to interface with other systems and drill down in the same way.

What This Means to the Micro-Business Owner

The reality is most entrepreneurs and micro-business owners will have to adopt a manual approach to creating and maintaining their Dynamic Results Dashboard, as this will be dictated by limited resources — particularly in the early days. The key thing is to focus on the most important numbers that tell you exactly what you need to know, when you need to know it. There is absolutely no point in investing huge amounts of time and money in developing an overly complex system that you can't feed with the appropriate data from which you can derive any benefit.

To start with, Brian focused on how effective his marketing was at attracting new visitors to his coffee shop. He's implemented a very simple response-based tracking mechanism to help them identify how effective his advertising is, by offering different rewards for each channel, or tool, he uses. So the number of free cookies shown on his till analysis will help track the effectiveness of his newspaper advertising and the number of free waffles shown on the till reports gives an indication as to the effectiveness of his radio advertising. He'll know what he's paying for both these sets of adverts and he can easily calculate the return on his marketing investment. Obviously, there's going to be a little bit of manual work involved here, but designing a simple spreadsheet with some formulas keeps his data entry to a minimum. He can even quickly benefit from seeing a graphical view of his data, if he so chooses, using the standard features of most spreadsheet packages.

If you're not so hot with spreadsheets, asking a friend who has slightly more advanced spreadsheet skills to help you is an easy option, to help create your Dynamic Results Dashboard.

In the early days, most of his attention is on training his staff and making sure they provide quality service and embody his core values, which are a reflection of his brand. He doesn't have a huge amount of time to spend on too many "numbers" and, in the first few months, he feels the numbers provided by the computerised till are more than sufficient. However, he must analyse these in association with the management accounts that Gemma produces on a monthly basis. By just looking at data from these two sources, they can quickly analyse the performance of the coffee shop and identify trends — which, by the way, is a very important insight, as they can accurately reflect changes in consumer behaviour, such as defecting to the market on Wednesday lunchtimes.

By having a combination of data that can be turned into useful information, Brian feels more in control and he sleeps better at night knowing everything is going in the right direction. As a micro-business owner, Brian is far more concerned with making sure the day-to-day activities are done properly, from attracting new customers and serving them quickly, to cleaning the coffee shop at the end of the day and accounting for the day's takings.

As his confidence grows, so does his confidence in the patterns he sees in his regular data, such as the total daily sales, the split between espressos, cappuccinos and lattes and his food sales, etc. He can begin to introduce more key performance indicators into his feedback system, update his Dynamic Results Dashboard and start to monitor other parts of his business.

A key point to remember is that a successful business works on the basis of continuous improvement and focuses on making the weakest link the strongest link. This is often referred to as the "Samurai Principle" because it's based on Japanese samurai warriors, who worked endlessly on making their weakest skill their strongest skill. They then repeat the process and work on the next weakest skill, to make it one of the strongest. It's a very simple but effective way to continually raise your standards and, most importantly, add resilience to the numerous factors that will have an impact on your business. The overriding benefit of this approach is that, as you strengthen your business, you inherently reduce the risk of not being up to coping with things when they go wrong — as they inevitably will!

Of course, as your business grows, a simple spreadsheet-based dashboard system may not be sufficient for your needs. Instead, you may decide a more sophisticated set of information reporting is required to manage your business efficiently and effectively. You'll know when you get to this point, because you'll be frustrated at the lack of visibility of some of your data. You should now have a basic appreciation of the challenges you're likely to face, should you choose to go down the route of developing a more complex system. However, if you focus on the three elements discussed earlier (visitors, conversions and sales) and incorporate these three elements into your simple Dynamic Results Dashboard, you'll have a very good start on which to build a more complex system and to adapt, as your business grows and your needs change.

Completing the Picture

We have now covered every element of the 21st Century Marketing System. We started by looking at "The Opportunity" which relates to defining your strategy; and the tool used here was the M.A.G.I.C. Marketing Matrix. We then moved on to "The Plan" focusing on the implementation of the strategy; and the tool we used here was the Seven Point Plan. The third piece of the jigsaw puzzle is "The Promise". Making a promise to your target audience is the communication section of the system; and here we use the Value Proposition Communicator. "The Operations" is the real activity of the business and the Operations Performance Optimiser can really help us understand the operational side of our business. Finally, we looked at "The Results" which collates information from all four pieces of the jigsaw puzzle, to provide detailed insights into your business.

One of the fundamental principles of the 21st Century Marketing System is that it implements the strategy you define at "The Opportunity" stage. Whilst the M.A.G.I.C. Marketing Matrix allows you to think about the whole of your business from a strategic perspective, it is actually more than that. Each component of the M.A.G.I.C. Marketing Matrix defines and forms the foundation of subsequent parts of the 21st Century Marketing System and, hence, completes the whole picture, as shown in figure 2.33.

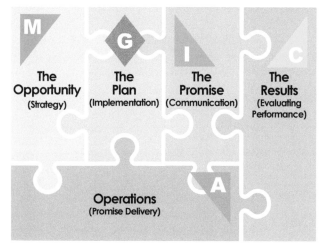

Figure 2.33 Applying the M.A.G.I.C. Marketing Matrix to the 21st Century Marketing System

When we think about "The Opportunity" our primary focus is the market (the "M") we intend to serve. What we are capable of doing —our Actions — are reflected in our operational capability. Therefore, the "A" (Action) part of the M.A.G.I.C. Marketing Matrix refers to the Operations part of the jigsaw.

As we think about implementing our strategy, we have to identify the various segments of interest and come up with a plan to talk to individual segments of our target audience. Therefore, the "G" (Group) element of the M.A.G.I.C. Marketing Matrix relates to the second half of the Seven Point Plan, where you define your business and marketing objectives, right down to the specific campaigns you will execute to achieve them.

When we make a promise to our target audience, we will ultimately want to influence them in some way and, hence, the "I" (Influence) component of the M.A.G.I.C. Marketing Matrix relates to communicating with your target audience and making that all-important "Promise". This is your chance to set realistic expectations about what you can deliver — and what you will be judged upon.

The fifth and final piece of the jigsaw puzzle is all about "The Results"; it focuses on the insights you need to answer your questions and, ultimately, control your business. The "C" (Control) element of the M.A.G.I.C. Marketing Matrix relates to "The Results" section of the 21st Century Marketing System.

Each component of the 21st Century Marketing System is supported by individual elements of the M.A.G.I.C. Marketing Matrix, as well as having a specific tool to develop it further and implement it in the real world. However, as I'm sure you now appreciate; the 21st Century Marketing System is far more than a set of tools based around a theory. It is a comprehensive, end-to-end solution to all your modern multi-channel marketing challenges, to make sure your voice is heard.

Stage	Matrix Element	Specific Tool
The Opportunity (Strategy)	**M** - Market	The M.A.G.I.C. Marketing Matrix
The Operations (Promise Delivery)	**A** - Action	Operations Productivity Optimiser
The Plan (Implementation)	**G** - Group	The 7-Point Plan
The Promise (Communication)	**I** - Influence	The Value Proposition Communicator
The Results (Insights)	**C** - Control	The Dynamic Results Dashboard

In conclusion, the 21st Century Marketing System enables you to build a comprehensive 21st Century Marketing Blueprint for your business, regardless of your individual requirements. It covers each area of your business, as well as supporting the entire business development cycle. Each component of the system has its own dedicated tool, which has been developed from both proven, well-established theory and best practice in the real world. Furthermore, each tool has been streamlined to cater for the specific needs of the entrepreneur and micro-business owner.

Every element of the system and each of the tools, support the underlying philosophy of modern marketing, which is reflected by the New Engagement Paradigm, discussed earlier in this book. The New Engagement Paradigm is far more than just a new way of thinking; it is an accurate reflection of how marketers actually need to respond to the challenges of a technically driven business and marketing landscape.

With the 21st Century Marketing System and its handful of supporting tools, you have absolutely everything you need to develop your own 21st Century Marketing Blueprint. You should now be able to consistently get your message in front of the right audience, at the right time, using the right tools and, ultimately, generate that all-important positive word-of-mouth for your business — to keep your brand top of your target audience's mind.

HOW to do it

Using the System

In Section 1, we looked at WHY 21st Century Marketing matters and how changes in the environment, consumer behaviour and technology have transformed the face of marketing forever. In Section 2, we took a detailed look at WHAT 21st Century Marketing is and examined each of the five pieces of the 21st Century Marketing System and their supporting tools.

Along the way, examples were given to show HOW to do 21st Century Marketing. In this section, we expand on that theme, using a detailed case study to show how the 21st Century Marketing System can be used to help you build your own 21st Century Marketing Blueprint.

Finally, we'll round off by explaining how to extend the 21st Century Marketing Blueprint, to include the extra elements to help you turn it into a full blown 21st Century Business Plan.

Pulling It All Together:
What the Complete System Looks Like from End to End

There are seven logical steps to implementing the 21st Century Marketing System.

Step 1 defines the strategic definition and the completion of the M.A.G.I.C. Marketing Matrix. This, effectively, serves as the introduction, or high-level overview, of your opportunity and how you intend to turn it into reality.

Step 2 defines the first three elements of the Seven Point Plan — your mission, vision and core values — which will affect everything else that you do. We'll complete the rest of the Seven Point Plan in step 5, but it is critical to complete these three elements properly before you move on.

Step 3 is to define the scope, or boundaries, of your operational capability using the Operations Performance Optimiser. Here, you will look at what resources, procedures, skills and manpower you will need and compare them to what you have access to. You should consider all the resources and everything else you will need to build your vision.

Step 4 is the reality check before you set your business objectives. It may be that you do not have all the resources you need at the beginning to achieve your ultimate mission and, at least in the short term, you may have to make some compromises and adjust your interim vision. It does not mean you should abandon your long-term vision, but you do need to make sure you set yourself realistic goals, as this will help you define SMART objectives. It doesn't mean to say that you shouldn't "aim for the stars"; it just means that whatever you decide you are going to set as your initial mission and vision, should be compatible (and congruent) with what you truly believe is actually achievable. The key thing here is to ensure that what you want to achieve and how you see yourself achieving it, is in line with the resources you have at the beginning and what you are likely to have as you progress.

In **Step 5**, we complete the second half the Seven Point Plan by defining your business objectives, then your marketing objectives, followed by your marketing communication objectives and, finally, designing your marketing campaigns to meet your overall business objectives.

Step 6 is to define and execute your individual marketing campaigns using the Value Proposition Communicator as your primary management tool and the Message Development Matrix to help you actually create your messages

Finally, in **Step 7**, you need to monitor your results, based on the key performance indicators you have defined in your Seven Point Plan and compare your results with what you ideally wanted to achieve. This will be an ongoing process because you need to continuously market your business and, hence, continuously monitor your results. It is only with this level of feedback that you can make well-informed decisions on how best to grow and build your business.

In the twenty-first century you need a customer focused business model. We call this your 21st Century Business Blueprint and we use the 21st Century Marketing System to create it.

This is summarised in figure 3.1 and you should refer to this on a regular basis as you design, build, operate, manage and refine your business. You can always go back and review the individual elements of the 21st Century Marketing System to refine your 21st Marketing Blueprint, to make sure you're achieving your overall objectives and progressing toward achieving your mission and vision.

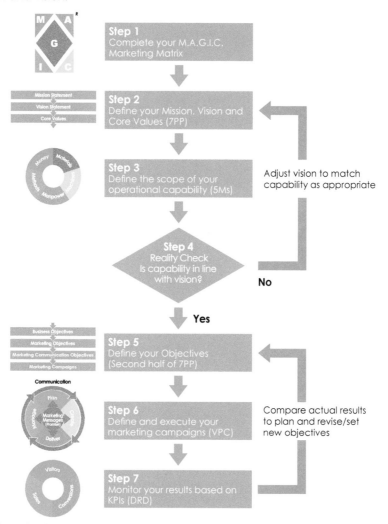

Figure 3.1 The Seven Steps to Creating Your 21st Century Marketing Blueprint

This case study has two parts. We'll start by pulling together everything Brian has done so far to get his business off the ground, so you can see how the 21st Century Marketing System all fits together. We'll then show how Brian used the system to further develop and enhance his marketing activities, once he's established and continues to build his business.

Case Study Part 1:
Brian's Coffee Shop (Start-Up Stage)

Step 1: The M.A.G.I.C. Marketing Matrix

Step 1 of the process is to complete the M.A.G.I.C. Marketing Matrix.

Brian's initial M.A.G.I.C. Marketing Matrix looks like this:

Market
Who do you consider to be your target market?

Customers	Primary target market is coffee drinkers who frequent the centre of town on a Monday to Saturday between 7:30 a.m. and 5:30 p.m. Several categories of customers have been defined and divided into: ▲ the early morning coffee drinkers who want a coffee on the way to work ▲ the mothers who drop off their children at school and want to chat to their friends on the way home ▲ the lunchtime crowd who want a sandwich/snack to go with their coffee ▲ professionals who want to hold a business meeting away from the office or use a laptop/tablet ▲ casual coffee drinkers who just want to enjoy a great coffee whilst taking a break from shopping.
Challenges	The main challenges that his target market faces is the lack of similar refreshment facilities in the town centre.
Competitors	There is limited competition as there are no major coffee chains in the area. The competition is currently limited to a couple of sandwich bars that also provide takeaway coffees and some of the local pub chains that open early to serve breakfast but don't provide a takeaway service.

Personas

What do the various segments of your target market look like?

Early Morning Workers	Nigel and Janice: Early morning coffee drinkers on the way to work:
	▲ Approx. age: Mid-thirties
	▲ Local professional office workers
	▲ Key attributes: Time poor
	▲ Requirement: Just coffee
	▲ Estimated spend per visit: £3
	▲ Consumption: In house and takeaway
	▲ Appreciates: Quality and speed of service
	▲ Primary motivation: Energy boost/self-time
	▲ Time: Visits between 7:30 a.m. and 9:00 a.m.
Morning Mothers	Sophie and Tracy: Morning mothers on the way home from the school run:
	▲ Approx. age: Late twenties to Mid-thirties
	▲ Local mothers whose children go to the local infants' school
	▲ Key attributes: Social coffee drinker with friends
	▲ Requirement: Coffee/cake/drink as well as a biscuit for a young child (preschool age)
	▲ Estimated spend per visit: £7
	▲ Consumption: In house
	▲ Appreciates: Social space to meet friends and somewhere to leave the pushchair
	▲ Primary motivation: Social interaction with friends
	▲ Time: Visits between 9:30 a.m. and 11:00 a.m. probably just once a week.
Lunchtime Snackers	Andy and Charlotte: Lunchtime coffee drinkers and snackers
	▲ Approx. age: Mid-twenties to late fifties
	▲ Local professional office workers
	▲ Key attributes: Time conscious
	▲ Requirement: Coffee/sandwich/hot snack/cake
	▲ Estimated spend per visit: £6
	▲ Consumption: In house
	▲ Appreciates: Quality and speed of service/clean and fresh environment
	▲ Primary motivation: High-quality and affordable lunchtime snack
	▲ Time: Visits between 12:30 p.m. and 2:00 p.m.
Business Meetings	Alistair and Rachael: Business meeting coffee drinkers:
	▲ Approx. age: Mid-thirties to late fifties
	▲ Local and travelling professionals
	▲ Key attributes: Time poor
	▲ Requirement: Just coffee and a good free Wi-Fi connection
	▲ Estimated spend per visit: £3
	▲ Consumption: In house
	▲ Appreciates: Quality and speed of service, quiet location at a table for meetings and to make phone calls with space for paperwork, laptop, iPad, or tablet
	▲ Primary motivation: Flexible meeting facility
	▲ Time: Visits between 10:30 a.m. and 12:00 p.m., 2:30 p.m. and 5:00 p.m.

Casual Shopper	Sam and Alice: Casual Shoppers
	▲ Approx. age: Retirees during the week and families on Saturday
	▲ Local shoppers
	▲ Key attributes: Usually more than one person in need of rest from shopping
	▲ Requirement: Coffee and snack
	▲ Estimated spend per visit: £5
	▲ Consumption: In house
	▲ Appreciates: Somewhere clean to sit down and rest, use of toilets, space for shopping bags and coats
	▲ Primary motivation: Social interaction and rest from shopping
	▲ Time: Primarily weekday afternoons and Saturdays.

Actions

What action can you take to satisfy the needs of your target audience?

Results	The results the target customers are looking for, is somewhere close to the centre town where they can get a decent cup of coffee and, possibly, a snack in clean, friendly environment any time during the day, six days a week.
Relevant	In Brian's case, the relevance is very closely related to the results his target audience are looking for, i.e. somewhere to get a great cup of coffee any time during the working day, six days a week, close to the centre of town, be it sitting down or takeaway.
Rare	Due to Brian's limited competition, his value proposition will be "rare" because he will be the only proper coffee shop in the centre of town. However, there will be other attributes that make him "rare", such as quality of his coffee and other products he offers, his opening times and any other combination of services he can offer to make his overall value proposition more unique and desirable, such as free Wi-Fi and spotlessly clean toilets.

From the personas defined above, Brian now needs to identify how he intends to interact with each of these groups. At this stage, all he really needs to consider is how he is going to get his message "out there" to attract the attention of the various segments of his target audience. He doesn't need to go into too much detail because he'll do that when he develops the "Group" element of his M.A.G.I.C. Marketing Matrix. The key thing is to capture all his ideas and make sure he doesn't forget anything important — he can always refine them later.

There will obviously be some overlap/duplication regarding which marketing tools he uses to communicate with each of the groups he's identified. What he now needs to do is identify which marketing tools he thinks will have the greatest impact at each stage of the customer's journey, so he knows where to invest his limited resources. Bear in mind that this is not a definitive list (or combination) as it may need to be changed over time as his business and understanding of the way his customers respond to his marketing efforts, develops. However, this is certainly a comprehensive list that he can talk through with his bank manager, investor, or business adviser when he's asked how he intends to market his business.

Group

How will you communicate with each segment of your target market at each stage of their customer journey?

Group 1	Early Morning Workers
Acquire	Radio and press advertising, PR, office posters
Convert	Posters at place of work, pavement sign outside coffee shop, promotional offers
Retain	Good face-to-face service and experience, various promotions including the loyalty card
Engage	Facebook page, blogging, tweeting

Group 2	Morning Mothers
Acquire	Radio and press advertising, PR, word-of-mouth
Convert	Flyers, pavement sign outside coffee shop, promotional offers
Retain	Good face-to-face service and experience, various promotions including the loyalty card
Engage	Facebook page, blogging, tweeting

Group 3	Lunchtime Snackers
Acquire	Website, radio and press advertising, PR, word-of-mouth
Convert	Posters at places of work, pavement sign outside coffee shop, word-of-mouth, promotional offers
Retain	Good face-to-face service and experience, various promotions including the loyalty card
Engage	Facebook page, blogging, tweeting

Group 4	Business Meetings
Acquire	Website, radio and press advertising, office posters
Convert	Posters at places of work, pavement sign outside coffee shop, word-of-mouth
Retain	Good face-to-face service and experience, various promotions including the loyalty card
Engage	Facebook page, blogging, tweeting

Group 5	Casual Shoppers
Acquire	Radio and press advertising, PR, flyers, word-of-mouth, pavement sign outside coffee shop
Convert	Flyers, pavement sign outside coffee shop, promotional offers
Retain	Good face-to-face service and experience, various promotions including the loyalty card
Engage	Personal interaction during the visit and continuous offline marketing activity

Whilst the Group element of the M.A.G.I.C. Marketing Matrix focuses on how we will communicate with the various segments of our target audience, the next section, "Influence", focuses on the messages that will be delivered to each of those groups at various stages of their customer journey.

For each specific group, Brian wants to deliver a consistent message across all marketing channels. Remember, in this section, the "tale" refers to the message, or story, Brian will tell in order to get his message across in the most effective and efficient manner. And, of course, these messages can be delivered by a number of marketing tools which will also be noted.

Influence

What will you say to each segment of your target market at each stage of their customer journey?

Target Audience	Early Morning Workers
Tale	When Brian first started his business, the key message he wanted to deliver to this segment of his target audience was that he is open from 7:30 a.m. every morning Monday to Friday and that he serves great coffee, which can be enjoyed either in house or by using his takeaway service for those who just want to "grab and go".
Tools	He has defined the primary tools during the acquisition and conversion stage as radio and press advertising, office posters, flyers and a pavement sign outside his coffee shop.

Target Audience	Lunchtime Snackers
Tale	Whilst Brian's physical offer of coffee and snacks is identical to all segments of his target market, he will need to communicate a different message to his lunchtime snackers than to his early morning workers. For example, he will need to communicate that his coffee shop is pleasant, clean and friendly and that he has plenty of seats and tables for his customers. He may also want to communicate that he has extra staff at lunchtime to ensure a speedy service, as they may be short of time.
Tools	His website, radio and press advertising, PR, word-of-mouth, posters and the pavement sign are the best combination of tools to convey this message.

Target Audience	Casual Shoppers (Market Day)
Tale	The message he wants to deliver to his casual shoppers' segment on market day will again be very different to the one he wants to deliver to his early morning workers. He will want to communicate that he actively supports his fellow small traders and wants to do something to enhance the market day shopping experience.
Tools	PR, flyers, posters and his pavement sign are all tools he could use to convey his message to this segment of his target audience.

The last section of the M.A.G.I.C. Marketing Matrix is the "Control" element and, here, Brian needs to decide what he's going to measure, how he's going to measure and monitor it and how to manage the control process as easily as possible. Therefore, with regard to the control element, all that needs to be defined at this stage is the type of data you will keep a close eye on, to keep your finger "on the pulse" of your business.

In Brian's case, it involves the prime numbers associated with running a successful coffee shop with, hopefully, a high turnover of regular low-cost items.

Control

What critical success factors and key performance indicators do you need to regularly monitor to ensure your success?

Measure	When Brian starts off, there will be a number of critical success factors that he needs to keep a close eye on, such as his daily takings, stock levels, how long people are staying in his coffee shop and occupying the tables, how long the queues are at the till and how long it takes to serve his customers.
	He will also have some very specific key performance indicators to measure that relate to each segment of his target market, such as the number of coupons redeemed for the promotional items, the average transaction value at various times of the day, the volume of advertising response codes redeemed (to identify his most effective marketing tactics) and any times of the day when his coffee shop is empty.
Monitor	He will need to decide how often he monitors his critical success factors and key performance indicators, for example, daily, weekly or monthly depending on their meaning within the business.
Manage	He's going to manage this data by collecting the necessary numbers from the till at the end of every working day and recording them in a spreadsheet, which he'll later summarise on a weekly and monthly basis. He'll then compare these actual figures to his original estimates, to see how he's doing and highlight any areas he needs to focus on.

Step 2: The Seven Point Plan (Part 1)

Brian now needs to refer to the first half of the Seven Point Plan, to define his mission and vision statements and his core values. His completed list looks like this:

Mission

Mission Statement	To serve great coffee and other hot drinks and quality snacks that people enjoy, savour and look forward to, in a relaxed, friendly environment where they feel cheerful, appreciated and at home.

Vision

Vision Statement	To become the leading independent chain of coffee shops and first choice for regular local customers in <his town> who want to enjoy quality hot drinks and supplementary products, in an environment they consider an extension of their home.

Core Values

Reliable	If he makes a promise, or says he's going to do something, he'll do it to the best of his ability. He more often than not achieves what he sets out to achieve, no matter how mundane and if Mary asks him to pick something up from the grocery store, he obliges without complaint.
Honest	Brian was brought up in a household with strong moral values and honesty and integrity are very important to him. He hates being lied to and can't help taking it personally.
Fun-loving	According to his friends, having a laugh and seeing the funny side of things is one of his greatest qualities. Although he doesn't exactly consider himself the "life and soul of the party" he does like people and is always smiling.
Motivated	Being a "self-starter" he finds it pretty easy to get up in the morning and get on with things. He hates lazy people and "doesn't suffer fools gladly".
Punctual	Timekeeping is high on his list and, if people don't turn up on time, he feels they don't respect him. One of his lifelong work habits is turning up for work ten minutes before he's due to be there and leaving ten minutes after the end of his shift.
Passionate	He's a firm believer in "If a job's worth doing, it's worth doing properly" and just cannot bring himself round to doing "half a job".
Respectful	"Treat others as you would wish to be treated yourself" is another favourite motto and. like most men, Brian likes to feel respected. He's also a great advocate of "manners don't cost anything".

Step 3: Capability

Step 3
Define the scope of your
operational capability (5Ms)

In Step 3 Brian uses the Operations Productivity Optimiser to define the scope of his operational capability. These are all the resources and processes he will need to employ, to ensure he creates and maintains a smooth-running operation that delivers on his promises to his target audience.

Operational Capability

Money	All businesses need cash, be it for initial start-up costs, working capital, or day-to-day cash flow to cover operational expenses. Every business will have a limit on the amount of cash actually available to them, which will set the financial boundaries of their operational capability. Some of this cash will be invested by the owners and other funds will be made available through various finance arrangements from banks, creditors, or other investors.
	Brian is fortunate to have sufficient capital without raising any from a third party. However, to manage his day-to-day activities he does need full access to money processing facilities, such as a debit and credit card machine, bank accounts, cash till as well as credit terms from his day-to-day suppliers. All of these need to be in place before he starts trading.
Materials	Brian's materials will mainly be the consumable items he purchases to resell, such as coffee, tea, hot chocolate, cold drinks, cakes, snacks and other items on the menu.
	He first has to find a suitable source of supply for everything he needs and then negotiate the appropriate terms, such as the regularity of delivery, the price, including any discounts, the acceptable level of quality etc. He will also potentially need to agree on a substitute/backup range of products if for any reason, his first choice becomes unavailable.
	He may decide to source all of his supplies from either one primary wholesaler to achieve the maximum volume discounts, or he may decide to spread his risk and deal with multiple suppliers.
Machines	Brian's business could not operate without a commercial coffee machine and the necessary power and water supplies to operate it. He will also need to consider maintenance and servicing contracts for all his equipment including other primary items, such as his display cabinets and fridges, his till and any oven or microwave used to heat the hot snacks.
	He will also have a range of cleaning equipment which he'll need to purchase, lease, or hire and, subsequently, maintain on a regular basis, in addition to any related consumables, such as bags and filters required by these items of equipment.

Manpower	Aside from himself and occasionally Mary, he also needs to make sure he has sufficient staff to cover the peak periods and allow for holiday cover and sickness. He will need to determine how much he needs to pay each person to get the level of staff he requires, in addition to covering all the other costs and responsibilities of employment.
	He also needs to make sure all members of his staff are fully trained to meet his customer service standards. Brian will have to cater for any legal requirements, such as food and hygiene training with appropriate government-approved training providers, to ensure his staff are suitably qualified to perform their designated roles.
Methods	Brian needs to decide exactly how he will do things to make sure his coffee shop runs smoothly. This includes everything from what he has to do and how long it takes to open the store at the start of every day, to what needs to be done at the end of the day to make sure his standards and operational capability are maintained.
	Other procedures also need to be clearly defined, such as what happens in the case of an emergency or a fire, what the reordering and restocking procedures are, the process for banking each day's takings and whatever processes are necessary to keep his premises spotlessly clean to provide a high-quality customer experience.
	There is actually quite a lot that he needs to consider and, perhaps, one way of viewing this to make sure he covers everything, is to define everything that should happen if he were not available to run the shop in person. For example, what would he have to tell somebody else in order for them to manage his coffee shop for him whilst he's on holiday?

Step 4: Reality Check

Step 4
Reality Check
Is capability in line
with vision?

Time for reflection! Step 4 in the process is taking a step back and conducting what is referred to as a "reality check". When starting a new business, we all have grand ideas about what we want to achieve and entrepreneurs have one common trait: we all believe we can achieve an awful lot in a short time. Nothing wrong with that!

But sometimes we do have to recognise that there are limits to what we can physically achieve. The point of reviewing our capability against our vision, at this stage in the process, is to make sure we do not over-promise in the second half of the Seven Point Plan, as that could result in negative word-of-mouth. We only want to commit to what we can actually achieve with the resources we have available to us.

That's not to say that we should question our vision or reduce our long-term "lofty" goals — far from it! It just means we should recognise the limit of our physical capability at a specific point in time. Every step we take in the early stages should directly contribute to the bigger steps we want to take in the longer term. By conducting this reality check here, it helps us focus on a tighter initial scope which will ultimately help us achieve our long-term goals.

When Brian actually sat down and thought about it, he decided that opening a second coffee shop within a year was probably going to stretch him a bit too far and put his business at far too great a risk. He, therefore, adjusted his plans to open a second outlet a year or two later — which means he won't get distracted by grandiose ideas in the early stages of establishing and growing his fledgling business.

Step 5: The Seven Point Plan (Part 2)

Having defined what he believes to be realistically achievable, although a little ambitious, Brian set himself a number of business and marketing objectives to achieve his goal and completed the second half of his Seven Point Plan as follows:

Business Objectives

Business Objective 1	To refine and document the business model for the first coffee shop by reviewing accurate monthly management accounts with a professional advisor (Gemma). This will also involve keeping a diary on at least a weekly basis, which will record all operational activity, challenges, decisions and changes to the model as it evolves, in addition to keeping the 21st Century Marketing Blueprint and M.A.G.I.C. Marketing Matrix updated at least once a quarter.
Business Objective 2	To break even within six months.
Business Objective 3	To be at 50% capacity for the early morning peak period (7:30-9:00 a.m. Monday to Saturday), taking an average of £3 per transaction by the end of month three, increasing to 75% by the end of month six.
Business Objective 4	To be at 50% capacity for the lunchtime peak period (12:30-2:00 p.m. Monday to Friday), taking an average of £6 per transaction by the end of month three, increasing to 75% by the end of month six.
Business Objective 5	To make sufficient profit by the end of the first year to be able to take a net personal income equal to 50% of his previous net annual salary from the Ford dealership.
Business Objective 6	To achieve a net profit of 200% of his previous annual salary by the end of the second year.
Business Objective 7	Open a second coffee shop funded by the profits of the first coffee shop by the end of year three.

Not all of Brian's business objectives will be supported by specific marketing objectives, as they will be the result of other activities, such as documenting his business model or breaking even within six months. Initially, he decides to focus his marketing activities on the early morning and lunchtime trade. If members of the other segments he has defined also pay him a visit, then that's a bonus — not an objective.

Marketing Objectives

Marketing Objective 1	To make 10,000 people aware his doors are open from 7:30 a.m. for a great cup of coffee on the way to work within the first six months.	Business Objective 3
Marketing Objective 2	To make 20,000 members of the local community aware his coffee shop has opened and has a £3 lunchtime special between 12:30 p.m. and 2 p.m. within the first six months.	Business Objective 4

Brian decides that his lunchtime trade is probably going to generate more cash flow than the early morning trade and, hence, he wants to focus the majority of his resources on this segment.

Marketing Communication Objectives (Lunchtime Snackers)

Marketing Communication Objective	Tool/ Channel	Description	Supports Marketing Objective
Marketing Communication Objective 1	Advertising	1) Place an advert in the local weekly newspaper with a coupon code for a free cookie to accompany every cup of coffee when the coupon is presented at the till. Objective is to redeem at least fifty coupons per week for the period of the six-week campaign.	Business Objective 2
		2) Place an advert in the local monthly community magazine with a different coupon code for a free cookie to accompany every cup of coffee when the coupon is presented at the till. Objective is to redeem at least forty coupons per month for the three months the campaign will run.	
		3) Running a series of radio adverts instructing listeners to quote "Radio XYZ" at the till to claim their free Belgian waffle, with the objective being to redeem at least one hundred waffles per week for the four-week radio campaign.	
Marketing Communication Objective 2	Printed Material	Personally distribute 240 flyers to local businesses during the first three months and speak to at least one person in each business.	Marketing Objective 2
		Hand out 1,000 flyers in the street every Saturday morning for the first month, with a 10% introductory discount code for purchases made that day on presentation of the flyer.	
		Hand out 2,000 date-stamped loyalty cards in the first month to every new customer served and keep a record of cards redeemed for a free drink.	

Brian really wants to keep his marketing activities as simple as possible so the majority of his resources will be focused on the lunchtime snackers' segment. However, he also wants to attract the early morning workers and decides to run a short and simple radio advertising campaign during the morning drive time. The salesperson from the local radio station has offered him a special deal on six fifteen-second slots between 6 a.m. and 9 a.m. every weekday morning for the first month and has advised him to run these directly after the news bulletin both on and half past the hour to attract his target audience's attention. He considers this to be a wise investment for not a lot of extra money, as it will also raise awareness with his prime target, the lunchtime snackers, while they drive to work. Therefore, his marketing communication objective for this group may look like this:

Marketing Communication Objectives (Early Morning Workers)

Marketing Communication Objective 3	Advertising	Run a radio advert on the local radio station between 6 and 9 a.m. to attract the interest of members of his target segment as they drive to work.	Marketing Objective 1

In a perfect world, Brian would only include one message in each piece of marketing communication. However, there are occasions when it actually makes economic sense to combine multiple messages — but with one proviso! Every piece of communication should have one primary message and if it can be supplemented by a secondary message, without detracting from the primary message, that can be a sensible way to optimise limited resources. For example, the majority of his PR and posters will be to attract the attention of the lunchtime snackers — i.e. that he has a great offer for the lunchtime snackers between 12:30 p.m. and 2 p.m. It will cost no extra to add a line or two at the bottom of the posters stating that he is open from 7:30 a.m. every morning for those who want to grab a great coffee on the way to work.

In this example, he delivers two very closely related messages to two closely related segments of his target audience, because the people he wants to talk to can actually be members of both segments at the same time. By contrast, it would not be appropriate to include an all-encompassing message to try and attract the morning mothers or market day pensioners, as this would ultimately confuse his primary target audience and his messages would be lost.

Where Brian wants to communicate with two very close segments (which could be collectively referred to as "local office workers") he has defined a few marketing communication objectives where, by using the appropriate tools, he can communicate more than one specific marketing objective and optimise his return on marketing investment.

Marketing Communication Objectives (Both Segments)

Marketing Communication Objective 4	Public Relations	Achieve one free PR article in the local print media per month for the first three months.	Marketing Objective 1 & 2
Marketing Communication Objective 5	Personal Selling	Hand out five posters per day (Monday to Friday) during the first six weeks to customers willing to display them in their offices or other public places they have responsible access to, such as a community centre, doctor's surgery, sports hall, etc. (Definitely not "fly posting"!)	Business Objective 2

Marketing Communication Objective 6	Website	Achieve an average length of stay of sixty seconds for new visitors to the website with 25% of visitors viewing an average of three pages per visit over the initial three-month campaign.	Business Objective 2
		Note: Brian has no real traffic generation strategy to start with and people will probably find his website by either typing in the URL advertised on his other marketing material or purely by accident. What he is interested in is that when they do arrive on his home page, they stay for a while and visit a couple of pages rather than just leave straight away. This will give him the comfort of knowing what he has to say is actually of interest to his target audience.	
Marketing Communication Objective 7	Facebook	Create one post per week for the first three months and achieve an average of ten "likes" per post and build a following of one hundred by the end of three months.	Marketing Objective 1 & 2

To make best use of his limited resources, Brian is actually running three "mini-campaigns" during the first three months of trading. The first is specifically targeted at the lunchtime snackers; the second is a short radio campaign aimed at the early morning workers; and the third campaign is directed at both segments.

It is a good idea to plan out the campaigns in the form of a Gantt chart or project plan (see figure 3.2) to give a visual, high level overview of what is happening and when. This is a very powerful, useful and yet simple management tool and really helps coordinate all activities and keep on top of things. You can create a campaign plan on paper, in a spreadsheet, or using one of the many project management software applications available on the internet, many of which are free to use.

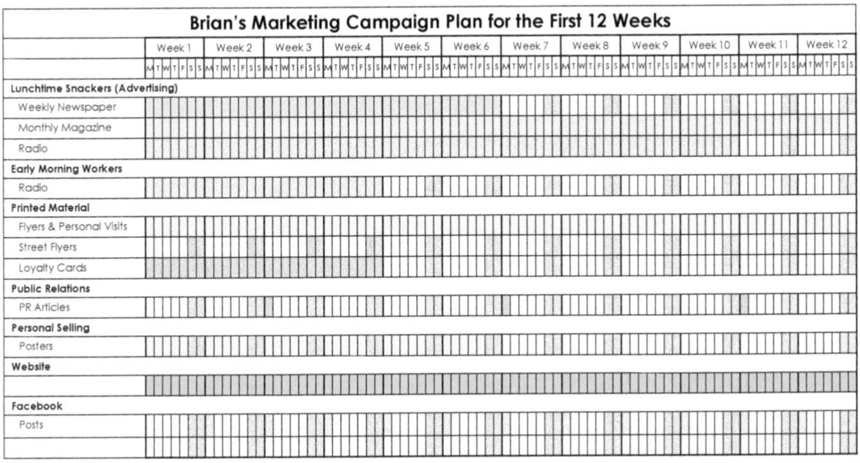

Figure 3.2 Brian's Campaign Plan

Step 6: Defining and Executing Marketing Campaigns

In Step 6, Brian focus exclusively on defining and executing his individual marketing campaigns using the Value Proposition Communicator. This relies on creating and developing highly relevant and targeted messages to deliver to specific segments of his target audience. You may want to deliver more than one version of your message over a period of time and, indeed, your message may be one of a sequence, if you have a long or complex customer journey.

In Brian's case, each message is really "short and sweet" given the nature of what he has to offer. Because he wants to keep things simple, he has decided to treat the early morning workers' segment as just a single segment at this stage. However, he does recognise there will be some behavioural differences between those who want to sit down and enjoy a coffee in his coffee shop and those who want to "grab and go". Therefore, he wants to create a highly relevant and targeted message for people like Nigel and a very similar message for Janice, but one which speaks to her specifically. He decides to create what is, effectively, two different messages (which can easily be used to create two separate adverts), which can be alternated during his radio and press adverts and, hence, serve the informational needs of both members of his target segment.

In this example, both messages are targeted at the morning workers; they have a common purpose and the outcome, as far as Brian is concerned, is identical. Using the TAPAS Message Development Framework discussed earlier, he has defined his campaign message as follows:

TAPAS Message Development Framework

Target Audience	Purpose	Action	Sequence
Early morning workers	Create the awareness that the coffee shop opens at 7:30 a.m. and it caters for those who want to sit in, as well as providing an early morning express takeaway service.	▲ Visit the coffee shop between 7:30 a.m. and 9:00 a.m. ▲ Redeem the special offer vouchers/ promotional codes.	This is the first message in the campaign sequence.

Finding the right words to say is usually the hardest bit; however, Brian has the Message Development Matrix at his fingertips and has broken his message down into the nine individual components. Based on the persona he has previously defined, he wants to create one message specifically to speak to Nigel and another very similar message to speak directly to Janice. As far as he is concerned, the outcome to his business is identical, i.e. selling coffee between 7:30 a.m. and 9:00 a.m. His objective is to sell as many as possible during this period and creating and delivering two separate messages will add a little variety to his campaign, which should make it more memorable in the minds of his target audience.

Message Development Matrix (Message 1: Nigel)

Headline	Do you need somewhere quiet to gather your thoughts before you start your day?
Sub-Headline	Sometimes all you need is a quiet half hour to gather your thoughts and plan your day before the mayhem starts.
Salutation	Dear Busy Professional
Problem	The phone rings and people clamour for your attention from the time you sit at your desk, which means you never get time to plan your day and achieve your goals. You often have to work late to catch up, but a little quiet time to plan at the start of the day would make all the difference.
Solution	Come to Brian's coffee shop on your way to work and plan your day, in peace, over a great cup of coffee.
Benefits	When you get to work you'll feel relaxed, in control and ready to face the day ahead.
Offer	Between 7:30 a.m. and 9:00 a.m. Monday to Friday you can get a free cookie or Belgian waffle to enjoy with your coffee.
Call to Action	Call in to Brian's coffee shop between 7:30 a.m. and 9:00 a.m. and sit down to enjoy a great morning coffee away from the office.
Summary	Enjoy a great coffee with a free snack, plan your day in peace and feel revitalised and in control when you take your first morning call.

Message Development Matrix (Message 2: Janice)

Headline	Never have time to catch your breath in the morning?
Sub-Headline	Do you arrive at your desk in the morning feeling like you've done a day's work before you even start?
Salutation	Dear Morning Hero
Problem	Mornings are always a rush trying to get the kids to school on time, you often never have time for yourself.
Solution	Come to Brian's coffee shop on your way to work and grab a great cup of coffee to enjoy in the office.
Benefits	If you don't have time for a decent cup of coffee at home before you leave for work, here's a great solution to help you start your day on a high note.
Offer	Fast takeaway service for those in a hurry between 7:30 a.m. and 9:00 a.m. Monday to Friday. Plus, you can get a delicious free cookie or Belgian waffle to enjoy with your coffee when you get to the office.
Call to Action	Call in to Brian's coffee shop between 7:30 a.m. and 9:00 a.m. on your way to work.
Summary	Enjoy a great coffee with a free snack the minute you arrive at your desk.

Whether Brian chooses to write the adverts himself or whether he gets some help from somebody else, he has thought through each element of the Message Development Matrix and given them plenty of material to write the final advertising copy. Not only that, the core messages that will be delivered to his target audience will be consistent across all tools or channels. This gives him the greatest chance of having his messages heard and remembered by his target audience.

Step 7: The Results

Step 7
Monitor your results based on
KPIs (DRD)

Finally, once his business was up and running, Brian kept a close check on his key performance indicators, which were reflected in a very simple Dynamic Results Dashboard that he built with Gemma's help in an Excel spreadsheet.

A good place to start is to consider the critical success factors and, for that, three key numbers are; visitors, conversions and sales. Quite often, as in Brian's case, a visitor may automatically convert into a sale, but for longer purchase cycles, such as a car or TV, visitors and conversions can take longer and may mean different things in different businesses. For example, if you sell double glazing, a visitor may equate to an enquiry and a conversion may equate to the initial home visit. If you have primarily an online business, a visitor may mean a visitor to your website and a conversion may be the exchange of an email address for a free report, which will enable you to collect the email address for future email marketing. It is important to understand what each piece of data actually means in your business context and in relation to your customers' journey.

Brian has decided that he wants to monitor the number of visitors to his coffee shop to gauge the "footfall" because he has very limited space and, hence, a limited number of tables and seats. An important number for Brian to monitor is the length of time customers spend in his coffee shop in relation to the amount of money they spend. As far as "conversion" is concerned, he wants to try and keep note of how frequently people walk into his coffee shop and walk out without buying anything and then try and assess the reason why. For example, if they walk out because they are in a hurry in the morning and the service is slow, he needs to adjust his serving process to minimise the waiting time. If they walk out because they merely change their mind, then there's probably not a lot he can do about it. It's going to be very difficult for Brian to gauge how many visitors do not convert to a sale given that the majority will, so the best he can probably do is to keep a note (either mentally or on a notepad by the side of the till) when he or any member of his staff notices that customers leave before being served. This is referred to as "exception reporting", i.e. reporting on the number of people who do not follow the standard process. On his Dynamic Results Dashboard, Brian will note these under the KPI of "leavers".

In a high-volume, small transaction value environment, maximising the number of transactions is a critical success factor. Therefore, he will need to keep a close eye on the number of sales he is making compared to his total capacity.

Thinking back to the Control element of the M.A.G.I.C. Marketing Matrix, Brian has decided what he wants to measure, how frequently he wants to monitor these key performance indicators and what he needs to do to manage them, as noted in the table below:

Dynamic Results Dashboard

Measure	Monitor	Manage	Data Source/ Comment
Total Sales	Daily	Record on management summary spreadsheet each day. Analyse weekly and monthly.	Till transactions / monthly management accounts.
Expenses	Weekly	Enter relevant transactional data into the accounting system on a daily or weekly basis. Transactional reporting from accounting system to provide necessary insights.	Accounting system/monthly management accounts.
Profit	Monthly	Part of month end accounting process with Gemma.	Monthly management accounts.
Stock costs	Monthly	Monitor supplier invoices with agreed contractual terms.	Monthly management accounts.
Stock levels	Daily	Manual stock control/usage monitoring process.	Physical stock on site/inventory recorded in accounting system and reorder frequency.
Number of "leavers"	Ongoing	Manual recording and review daily. Observation of queue length at the till and time of the day.	Notepad by the side of the till.
Percentage occupancy	Ongoing observation/ transactional till data	May take samples during the day and record in a notebook - probably best "guesstimate" based on what's observed in real time.	Manual recording and data from the till relating to the number of sales consumed on the premises.
Average time per visit	Ongoing observation	May take samples during the day and record in a notebook to estimate average time per visit.	Notebook/till data.
Number and type of takeaway sales vs. in-house consumption	Daily	Record these figures daily and if possible note the time of day the peak consumption period occur for each type. This data needs to be analysed frequently for maximum insights.	Till data.

Using the 21st Century Marketing System Brian built a fairly comprehensive but, most importantly, a usable 21st Century Marketing Blueprint for his new business. One of the primary benefits is that Brian feels totally in control of his new venture (and, hence, his destiny) because it allows him to easily manage every aspect of his daily activities whilst keeping one eye firmly focused on the bigger picture. By monitoring the most important critical success factors and key performance indicators, he significantly reduces his personal risk and, hence, increases his overall chance of success.

Case Study Part 2:
Brian's Coffee Shop (Established Stage)

This is the second part of the case study on Brian's coffee shop. He's now been running for about eighteen months and, whilst things are now going quite well, it's been a bit of a roller coaster ride and certainly a very steep learning curve. Since he opened, he has been working diligently with Gemma to keep a close eye on all the important numbers. He's also now got a good team around him who all enjoy working in the coffee shop and he has a decent number of regular customers who seem to like what he has to offer.

Of the original five segments he defined when he first developed his 21st Century Marketing Blueprint, he has managed to build his regular trade around all but one: the "business meetings" segment. He made a concerted effort to attract these business people but found that they were dissatisfied mainly by the noisy environment caused by all his other happy customers. He quickly realised that the morning mothers and their young children were not really a compatible combination with those trying to talk over technical or business-related matters or make important business phone calls. He talked to the "business meeting" people and they told him what they needed. This was a very valuable exercise in customer feedback and a crucial part of his environmental scanning process. The net findings were that they all loved his products but the environment didn't work for them.

He held a focus group with several of his regular business customers after work one evening where he gave them free coffee and cakes in exchange for an hour of their time. They talked about the kind of facility they wanted and came up with the concept of "Brian's Business Lounge — a coffee shop dedicated to the business professional on the go". This was quite a radical departure from Brian's original idea and a concept that excited him and Mary, as well as the business meeting crowd. All agreed it had to be done properly and Brian suggested it would take about a year to find suitable premises, set things up, train new staff and get everything ready to go. Fuelled with the success of his first coffee shop, Brian's entrepreneurial mind started working overtime before Gemma brought him back to earth. "Yes, it's a great idea", she tells him, but warns, "It may divert critical resources from your first venture and you need to consolidate your existing operations before you expand".

Both he and Mary agree that it's good advice and revisit their 21st Century Marketing Blueprint. Whilst they've been bubbling along quite nicely for some time now, what they lack is a customer retention strategy and they realise they should create and implement one, before they focus all their attention on their second venture. By strategically and actively engaging with their existing customers they should build a more loyal customer base, which will give Brian a little "insurance" if a competitor comes onto the scene and tries to steal his customers.

Having refreshed himself on the 21st Century Marketing System and some of the underlying theory, Brian reviews his business data and estimates that about 70% of his business comes from his established customer base. This obviously means that 30% are still new customers so he cannot completely stop his customer acquisition marketing activities. He also realises that it costs up to twenty times more to acquire a new customer than retain an existing one, so he decides to scale back and allocate 20% of his marketing budget to his customer acquisition marketing activities and the remaining 80% to develop and implement a customer retention marketing strategy.

Whilst Brian has learnt an awful lot about marketing since he started his business, customer retention is completely new to him. Gemma persuades him to seek the help of a marketing professional and recommends Alex, one of her other accountancy clients. Brian agrees to start with one day's consultancy to "test the waters" and explore some ideas. Alex runs a small local marketing agency and quickly gets to grips with what Brian is trying to achieve. Brian learns that a full-blown customer retention strategy can be very resource-intensive and requires quite a bit of specialist IT and marketing skills.

Fortunately, Brian understands the importance of relationship marketing and that he needs to stay in continuous contact with his customers to keep his business and brand "top of mind". Alex recommends Brian builds a customer database, so he can market to individuals on a more personal level and deepen the relationship with members of each segment of his target market.

This will mean capturing some key details, such as the first name, surname, email address, telephone number and a number of other details about his customers and managing them in some type of "customer relationship management system" (CRM) so Brian can personalise his marketing. They agree the best way to implement this is with a loyalty card scheme, where he will offer every customer the opportunity to receive points that can be redeemed against future purchases from his coffee shop. This type of scheme is very common in the retail sector and, with a modest investment in IT, can facilitate ongoing engagement with existing customers and encourage repeat purchases.

One of the significant, technological advancements in recent years has been the proliferation of complex services available via the web. There are many software companies who provide their business solutions on a "software as a service" (SaaS) basis i.e. pay-as-you-go. These solutions are often scalable and can be easily integrated with existing websites with just a little development effort. The ongoing maintenance and development costs are the responsibility of the software providers and the cost to clients, such as Brian, can be as low as just a few hundred dollars per month (depending on the extent to which he uses their service).

Note: Pricing for these types of systems tends to be in USD, as many software vendors are based in the US and have a huge home-based target market. At the time of writing, a solution costing $199 pcm equates to around £150 pcm or £1,800 pa, which, of course, is a tax-deductible business expense.

Brian is no techie and certainly does not want to get involved in any IT-related development. He does, however, appreciate the benefits of what the IT solution recommended by Alex will do for his business and they agree that this is an ideal opportunity to redevelop Brian's website now that he knows more about what he really needs. He agrees to appoint Alex as his project manager to work with a local website company to develop and implement his new website, with CRM and loyalty card system integration. This gives Brian the technological infrastructure he needs to progress to the next level, at a realistic level of investment and at minimal risk.

A couple of months later, Brian has his new fully integrated website up and running and continues to work with Alex to develop the rest of his customer retention marketing strategy. Brian realises that whilst hiring a consultant may be an expensive undertaking, the benefits they bring to his business can be immense and quickly show a return on his investment. Alex's primary role is to develop the customer retention strategy and train Brian and his key staff on how to implement it and keep it up-to-date on a regular basis. Gemma has strongly recommended that Brian keep Alex on a monthly retainer for at least six months after the project has finished, to provide any additional support and training whilst he fully gets to grips with his new system.

If Brian is to achieve his longer-term goal of opening his second shop, the business lounge, he needs to free himself up from the day-to-day operation of his existing business. Having taken advice from both Gemma and Alex, he agrees it will be a sensible idea to appoint a manager to take over the running of his existing coffee shop. Sally, one of their two full-time members of staff, is an ideal candidate as she is ambitious, hardworking and gets on well with all the customers. They also agree that it will take several months for Sally to become comfortable in her new role and for Brian to train her sufficiently and "hand over the reins".

Moving on, Brian reviews the seven steps to implementing the 21st Century Marketing System with Alex and they agreed there is very little to change in terms of the M.A.G.I.C. Marketing Matrix. In fact, it's just the "retain" and "engage" elements of the "Group" section that they need to focus on in Step 1.

There is nothing to change in step 2 and Alex has made a significant contribution to addressing the issues relating to the machines, manpower and methods in step 3, thus giving Brian the extra operational capability he needs to actually implement a customer retention strategy. With this extra operational capacity, the reality check in step 4 is satisfied and they can now move on to step 5, where they set some new business, marketing and marketing communication objectives as well as define the associated marketing campaigns to achieve them.

Brian has been talking to a number of his regular customers to find out what they like about his service, why they keep coming back and what he can do to improve their customer experience. The early morning workers, like Nigel, who enjoy their morning coffee at one of Brian's tables seem very happy and, in particular, enjoy their morning snacks, such as a bacon sandwich. However, feedback from Janice and a few of her colleagues, who just want a takeaway, suggests that they occasionally get frustrated by the slow service when they're in a desperate hurry to get to work on time.

When reviewing the various segments of his target audience, Brian decides he actually wants to split his early morning workers segment into two: one for customers like Nigel who want to sit at a table and one for customers, like Janice, who prefer a takeaway to drink at the office. He now wants to treat them separately and deliver different messages to each subgroup and thinks he can now provide a superior service (now that he understands his customers better) by creating two separate and distinct personas.

The morning mothers also seem quite happy, although several suggest there could be a wider range of drinks and healthy snacks for their young children. A couple have also suggested it would be nice to be able to talk to their friends, without worrying about the young children for half an hour whilst they drink their coffee and chat. They suggest some form of crèche would be a good idea, although they do appreciate that in the coffee shop that's somewhat impractical. Feedback from the lunchtime snackers is also very positive, although several did comment that they would like a wider variety of food choices, which would encourage them to come more frequently.

As for the casual shoppers, many of them are quite cost-conscious and, whilst they do enjoy more than one cup of coffee, Brian's speciality coffee prices stretch their budget beyond a second cup. The shoppers who come on market day have begun to use Brian's coffee shop as a social meeting place to meet their friends and would prefer something a little more substantial than just a snack on their weekly outing. For some, it's one of the highlights of their week and they look forward to their weekly treats.

Brian decides to leave the personas for the morning mothers, lunchtime snackers and casual shoppers exactly as they are. However, as he is now getting a significant amount of trade on market day, due to specific marketing promotions he's run, he decides to create a persona for this new segment.

It's clear from the feedback from his "business meetings" segment that he cannot meet their needs. So he decides it's best if he removes them from the groups within his target audience to whom he actively markets. This does not mean he won't market to them in the future — he will when he opens his business lounge — but, for now, it is just not appropriate to market to them specifically. If he does, he's wasting his money and potentially damaging his reputation. He wants to avoid any negative word-of-mouth, however minor, deciding even comments like "Brian's coffee shop is rather noisy" sprinkled over social media, are best avoided.

Retention Objectives

The introduction of a customer retention marketing strategy is a significant enhancement to Brian's original business model. He, therefore, needs to set some associated business objectives which, in turn will have a number of critical success factors. These are summarised in the table below:

Business Objectives

Business Objective BR1	Develop and implement the new website with CRM and loyalty card integration within three months.
Business Objective BR2	Train Brian and other key members of staff to be totally competent and confident in the use of the new system and self-sufficient within six months.
Business Objective BR3	Split the morning workers into two separate segments: one for those that drink in — and one for the "takeaways".
Business Objective BR4	Achieve at least 500 "sign-ups" to the new loyalty system within the first month, increasing to 2,000 members by the end of the third month and capture sufficient customer details, to facilitate at least personal marketing by email.
Business Objective BR5	Increase the proportion of business coming from repeat customers to 80% of total takings within six months of introducing the new loyalty card–based system.
Business Objective BR6	Achieve 0.5% of total sales attributable to the redemption of loyalty card points within six months of launching the system.

The next step is to define the marketing objectives to support these business objectives. However, as before, there are a number of business objectives that do not lend themselves to the creation of specific marketing objectives, for example, the development and implementation of the new system or training the staff in how to use it. Other business objectives, such as the number of sign-ups to the new loyalty card system, are very specific and SMART. The success of Brian's customer retention strategy relies on its rapid adoption by all customers, both new and existing. Therefore, the majority of his marketing focus will be on promoting the scheme and encouraging sign up.

Marketing Objectives

Marketing Objective	Description	Supports Business Objective
Marketing Objective MR1	Make every customer aware of the new loyalty card scheme and the benefits it offers and achieve 2,000 members within three months.	Business Objective BR4 & BR6
Marketing Objective MR2	Generate at least two sales per week for 50% of the loyalty scheme members within the first three months.	Business Objective BR5
Marketing Objective MR3	Engage more proactively with social media marketing and email marketing. Send out emails and post on at least two social media platforms several times a week within a month of implementing the new system.	Business Objective BR5 & BR6
Marketing Objective MR4	Capture as many details as possible to populate the new CRM system, to allow detailed reporting by segment.	Business Objective BR4

Again, the marketing objectives translate into a number of marketing communication objectives, which should all ultimately support one or more business objectives. But first Brian, once again, refers to the New Engagement Paradigm to select the most appropriate traditional, digital and social media tools to complete his marketing communication objectives, as shown in figure 3.3.

Figure 3.3 Retention Tools of the New Engagement Paradigm

Retention Marketing Communication Objectives

Brian will have to split his marketing communication objectives into two phases. Phase 1 will be to promote the loyalty card scheme and encourage as many sign ups as possible. Once people have signed up and given him their contact details, he can send them more personalised messages. Phase 2 will then focus on delivering personalised segment-specific messages.

The practicalities of how the scheme will work are as follows: Customers will be given or will take a leaflet containing a loyalty card and instructions on how to register on the website. The objective is to link the pre-printed membership ID number on the card with a physical person in the CRM database and for this to occur the customer needs to register their details on the website. If they don't want to do it themselves, they can complete the form on the leaflet and give it to Brian's staff. Brian has also purchased a small, cheap laptop he can lend to customers whilst they are in the shop to encourage them to sign up immediately. His IT support chap has restricted online access to just Brian's sign up page, so customers don't use it to surf the Web and only use it for a few minutes at a time.

His first marketing objective is: "Make every customer aware of the new loyalty card scheme and the benefits it offers from the launch day and achieve 2,000 members within three months". His target audience for these messages are his existing customers and, because he does not know them by name (at least as far as his IT system is concerned), he will have to use the channels they currently communicate through to deliver this new message. This means he will have to develop a couple of very specific marketing communication objectives.

Marketing Communication Objectives (All Segments)

Marketing Communication Objective	Tool/ Channel	Description	Supports Marketing Objective
Marketing Communication Objective 1	Printed Material	Place printed leaflets on every table next to the menu and print details of the loyalty scheme on the menus themselves. Print new posters to advertise the scheme in the coffee shop window and to give to some of the regular customers to put up in their offices, to replace the original posters.	Marketing Objective MR1 & MR4
Marketing Communication Objective 2	Personal Selling	Inform every customer of the new loyalty scheme at the point of sale and offer them a leaflet detailing the scheme.	Marketing Objective MR1 & MR4
Marketing Communication Objective 3	Website	Add a new section on the home page of the website advertising the new loyalty card scheme and direct visitors to register on the new landing page.	Marketing Objective MR1 & MR4
Marketing Communication Objective 4	Facebook	Add a comment at the bottom of each post informing customers about the new loyalty card scheme with a link to the new membership sign up landing page on the website.	Marketing Objective MR1 & MR4

This will be an ongoing campaign and the numbers of leaflets and posters taken will be an indication of the success of communicating his awareness message about the scheme, as will the number of actual sign ups.

Once Brian has persuaded a number of his regular customers to engage in the loyalty card scheme, he will have to communicate with them regularly to keep them engaged and to see a return on his investment.

Early Morning Workers ("Takeaway")

Looking at the feedback from each segment, Brian first decides he needs to improve the service for "Early Morning Workers (Takeaway)" customers, such as Janice. He needs to identify exactly who these people are and capture them in his database, marking them with a flag signifying which segment they belong to. He's not quite sure how to cater for their specific, quick service needs and decides the best way he can find out is by talking to them individually. Now that he has their contact details, he can talk to this specific segment by email and ask for the suggestions — perhaps even using a short survey from an online survey tool such as Survey Monkey. Email marketing for this segment will be one of his primary retention tools at this stage.

Once he has the replies and has considered the responses, he may decide that for a couple of weeks from 7.30am to 9.00am it's worth trying having a separate service area by the door that only serves a limited selection of drinks, such as filter coffee (rather than the speciality coffees). He needs to communicate this to his "Early Morning Workers (Takeaway)" customers and, again, email is a sensible tool to achieve this marketing communication objective. He will send out the survey request twice, just in case some people don't reply, but he will be careful not to send the survey a second time to those who have already replied, as that would really damage his brand!

Marketing Communication Objectives
Segments: Early Morning Workers (Takeaway)

Marketing Communication Objective	Tool/ Channel	Description	Supports Marketing Objective
Marketing Communication Objective 5	Email	Send an email to all members identified as belonging to the "Early Morning Workers' (Takeaway)" segment asking them to complete a short survey. Objective is to achieve a 25% response rate within three days.	Marketing Objective MR1 & MR4
Marketing Communication Objective 6	Email	Email all members of this segment with details of the new "Grab & Go" morning service for a limited selection of the menu and repeat it once per week for the duration of the campaign. Objective is to achieve a 50% open rate within three days.	Marketing Objective MR2 & MR3

Morning Mothers

For the morning mothers, email may not be the best tool as many have said they don't actually get time to check their emails very frequently. Instead, they preferred to rely on Facebook and other social media platforms to communicate with their friends. This is more than sufficient information to convince Brian he needs to actively engage with Facebook and Alex recommends that he set up a Facebook page dedicated to this group of customers. His biggest challenge now is to get the morning mothers visiting his new Facebook page on a regular basis and sharing it with their friends. On all of his promotional materials in the coffee shop, such as the menus, till receipts and even the loyalty cards, he asks them to "like" Brian's coffee shop on Facebook and "share" with their friends. This at least gives him a small social media following to encourage a conversation. His primary use of Facebook, in this example, is to promote special offers and communicate any other information that might be of interest to this specific segment.

One particular idea he wants to try is to employ two qualified child-minders for two hours on a Tuesday morning, to entertain and look after the younger children at a couple of tables in the corner of the coffee shop. His idea is to have them within full view of their mothers, but have his two professionals look after up to three children each. This will take up the space of a few tables for just two hours a week and give the mothers a reason to use his coffee shop as their regular meeting point. Brian plans to make a small charge per child to cover his additional costs. He's asked Alex to help him create some "remarkable" content that will generate buzz on social media and get some free PR.

Marketing Communication Objectives
Segments: Morning Mothers

Marketing Communication Objective	Tool/ Channel	Description	Supports Marketing Objective
Marketing Communication Objective 7	Printed Material	Print the details of his Facebook page on all offline and online marketing material asking them to "like" his page.	Marketing Objective MR2 & MR3
Marketing Communication Objective 8	Facebook	Post a special weekly offer targeted at this segment on Facebook once per week, giving a promotional code for a free child's drink to be redeemed at the till when the loyalty card is presented.	Marketing Objective MR2 & MR3
Marketing Communication Objective 9	Facebook	Write a fresh post once per week promoting special events the Morning Mothers may find attractive, such as the crèche facility between 9:30 a.m. and 11:30 a.m. Additionally, at the end of each Tuesday, post regular pictures of the children having fun, to keep the information fresh and encourage "sharing". Of course, he'll need the mothers' permission to take and share the photos, but if he can get them to take them on their smart phones and share them themselves — all the better.	Marketing Objective MR2 & MR3

Lunchtime Snackers

He anticipates that not all of his lunchtime snackers' segment will bother with the loyalty card and that he must communicate with them in a different way. He is also aware, because he's talked to his customers, that many companies block the use of social media sites at work. Therefore, anything he puts on Facebook is highly unlikely to reach this target audience, unless they use Facebook on their personal smartphones. They do, however, have access to his website and he decides it is far better to utilise this medium to communicate with the majority of his lunchtime snackers' segment. There will, of course, be several members of this segment who do have access to social media during normal working hours and Alex advises him to merely use Facebook and Twitter to direct members of his target audience to his website who are active on these platforms. For example, a short tweet saying, "Click here to see today's lunchtime special at Brian's coffee shop", is all he needs. The link will take them to the website landing page.

Marketing Communication Objectives
Segments: Lunchtime Snackers

Marketing Communication Objective	Tool/ Channel	Description	Supports Marketing Objective
Marketing Communication Objective 10	Website	Post the "weekly lunchtime special" menu on the appropriate landing page of the website every Monday morning with a picture of the daily dishes and attract at least 250 views per week within three months.	Marketing Objective MR2 & MR3
Marketing Communication Objective 11	Facebook	Write a daily post each morning encouraging customers to view and "like" today's daily special on the website.	Marketing Objective MR2 & MR3
Marketing Communication Objective 12	Twitter	Write a daily tweet each morning to encourage customers to view today's daily special on the website and share it with their followers.	Marketing Objective MR2 & MR3

Casual Shoppers

Brian wants to encourage as many of his regular customers as possible to sign up for the loyalty scheme and decides the best he can do for the casual shoppers, partly because he doesn't really understand how to communicate with them, is to rely on in-store promotions and just talk to them face-to-face to get their feedback. Many have quite a bit of time to spare and come into the coffee shop when Brian actually has the time to have a chat with them. They see the coffee shop as part of their social scene and are not in any particular hurry, which gives Brian the opportunity to get to know them and what they require much better. He decides his best communication strategy with this segment, as far as his retention strategy is concerned, is face-to-face during the normal course of business and, therefore, cannot define any specific marketing communication objectives at this stage for this segment. This may change in the future if he decides to do any special promotions, but his primary objective is to get as many people signed up to the loyalty card scheme as possible. This is covered by previously defined, more generic marketing communication objectives.

Market Day Shoppers

His market day shoppers are just a little different. Alex suggests that many of them will not have access to the Internet or social media, particularly whilst they are wandering around the market, but points out nearly all of them have a mobile phone. The objective is to prompt them to visit Brian's coffee shop whilst they are in town on market day and Alex also suggests that a simple SMS-based marketing text could encourage them to visit Brian's coffee shop, if they receive the text whilst shopping. Location-based, mobile marketing could be an option, where a text can be sent to every mobile phone within, say, a mile of Brian's coffee shop, but this will target every mobile phone within that location. Alternatively, he could build a list of his regular market day customers' mobile phone numbers within his CRM system and just send them a personalised text once a week. The printed material and personal selling will play a key role in communicating with this segment once they are in the coffee shop, but to get them through the door, SMS will be the primary tool.

Marketing Communication Objectives
Segments: Market Day Shoppers

Marketing Communication Objective	Tool/ Channel	Description	Supports Marketing Objective
Marketing Communication Objective 13	SMS	Send a text at 10 a.m. every Wednesday (market day) to the segment identified as "Market Day Pensioners" that contains a discount code inviting them to select from the Market Day Menu when they present their loyalty cards and achieve a 30% response rate within three months.	Marketing Objective MR2 & MR3

Retention Campaigns

The purpose of planning the campaigns this way is to ensure Brian has a good high-level understanding of all of the marketing communications activities he needs to perform in order to make sure he services the individual needs of each segment. One of the key aspects of a marketing retention campaign is to keep up the communication levels with members of the target audience — between the actual transactions. Once the customers are back in Brian's coffee shop, it's very easy for him, or any member of his staff, to talk to them and build on, or recreate, that "feel-good factor".

However, whilst they are away from the coffee shop, he wants to encourage them to think fondly about his value proposition and plan their next visit. If you cast your mind back to the discussion earlier in this book on commitment and trust, you may remember that loyalty and commitment are built as a result of numerous satisfactory transactions. These transactions are not just the physical transactions where cash is exchanged for services; they also include what could be referred to as "communication transactions". This is why it is very important for Brian to keep "paying the rent" on that piece of his customers' minds that associates a great coffee experience with his coffee shop.

Based on Brian's marketing communication objectives, described above, his overall retention marketing campaign is made up of several sub-campaigns, one for each segment. His complete retention marketing campaign plan for the first twelve weeks is shown in figure 3.4.

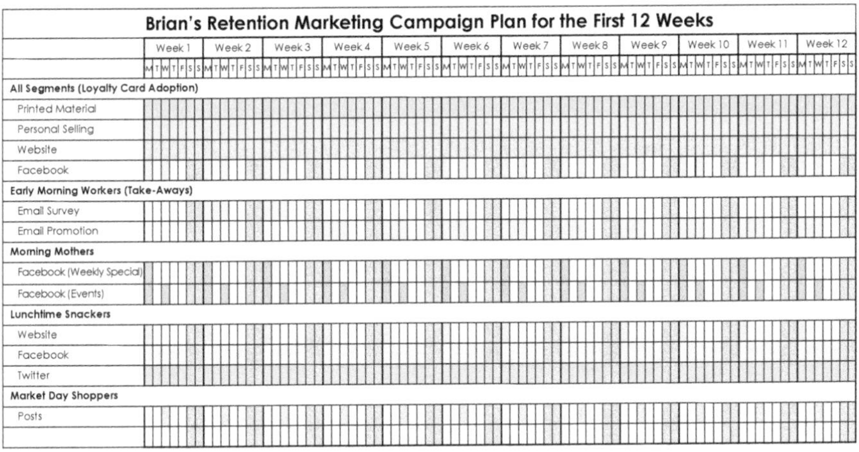

Figure 3.4 Brian's Retention Marketing Campaign Plan

Retention Messages

Brian now has to think very carefully about the specific messages he wants to deliver to each segment, to ensure he gets a consistent message across, using all the channels available to him. The first message he wants to deliver at this stage is to promote the introduction of the loyalty card scheme. He develops his message using the TAPAS framework and Message Development Matrix from the Value Proposition Communicator to ensure he develops and delivers a clear and consistent message.

Message 1: All Segments

TAPAS Message Development Framework

Target Audience	Purpose	Action	Sequence
All segments	Create awareness of the new loyalty card scheme and encourage as many sign ups as possible	▲ Take the leaflet and loyalty card and use it straight away with their current purchase ▲ Register their card online or via the form on the leaflet and enter at least the minimum details into the CRM system via the website	This is the first message in the campaign sequence

The message Brian wants to deliver to all his existing customers and he uses the Message Development Matrix to plan the key elements of his message:

Message Development Matrix

Headline	Enjoy the benefits of the Coffee Club — join today and collect points with every purchase.
Sub-Headline	Rewards for regular customers! Join the loyalty card scheme today and start collecting point toward your FREE lunch today!
Salutation	Dear Coffee Connoisseur
Problem	In the hustle and bustle of today's busy world, it's sometimes difficult to get the service you deserve that makes you feel special.
Solution	Join the Coffee Club loyalty scheme today and start collecting points toward your special treat.
Benefits	Start collecting points on every purchase and spend them on anything on our entire menu.
Offer	Sign up today and register your details to receive double points on your first purchase.
Call to Action	Log onto our exclusive members area at < Brian's website URL > and register your details to make sure your rewards are recorded.
Summary	Join the Coffee Club and reap the rewards! Don't delay — join today and start collecting points straight away!

Message 2: Segment — Early Morning Workers ("Takeaway")

There are two parts to the campaign for this segment. The first is to capture feedback via a survey and the second is to communicate how Brian intends to meet their needs, as a result of receiving their feedback.

TAPAS Message Development Framework

Target Audience	Purpose	Action	Sequence
Early Morning Workers (Takeaway)	Ask members of this segment to complete an online survey	▲ Ask members to complete the online survey referred to in the email to capture their feedback	This is the first message in the campaign sequence designed to capture feedback

He uses the Message Development Matrix to plan the key elements of a request for help message:

Message Development Matrix

Headline	In a hurry? Please tell us how we can serve you better.
Sub-Headline	We've noticed some of our customers may be waiting too long for their early morning takeaway.
Salutation	Dear Morning Hero
Problem	If you're running late and racing to get to work on time, the last thing you want is to wait ages for your morning coffee.
Solution	A faster service that allows you to grab and go as quickly as possible without having to queue.
Benefits	Don't waste time queuing to place your order, when you should be racing to the office.
Offer	If you tell us how we can serve you better and what will get your morning off to a great speedy start, we'll do everything we can to accommodate you.
Call to Action	Please complete the attached survey as soon as you can; it will only take two minutes and we really value your input.
Summary	By completing the attached survey, we can tailor our service to suit your specific needs, particularly if you're in a hurry first thing in the morning.

And now for the second part…

TAPAS Message Development Framework

Target Audience	Purpose	Action	Sequence
Early Morning Workers (Takeaway)	To communicate the launch of the new service specifically designed for this segment	▲ Ask members of the target audience to come and try this new service and provide their feedback	This is the second message in the campaign sequence designed to improve speed of service to this segment

Brian uses the Message Development Matrix to plan the key elements of a message announcing this new service:

Message Development Matrix

Headline	We've listened to you and have something new you might like to try
Sub-Headline	Come and try our new early morning express takeaway service and avoid queues.
Salutation	Dear Morning Hero
Problem	If you're running late and racing to get to work on time, the last thing you want is to wait ages for your morning coffee.
Solution	A faster service that allows you to grab and go as quickly as possible without having to queue.
Benefits	Don't waste time queuing to place your order when you should be racing to the office.

Offer	Grab your coffee in seconds and avoid the queue.
Call to Action	Come and try Brian's new early morning express takeaway service and tell us if we've got it right.
Summary	Designed specifically for those who don't have time to spare, come and try Brian's early morning express takeaway service and enjoy a great coffee as soon as you get to work.

In this example, the salutation, problem, solution, benefits and offer will be very similar because the same need is being addressed in both messages. This example shows how focusing on one segment of your target market can help you design and deliver a highly targeted message, which will resonate with them as if you were talking to them one-on-one.

Message 3: Segment — Morning Mothers

TAPAS Message Development Framework

Target Audience	Purpose	Action	Sequence
Morning Mothers	To promote the weekly special offer to this segment	▲ Use this promotional code to redeem against your purchase	This is the first message in the campaign sequence

Using the Message Development Matrix, Brian wants to develop two messages for this target audience. The first is that they are welcome in his coffee shop on the way back from the morning school run and he encourages them to bring in their toddlers between 9:30 a.m. and 11:30 a.m.

Message Development Matrix

Headline	Meet your friends and treat your toddler
Sub-Headline	Take advantage of a free healthy drink for your toddler whilst you share a coffee with your friends.
Salutation	Dear Busy Mum
Problem	Do you need a little "me time" to spend with your friends?
Solution	Meet them at Brian's coffee shop on Tuesday morning.
Benefits	Enjoy a coffee with your friends, away from the house.
Offer	Enjoy a great coffee in a child-friendly environment and treat your little one to a free healthy drink.
Call to Action	Meet the girls at Brian's coffee shop on Tuesday morning to catch up and chat.
Summary	Come to Brian's coffee shop between 9:30 a.m. and 11:30 a.m. on Tuesday mornings to enjoy a great coffee with your friends and treat your toddler to a free healthy drink.

The second message Brian wants to communicate is that the morning mothers can chat to their friends for half an hour whilst professional child-minders watch their toddlers just a short distance away.

TAPAS Message Development Framework

Target Audience	Purpose	Action	Sequence
Morning Mothers	To promote the weekly toddler supervision event	▲ Bring your toddler to join in the fun whilst you chat with your friends	This is the second message in the campaign sequence

The message Brian wants to deliver here is that the kids are safe, because they are being watched by professionals just a short distance away, meaning the morning mothers can relax and enjoy themselves whilst still being on hand.

Message Development Matrix

Headline	Toddler time at Brian's coffee shop
Sub-Headline	Let us look after your toddlers for half an hour whilst you enjoy a coffee and a chat with the girls.
Salutation	Dear Busy Mum
Problem	Do you need a little "me time" to spend with your friends without worrying about your toddler?
Solution	Meet your friends at Brian's coffee shop on Tuesday morning and let our professionally qualified child-minders watch the kids.
Benefits	Relax with a coffee and a chat whilst someone else watches your toddler.
Offer	Enjoy a great coffee in a child-friendly environment where both you and your toddlers can have some fun.
Call to Action	Meet the girls at Brian's coffee shop on Tuesday and let us watch the kids.
Summary	Come to Brian's coffee shop between 9:30 a.m. and 11:30 a.m. on Tuesday mornings to enjoy a great coffee with your friends whilst we watch the kids.

Message 4: Segment — Lunchtime Snackers

The primary purpose of this message is to promote the "specials" menu, which Brian changes on a weekly basis to maintain interest in his selection and keep the menu fresh.

TAPAS Message Development Framework

Target Audience	Purpose	Action	Sequence
Lunchtime Snackers	To communicate the weekly "specials" lunchtime menu to this segment	▲ Visit the coffee shop and order from the weekly specials lunchtime menu	This is the first message in the campaign sequence

To raise awareness and interest in his "specials" lunchtime menu and to encourage take up and use of the loyalty card scheme, Brian decides to offer double reward points from this menu for the three-month promotional period, to try and determine the types of food his customers prefer. This will inevitably lead to greater satisfaction and, hence, loyalty, as well as minimising waste from unsold food with a very short shelf life.

Message Development Matrix

Headline	What will you try from this week's specials?
Sub-Headline	Fancy something different this week? Which one's your favourite day?
Salutation	Dear Lunchtime Diner
Problem	Limited menus can be boring.
Solution	Try something different from our ever-changing weekly specials' menu.
Benefits	There is always something new to try in addition to the regular choices.
Offer	Collect double reward points this week on every item from our special menu.
Call to Action	Visit Brian's coffee shop and select from a great variety of lunchtime treats and collect double points all this week.
Summary	There is something different to try every day on the lunchtime specials' menu at Brian's coffee shop. Earn double points to redeem against your next free lunch.

Message 5: Segment — Market Day Pensioners

Brian has just one small challenge on market day, because he doesn't want to attract market day shoppers at the expense of his usual lunchtime trade. He's noticed that many shoppers prefer to spend quite some time around the market before coming in a little later than the usual lunchtime crowd. Most cafes and other eating establishments around the town stop serving their lunchtime menu around 2 p.m. Brian sees this as an opportunity and wants to encourage his market day shoppers to come as late as possible, so they don't clash with his regular lunchtime trade. He, therefore, decides to offer an incentive for those who want to dine just a little later.

TAPAS Message Development Framework

Target Audience	Purpose	Action	Sequence
Market Day Shoppers	To attract the market day shoppers and encourage them to return every week	▲ Respond to the SMS marketing text by visiting the coffee shop after 2 p.m.	This is the first message in the campaign sequence

Alex recommended that this message be delivered by SMS, so it has to be very short and sweet. In terms of developing the message using the Message Development Matrix, it's done in exactly the same way because the thought process in developing targeted messages is the same, regardless of how long they are. An SMS is a good example where just using one or two components of the Message Development Matrix are used to deliver the entire message through a short message medium. The same applies to tweets.

Message Development Matrix

Headline	Are you tired after all that market day shopping?
Sub-Headline	Why not enjoy a late lunch from Brian's market day special menu and earn double points toward your next free lunch?
Salutation	Dear Market Day Shopper
Problem	Having to rush to complete their shopping in order to make sure they have the choice of a full menu before the lunchtime session closes.
Solution	Come to Brian's coffee shop where the lunchtime period is extended on Market day.
Benefits	You don't have to rush your shopping to get your lunchtime meal on your weekly trip to the market.
Offer	Take your time to complete your shopping and receive double points with a late lunch on market day at Brian's coffee shop.
Call to Action	Come to the market day party at Brian's coffee shop between 2 p.m. and 4 p.m. and enjoy a full late lunch from our market day special menu.
Summary	Don't fight the lunchtime crowds. Take your time around the market and then relax at Brian's coffee shop with a full late lunch served from 2 p.m. to 4 p.m. every market day.

For example, the text might read "Fancy a late lunch? Earn double points on Market Day specials served from 2-4pm at Brian's coffee shop on the High Street" (121 characters).

Retention KPIs

The Dynamic Results Dashboard will be developed in exactly the same way for retention-based objectives as it is for acquisition-based objectives. Again, the key point is to focus on a few things that matter the most and can make the biggest difference, with particular focus being given to the number of visitors, the conversion rate and the number of sales.

In the following table, the column MCO refers to the specific marketing communication objective defined earlier; the column labelled MO refers to the marketing objective each marketing communication objectives supports; and the final column labelled KPI, refers to the type of data that needs to be measured, monitored and managed to ensure each marketing communication objective is actually achieved.

All Segments

MCO	Tool	Description	MO	KPIs
1	Printed Material	Place printed leaflets on every table next to the menu and print details of the loyalty scheme on the menus themselves. Print new posters to advertise the scheme in the coffee shop window and to give to some of the regular customers to put up in their offices, replacing the original posters.	1 & 4	▲ Number of leaflets and posters consumed
2	Personal Selling	Inform every customer of the new loyalty scheme at the point of sale and offer them a leaflet detailing the scheme.	1 & 4	▲ Number of leaflets distributed at the till ▲ Number of customers actually signing up to the scheme
3	Website	Add a new section on the home page of the website advertising the loyalty card scheme and direct visitors to register on the new landing page.	1 & 4	▲ The number of visitors to the website ▲ The number who click through to the landing page ▲ The number of completed customer records in the CRM system
4	Facebook	Add a comment at the bottom of each post informing customers about the new loyalty card scheme with a link to the new membership sign up landing page on the website.	1 & 4	▲ Number of "click-throughs" to the website landing page from Facebook ▲ Segment: Early Morning Workers (Takeaways)

Segment: Early Morning Workers (Takeaways)

MCO	Tool	Description	MO	KPIs
5	Email	Send an email to all members identified as belonging to the "Early Morning Workers (Takeaway)" segment asking them to complete a short survey. Objective is to achieve a 25% response rate within three days.	2 & 3	▲ Number of emails sent ▲ Number of emails opened (open rate) ▲ Length of time between sending the email and receiving a response ▲ Number of survey responses received
6	Email	Email all members of this segment with details of the new "Grab & Go" morning service for a limited selection of the menu. Repeat it once per week for the duration of the campaign. Objective is to achieve a 50% open rate within three days.	2 & 3	▲ Number of emails sent ▲ Number of emails opened (open rate) ▲ Length of time between sending the email and receiving a response ▲ Number of customers using the service (probably from till data)

Morning Mothers

MCO	Tools	Description	MO	KPIs
7	Printed Material	Print the details of his Facebook page on all offline and online marketing material asking them to "like" his page.	2 & 3	▲ Number of visitors to the Facebook page ▲ Number of "likes" generated per post
8	Facebook	Post a special weekly offer targeted at this segment on the Facebook page once per week giving a promotional code for a free child's drink, to be redeemed at the till when the loyalty card is presented.	2 & 3	▲ Number of visitors to the page per week ▲ Number of purchases resulting from the promotional codes ▲ Number of free drinks given out ▲ Number of loyalty cards presented from 9:30 a.m. to 11:30 a.m.
9	Facebook	Write a fresh post once per week promoting special events the Morning Mothers may find attractive, such as the crèche facility between 9:30 a.m. and 11:30 a.m. Additionally, at the end of each Tuesday, obtain permission and post pictures of the children having fun to keep the information fresh and encourage "sharing".	2 & 3	▲ Revenue from the crèche facility ▲ Number of toddlers catered for ▲ Average length of stay ▲ Number of sales during these events

Lunchtime Snackers

MCO	Tools	Description	MO	KPIs
10	Website	Post the "weekly lunchtime special" menu on the appropriate landing page of the website every Monday morning with a picture of the daily dishes and attract at least 250 views per week within three months.	2 & 3	▲ Number of visitors to the lunchtime specials landing page
11	Facebook	Write a daily post each morning encouraging customers to view and "like" today's daily special on the website.	2 & 3	▲ Number of views of these daily posts ▲ Number of likes generated
12	Twitter	Write a daily tweet each morning to encourage customers to view today's daily special on the website and share it with their followers.	2 & 3	▲ Number of followers ▲ Number of retweets ▲ Number of meals from the "specials" menu purchased each day ▲ Number of "specials" recorded on the same days in the loyalty card system

Market Day Shoppers

MCO	Tools	Description	MO	KPIs
13	SMS	Send a text at 10 a.m. every Wednesday (market day) to the segment identified as "Market Day Shoppers" that contains a discount code, inviting them to select from the Market Day Menu when they present their loyalty cards and achieve a 30% response rate within three months.	2 & 3	▲ Number of SMS sent ▲ Number of SMS-based discount codes redeemed ▲ Number of customers between 2 p.m. and 4 p.m. on market day ▲ Number of loyalty card transactions during these periods ▲ Average spend per transaction

The whole purpose of the Dynamic Results Dashboard is to keep a close eye on the most important numbers that make the biggest difference. It is also important to remember that it is a very flexible format and should reflect actual business needs rather than follow a prescriptive design. In the table above, Brian has identified the key performance indicators that will help him achieve each particular marketing communication objective and, in turn, their associated marketing objectives and business objectives.

Turning Your 21ˢᵗ Century Marketing Blueprint into a Business Plan

In this section, we'll turn your 21st Century Marketing Blueprint into your 21st Century Business Plan. It's important to remember that the purpose of your 21st Century Marketing Blueprint is to help you build and manage your business on an ongoing basis. Think of it as your "business building" tool. Your business plan, on the other hand, is typically used to secure the resources you need when you start your business, or when you need to expand, or if you need to refinance to achieve a specific outcome.

The key differentiator between the two is that the audience for your business plan is typically somebody outside of your business, such as your bank manager, investor, or suppliers from whom you are trying to secure a line of credit. Its primary focus is to help you secure the resources you need, so that you can start or continue to build your business. Business plans, therefore, tend to be quite formal documents and need a structure that communicates specifically with their intended target audience. By their very nature, this makes them quite unsuitable as a basis on which to run your business day-to-day, month-to-month.

What typically happens is, entrepreneurs and small business owners write their business plan because they have to, in order to secure the resources they need. Once they're up and running, they rarely look at their business plan again, although they "keep meaning to update it soon". This was certainly very prevalent in my research. It also reflects my own personal experience!

The reality is that the day-to-day pressures take over and all these good intentions go out the window. Entrepreneurs and micro-business owners, generally speaking, have a habit of becoming very tactical and reactive — particularly in terms of their marketing. They often adopt a "strategy" of trial and error, which actually increases their risk of failure massively, as evidenced by official research and the government start-up business failure rate statistics!

We typically find very formal business and marketing plans in larger, more established businesses where they have the resources and need to manage things from a very strategic perspective. At the other end of the scale, entrepreneurs and, particularly, micro-business owners, tend to react to their ever-changing business challenges with a seemingly carefree gusto, which makes them — well, entrepreneurs! There's nothing wrong with being creative and innovative; however, we could be a bit more structured about how we go about it, which increases our chance of success.

What I am critical of, is that the carefully planned strategic approaches to business development, used by bigger and well-established businesses, are too resource-intensive and, hence, impractical during the innovative start-up and early growth stages of new micro-business development. A more flexible and practical approach is needed. What fuels entrepreneurs and micro-business owners and keeps us awake at night is working out how we can craft and shape opportunities and turn them into reality. We rarely derive immense pleasure from writing long wordy documents, just to "get permission" to have a go at fulfilling our dreams!

Don't get me wrong — I'm not saying strategic planning is a bad thing. Far from it! However, I'd advocate that it just needs to be fit for purpose, to add value to the micro-business development process and not detract from it with a "one size fits all" approach.

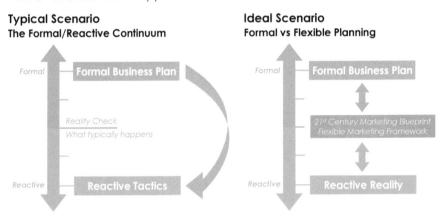

Figure 3.5 The Formal/Reactive Planning Continuum

The 21st Century Marketing System has been designed specifically to address this problem and, therefore, fits somewhere between the two extremes of the formal/reactive continuum, as shown in figure 3.5.

Depending on the nature of the business and the resources you require, your business plan may be either very formal (and, hence, closer to the top end of the complexity scale), or, if you don't need to secure a lot of resources, you may be able to manage with something nowhere near as complex or

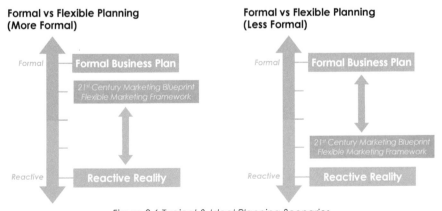

Figure 3.6 Typical & Ideal Planning Scenarios

detailed and, hence, less formal (towards the lower end of the complexity scale), as shown in figure 3.6.

It's obviously for you to work out what's appropriate in your particular situation, but whatever you decide, you should develop your 21st Century Marketing Blueprint first and then develop your 21st Century Business Plan. The reason for this is that your business plan should accurately summarise your (real) intended business activities, which you've carefully thought through and documented in detail as you've prepared your 21st Century Marketing Blueprint. Hence, why we present this chapter at the end of the book, not the beginning!

How complex you make your 21st Century Marketing Blueprint will be determined by what you want to achieve and when you want to achieve it. It is perfectly acceptable to start building your 21st Century Marketing Blueprint and implement it, one small step at a time. Certainly, in the early stages, you may want to focus on something that is not too detailed or too rigid. As you learn more about your marketplacé and adapt your business to capitalise on the opportunities you identify, you can extend your 21st Century Marketing Blueprint as you see fit and, over time, build something that is much more comprehensive.

Whatever you decide, your 21st Century Marketing Blueprint should focus on what **you** need, not what someone external to your business, such as a bank manager or investor, may require. That comes later. Their information needs will be very different to yours, although there will inevitably be some overlap. If you start by satisfying your needs first, their needs will be easier to satisfy — which means you should actually find it easier to secure the resources you require, as you'll have a much more solid and "bulletproof" plan.

By now, you should have spent quite some time defining your 21st Century Marketing Blueprint and thought about many areas pertinent to how you will build, manage and promote your business to attract your ideal customers. If you have been very diligent and completed it as suggested in this book, your plan should look like figure 3.7.

Opportunity
- ▲ Market
- ▲ Action
- ▲ Group
- ▲ Influence
- ▲ Control

Seven Point Plan
- ▲ Mission
- ▲ Vision
- ▲ Core Values
- ▲ Business Objectives
- ▲ Marketing Objectives
- ▲ Marketing Communication Objectives
- ▲ Campaign Objectives

Promise
- ▲ Value Proposition Communicator
- ▲ Message Development Matrix

Operations
- ▲ Materials
- ▲ Machines
- ▲ Manpower
- ▲ Methods
- ▲ Money

Results (KPIs)
- ▲ Measure
- ▲ Monitor
- ▲ Manage

Figure 3.7 The 21st Century Marketing Blueprint

As an entrepreneur or new business owner starting out, how formal and how comprehensive you make your business plan will be determined by somebody else's information needs. Some organisations, such as banks or business start-up support schemes, may have a particular format they require and may even have a template you can use. However, more often than not, you'll be left to your own devices and will have to create something from scratch. If you cannot find out exactly what the person you're pitching your ideas to requires, then you're going to have to make an educated guess. You can use the 21st Century Business Plan as your starting point and adapt it to suit your specific needs.

Building Your 21ˢᵗ Century Business Plan

If you look on the Internet or in a book shop, you'll find a huge number of books suggesting how a business plan should look. One thing I've noticed over the years is that when I present a bank manager or venture capitalist with a comprehensive business plan that's taken me many days or even weeks to prepare, they are not that interested in reading it. What they are interested in is fishing out the information that helps them evaluate your requirements and determine whether or not they are able to give you the resources you request. It, therefore, makes absolute sense to present your business plan in a format that provides them with the exact information they want, so they can review your proposition quickly and easily. This is particularly important if you are looking for investment from a venture capitalist or other private investor, because they tend to get a very large number of propositions across their desk every day and have to filter them based on their initial impression.

The reality is that you only have, maybe, thirty seconds to get your message across to your potential investor, although your bank manager may have a little more time. Either way, your business plan needs to start with a bang! The 21st Century Business Plan has been designed to achieve exactly that and is shown in figure 3.8.

Table of Contents

Executive Summary
- ▲ What we want to do
- ▲ Total resources identified
- ▲ Resources currently available
- ▲ Resources still required
- ▲ Return on investment

Main Body of Business Plan

Business Opportunity

Internal Capability

Target Customers

Marketing Plan

Critical Success Factors

Financial Forecasts

Financials
- ▲ Income Statement (P&L)
- ▲ Balance Sheet
- ▲ Cash Flow Forecast
- ▲ Investment/Borrowing Requirements
  - ▲ Money
  - ▲ Time
  - ▲ Risk

Supporting Information

Appendices

Figure 3.8 The 21st Century Business Plan

Remember that your reader or listener may well be time poor and it is your responsibility to "market" your ideas as effectively as possible. The Message Development Matrix, introduced in the chapter on "The Art of Effective

Communication" (see figure 2.21), is a great tool to help you develop and deliver a compelling message effectively and efficiently.

If you succeed in attracting an investor's attention at the very early stage, it then becomes absolutely vital that everything detailed thereafter is consistent, congruent and supports your initial claims. Having grabbed your reader's attention in the opening section, there is a reasonable chance they will proceed to the second stage, which is to quickly skim, or speed read, the rest of your document. They may commit three to five minutes of their precious time to see whether what you have to say is actually of interest to them. If you're lucky enough to proceed to the "consider further" pile, you're probably in the top 1% of the investment opportunities that pass across their desk.

The third and, probably, final pass is your last opportunity to really impress your reader. Here, they will read your business plan in a reasonable amount of detail from beginning to end — so it is absolutely crucial that the promises you made in your introduction are delivered upon throughout the rest of the document. At this stage, your reader will have a number of questions (which you must anticipate) and they are reading your document to find the answers to those questions. However, you are not in the room or sat across the desk, so the only place they can get the answers to their questions is from your written document.

Your bank manager may take a slightly different tack. They will start with the introduction, to get the "flavour" of your document and then go straight to the cash flow section, to find out how much you want. If what you're asking for is within their remit, they will probably skim read the whole document; if not, they'll at least know who to pass it on to.

The important thing to bear in mind is that whoever you are trying to impress, they will probably skim read your document — which means you have to make it easy to skim read! Let's take a look at each section in a bit more detail.

Setting the Stage

When your reader opens your business plan, they will be looking to answer a few key questions:

- ▲ What do you want to do?
- ▲ What are the total resources required to do it?
- ▲ What resources do you already have available to you?
- ▲ What resources will you need to complete the picture (and, in particular, what funding is required)?
- ▲ What will the return on their investment be?

If you're seeking investment from a private investor, this may be the return on their capital investment in addition to a shareholding. If you're looking for funding from a bank, then your bank manager needs to be sure you can afford to repay whatever you borrow, plus interest and other fees.

The purpose of this first section is to answer these questions at a high level very quickly so that you capture their attention. Executive Summaries should be short and sweet — ideally no more than half a page. At this stage in the game, you are not giving the full details of your proposal; you are merely given the headlines. If you think about the beginning of the evening news, they normally give you a quick overview of what's coming in the programme. Your Executive Summary should do the same job for your business plan. By the time they get to the end of this section, they should have a pretty clear idea of your requirements.

Although the Executive Summary comes at the very front of the document, it will probably be the last section you write, because until you've completed the rest of the document you don't know what you will be summarising.

If you have completed your 21st Century Marketing Blueprint fully and paid attention to all the important details, you will have plenty of information on which to base your 21st Century Business Plan.

Most of the work required now is to map what you created in your 21st Century Marketing Blueprint across to the relevant sections in your 21st Century Business Plan. Your mission and vision statements, core values and business objectives can be summarised to create the section entitled "What we want to do". This should be no more than one paragraph, so your job is to summarise these elements and include them as the first paragraph of your Executive Summary, as shown in figure 3.9. You may choose to give each section within your Executive Summary its own appropriate title. This will break up the text and help with speed reading.

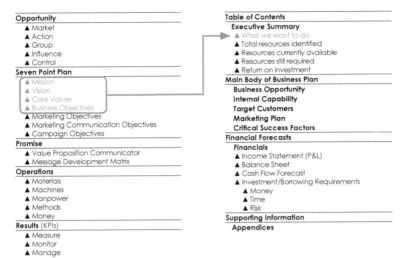

Figure 3.9 Mapping the Executive Summary (Part 1)

The section on resources should come from the Operations section of your 21st Century Marketing Blueprint (see figure 3.10). You should aim to summarise your operational resources in just a couple of paragraphs. If you follow the format here and lay out your discussion as "This is what it's going to take to achieve our goals, this is what we already have and this is what we're looking for", it's got a nice smooth and logical flow. Your reader will also be able to very quickly understand the level of risk that's involved because, for example, if you have nothing and are looking for the bank to provide everything, you're effectively asking them to take all the risk. However, if you already have your premises and some of your equipment, you will be sharing the risk, which will affect the outcome of your requests for resources. The earlier in the process you identify all of the risks, the more likely you are to get a quick decision — even if it's a no!

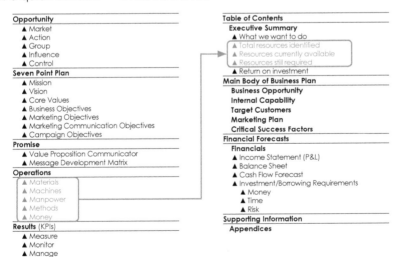

Figure 3.10 Mapping the Executive Summary (Part 2)

Once you've completed all of your financial calculations and worked out your cash flow, etc., you will be able to work out your borrowing requirements and then return on investment. This should be summarised as the last piece of the Executive Summary, so your reader knows exactly what you're asking for up front, as shown in figure 3.11.

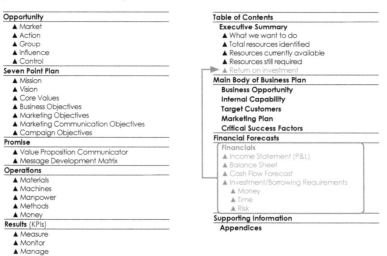

Figure 3.11 Return on Investment

Your Executive Summary should pretty much allow your reader to make a decision based solely on the information it contains. The rest of the document just backs up everything you've said here and gives them comfort that they've made the right decision (for them).

Main Body

The bulk of the Main Body in your business plan will come from the first section of your 21st Century Marketing Blueprint because all the work you did to diligently define your business in terms of the M.A.G.I.C. Marketing Matrix will be extremely useful here, as shown in figure 3.12. In fact, you could more or less cut and paste everything you've already done into this section and then "tidy it up" so it's appropriate for your target reader. You will need to ask yourself a series of questions, to help identify your reader's objections and to make sure you address and answer them in this section. If you're struggling to think what questions or objections you may get, explain your ideas to a friend or colleague and ask them to play "devil's advocate" and critique your ideas. They say "the devil is in the detail". Here is your chance to provide that detail.

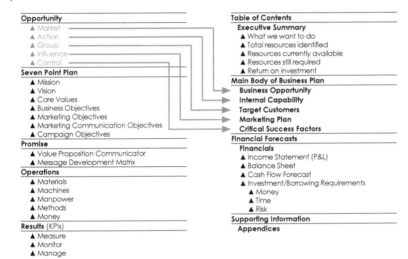

Figure 3.12 Mapping the M.A.G.I.C. Marketing Matrix

Financials

There is absolutely no doubt your bank manager or investor will be particularly interested in the financials. At the end of the day, they are primarily interested in knowing that their money is safe and how much they are going to make. Therefore, the sort of questions they will be looking for answers to include: How much do you need? For how long? Can you afford to repay it within the required timeframe? What are the risks? What guarantees are there that their money is safe? What happens if it all goes wrong? How and when do they get their money back?

Quite often, your target reader will have at least some form of accounting training and, when making financial decisions, they will think in terms of the standard financial statements. These are the Income Statement (which shows trading activity (profit/loss) over a period of time), the Balance Sheet (which shows a business's net worth at a particular point in time) and the Cash Flow Forecast (which identifies how much cash the business needs and when it needs it, so it can pay all its bills on time).

With the best will in the world, all your financial predictions will be your best guess, based on a series of assumptions. However, this does not preclude you from presenting your projections, using the same reporting mechanisms as if they had actually happened. In fact, these three financial statements are very useful management tools and can be used to great effect to present your projections in a well-established and recognised format. This also demonstrates that you can "speak the same financial language" as your target audience, which will inherently instil a level of confidence in your ability to run a business. If you feel exposed in this area, then you'd be well advised to get some help from your accountant in preparing them. Using these three statements to articulate how you anticipate your business performing also makes you think in detail about the financial implications of your tactical business activities.

In building up your 21st Century Marketing Blueprint, you identified a number of critical success factors and key performance indicators, all of which will help you manage and build your business. You have also considered what resources you will need, in order to physically operate your business using the Operations Performance Optimiser (the 5Ms) and these will need to be paid for. These will also form part of your investment and borrowing requirements. You can therefore take a significant amount of what you have already thought about and documented and use this information to generate your projected financial statements. For example, in step 6 of the Seven Point Plan, Brian identified a number of marketing communication objectives, some of which required advertising on the radio and in the local press. He will know what these cost and when they need to be paid and can, hence, "plug them in" to the appropriate sections on the Expenses side of his Income Statement. He will have also defined his target daily sales revenue figures and can build these up into monthly and quarterly revenue projections on the Income section of his Income Statement. He will know when he expects to get this income and when he needs to pay his suppliers and can plug these figures into the relevant sections on his Cash Flow Forecast. Brian's second business objective is "to break even within six months" which is another useful piece of information he can use in this section and, if he mentions this in his Executive Summary, it also needs to be accurately reflected in the Financials of his business plan. Figure 3.13 shows how to map this information from your 21st Century Marketing Blueprint to your 21st Century Business Plan.

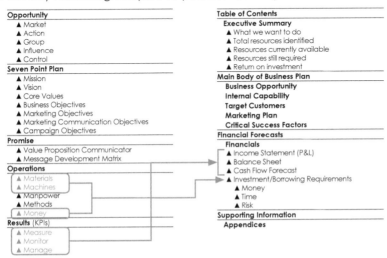

Figure 3.13 Mapping the Financials

There are three key elements that your target reader will be especially interested in: how much money you need, how long you want it for and what risks are involved. The majority of their objections will be centred on

Key Investment Questions

Money
▲ How much money do you want?
▲ Can you afford it?
▲ How much return will they make on their investment?

Time
▲ How long do you want it for?
▲ When do you need it?
▲ When do they get it back?

Risk
▲ Who is managing the risk?
▲ What happens if it goes wrong?
▲ How do they get their money back?

Investment Considerations

these three investment considerations and you need to make sure that what you said in the body of the report is accurately reflected in terms of the financial statements, to make sure they are congruent.

Each of these three elements will have an impact on the other two. For example, if you want a lot of money, it's likely to take you a long time to pay it back. Therefore, the lender is at greater risk than if were repaid quickly. If your loan repayments are, say, 25% of your revenue, then the lender is at far greater risk than if your repayments equate to 5% or 10% of your profit. If you have a large funding requirement and it is being provided by a single source, that single lender will be taking all the risk. They may find your proposal more palatable if the risk is spread between two or three separate lenders. Whoever you are looking to finance your business with, they will want to know the whole picture, so they can accurately assess their overall risk exposure.

Evaluating the overall risk will be a very large part of the decision-making process. They will be looking at who is managing the risk and what experience they have, in terms of business experience as well as risk management. If you are prepared to share the risk by, for example, investing a significant amount of your own money alongside theirs, they will feel a lot more confident. And this is a key point: any kind of investment is all about the "C" word — confidence! Ultimately, the whole of your business plan must instil a high degree of confidence in the reader if you're going to be successful in securing the resources you need — hence, why a robust and structured approach is required.

Lenders are very keen to reduce their risk as far as possible and every bank I've dealt with was also looking for some kind of security against which to secure any lending facility. I often felt that they were more interested in how much equity I had in my home than the potential of my business propositions. Put bluntly, if you have, say, £100,000 equity in your family home, they may lend you 50% or 60% (or whatever their percentage risk factor is). If your business fails they are perfectly entitled to sell your home to get their money back. So if you borrow £60,000 secured against your £100,000 equity and it all goes wrong, by the time they've added their fees and charges (let's just say £10,000 for the sake of argument), if you don't have £70,000 in your back pocket, they can force you to sell your house for less than what you'd like and you end up losing big time. I knew a chap who was forced to sell his house to pay all the business debts back and, unfortunately, it was in a down market where house prices were collapsing. He had to sell it at a huge loss and, when the bank took all his equity, he still owed them £25,000. Result? No home, no business (and no job) and still £25,000 in debt. Ouch!

Here's the best example I have from my own experience: When I asked one particular bank to lend me £250,000 to help buy and refurbish a commercial property, they wanted me to put up £250,000 in cash as security against the loan, in addition to taking a first charge over the property I was purchasing. I mean, why would I even bother? It would be cheaper and far less hassle to use my money. Coincidently, I still have this letter on file as a keepsake. The bottom line is this: "banks don't like risk". Those were the exact words I heard from one bank manager!

Just to sum up: the main thing you have to do in the financials section of your business plan is to convince your investor/target reader that you fully understand the financial side your business and the risks you're prepared to take to secure their support. Talking to them in their language, i.e. financial statements, is a good way to show that you understand the finances and generate confidence in your proposal. You need to articulate your financial requirements clearly and concisely and back them up with as much evidence and coherent explanation as possible.

Appendices

If you have any supporting information, it should be included in your appendices. For example, if you have discussed potential premises you want to buy or lease, then including the estate agent's information sheet may help the reader appreciate (and picture) exactly what you're talking about. Other things you may consider including are; the specifications of any equipment, a cost-benefit calculation and other evaluations you have mentioned in the body of your business plan. Other useful appendices may include any staff CVs/résumés — particularly if the career histories of any potential board members support your discussions on the skills available to your business venture. Anything that can support your main argument, but would be too much detail in the main body of your document, should go into the appendices as a separate section, so they can be quickly and easily identified.

For example, the appendices to Brian's business plan may include the following:

Supporting Information

Appendices
- ▲ Appendix 1: Potential Premises
- ▲ Appendix 2: Equipment Specifications
  - ▲ Appendix 2.1: Coffee Machine
  - ▲ Appendix 2.2: Fridges
  - ▲ Appendix 2.3: Cleaning Equipment
- ▲ Appendix 3: ROI Calculations
- ▲ Appendix 4: Owner's CV/Business Profile

That's how you use your 21st Century Marketing Blueprint as a basis for your 21st Century Business Plan. And remember: your 21st Century Marketing Blueprint is your business development tool and should be something you create and keep up-to-date as you build your business. It is for your internal use and serves your information and control needs. By contrast, your 21st Century Business Plan is something you create when you need to secure resources from others. Its sole purpose is to serve their informational needs and help them make a decision regarding providing the resources you require.

What Next?

Thirty years ago, I was just like so many other new entrepreneurs and micro-business owners: I thought I had a great idea and a fantastic product. I was full of hope and optimism. The world was my oyster and I convinced myself my product was so great that the world would beat a path to my door and it would sell itself. However, the reality speaks for itself! I didn't have a clue about marketing — I mean real marketing — and that's what led me to the banker's lair and that fateful meeting with Cleason on the 4th July 1990.

As I look back, with the benefit of hindsight, I now realise this was an important turning point in my life and the start of the journey that would define my destiny.

Like so many entrepreneurs, I was driven by my desire to provide well for my family, make a positive contribution to society, leave a legacy and enjoy life. But the path to success is both full of opportunity and littered with obstacles. It has many mountains to climb and valleys to enjoy. It's also full of many people who will cross your path for a reason — good or bad — or join you on your journey for a season, or even a lifetime. There will be many highs and many lows, as you, as a fellow entrepreneur and business owner will know better than anyone else.

There are no shortcuts to success, but your current path can be smoother when guided by others who have travelled before you. I hope I have encouraged you to study success as you chart your course to your ultimate destination — and let's not forget, we can also learn very valuable lessons from the failures of others, too.

Recent research reveals most business failures can be attributed to management mistakes rather than misfortune or market forces. The single biggest mistake cited by most failed entrepreneurs and business owners was the lack of a marketing focused business plan — one they could quickly adapt to changing market forces to profit from new opportunities. It seems many modern entrepreneurs and business owners still make the same mistakes I made thirty years ago.

With advances in technology and more fickle and demanding consumers, the need for a flexible marketing-focused planning framework has never been greater. Now you have finished this book, you have the 21st Century Marketing System in your hands and all the supporting tools you need to create your own 21st Century Business Blueprint, tailored to your own specific business needs.

I hope you now appreciate the power of the 21st Century Marketing System and, in particular, the New Engagement Paradigm and how it can be used to truly engage with your target audience. By following the 21st Century Marketing System step-by-step as described in this book, you have everything you need to turn your opportunities into reality and make a real difference to those you care about most. But it doesn't stop there. Additional resources and training are available on the 21st Century Marketing Academy website, www.Academy.21stCentury.Marketing where you can also register your copy of this book.

This will automatically qualify you for FREE Membership to the 21st Century Marketing Academy where you'll be able to access a number of free resources to help you get the best out of your training investment. Your Membership is absolutely FREE — you do not need a credit card and no payment is necessary. It is simply our way of saying "Thank You" for investing in this book and placing your trust in us. You'll also be the first to hear about the next books in the 21st Century Marketing series — so why not drop by and sign up today?

Whether you already run your own business, or whether you plan to start one in the future, there is a wealth of knowledge, experience and practical advice available in the Academy to help you succeed in your business venture and live the life of your dreams.

If you want to continue your marketing and entrepreneurial education, you'll also be able to preview all the courses in the 21st Century Marketing Academy. These courses have been specifically designed to help entrepreneurs and micro-business owners fully engage their target audience by making sure they deliver the right message, at the right time, using the right tools.

This book is the start of a very exciting journey. May I wish you every success in your entrepreneurial ventures and make sure you register and become part of the 21st Century Marketing community at:

www.Academy.21stCentury.Marketing.

Good luck!

* * * * *

Bibliography

Carmody, D. P. and Lewis, M. (2006) "Brain activation when hearing one's own and others' names." Brain Research. Elsevier, 1116(1) pp. 153–158.

Google (2013) Mobile Search Moments: Understanding How Mobile Drives Conversions. [Online] [Accessed on 23-7/15] www.thinkwithgoogle.com/infographics/creating-moments-that-matter-infographic.html.

Halligan, B. and Shah, D. (2009) Inbound Marketing: Get Found Using Google, Social Media, and Blogs. John Wiley & Sons.

Hess, J. and Story, J. (2005) "Trust-Based Commitment: Multidimensional Consumer-Brand Relationships." Journal of Consumer Marketing. Emerald Group Publishing Limited, 22(6) pp. 313–322.

Hill, N. (1937) Think and Grow Rich. The Ralston Society.

Maslow, A. H. (1943) "A Theory of Human Motivation." Psychological Review. American Psychological Association, 50(4) p. 370.

Mobile Marketing Association (2013) The Mobile Marketing Roadmap. [Online] [Accessed on 27/3/14] www.mmaglobal.com/documents/mobile-marketing-roadmap.

Morgan, R. M. and Hunt, S. D. (1994) "The Commitment-Trust Theory Of Relationship Marketing." The Journal of Marketing. JSTOR pp. 20–38.

Zyman, S., Harris, R., Strupp, D. and MacMurray, S. (1999) The End of Marketing As We Know It. HarperBusiness New York.